Qigong Empowerment

A Guide to Medical, Taoist, Buddhist, and Wushu Energy Cultivation

By

Master Shou-Yu Liang

&

Wen-Ching Wu

Edited by

Denise Breiter-Wu

 The Way of the Dragon Publishing, Rhode Island, U.S.A.

Published by:

The Way of the Dragon Publishing

P. O. Box 14561

East Providence, RI 02914-0561

United States of America

Publisher's Cataloging-in-Publication Data

Wu, Wen-Ching, 1964-

     Qigong empowerment: a guide to medical, taoist, buddhist, and wushu energy cultivation / by Wen-Ching Wu and Shou-Yu Liang

     illus. p. cm.

     Includes bibliographical references and index.

     ISBN 1-889659-02-9

     1. Qigong--Health aspects. 2. Medicine, Chinese. 3. Taoism. 4. Buddhism. 5. Chi (Chinese philosophy). 6. Martial arts--Training. I. Title. II. Liang, Shou-Yu.

GV505.LW8   1997   613.7'1   96-61197

Table of Contents

Acknowledgments

As it is with every project, there are always individuals, beside the obvious, that contribute to the completed work. This volume is no exception. Many people have helped the authors in making this volume as complete and user friendly as possible.

Thanks to **Bill Pyne**, **Frank Whitsitt-Lynch**, **Mike Bernier**, and **Vincent Wu** for helping and answering many computer related questions. Thanks also to **Joe Sousa, Nancy Passmore**, **The Bravo Family**, **The Pereira Family, Gary Metz, Dr. Lynn Carter, Siu-Hung Huen**, and **Mo Hui** for general help. A special thanks to **Sarah Alexander** for her exact proof reading. Also thank you to all the friends and students at The Way of the Dragon for their continuous support through the years.

Dedication

To my Grandfather, who initiated my qigong training, to all my teachers, and all my friends that have helped and supported me.

To my parents, my wife, and my beautiful children, Helen and Maria, for supporting my career.

To my uncle, Jeffrey D. S. Liang and my aunt, Eva, for sponsoring my immigration to North America, for always being there for me, and for providing the opportunity for me to prosper in North America.

To all qigong enthusiasts, all the people that are engaging in the research and fulfillment of qigong, and to all my students.

Liang, Shou-Yu

Fall 1996

To my grandparents, my parents, and my wife for loving me, for supporting me, and for being my inspiration.

To my beautiful son, Andrew, and everyone in his generation. May they use this knowledge to make the world a better place to live in.

Wu, Wen-Ching

Fall 1996

Warning-Disclaimer

The exercises in this book may be too mentally and physically demanding for some people. Readers should use their own discretion and consult their doctor before engaging in these exercises. The authors and the publisher shall have neither liability nor responsibility to any person or entity with respect to any loss or damage caused, or alleged to be caused, directly or indirectly by reading or following the instructions in this book.

If you do not wish to be bound by the above, you may return this book to the publisher for a full refund.

Foreword:

by Dr. Wu, Cheng-De

I met Mr. Liang in China. He currently resides in Canada. Mr. Liang came from Sichuan, China, a highly spiritual place with extraordinary and remarkable individuals. Mr. Liang has a flourishing love for wushu and qigong, and has an earnest effort to promote the precious Chinese treasures — wushu and qigong — in the United States, Canada, and all over the world.

Upon arriving to the United States, I met Mr. Wu during a U.S. National Chinese Martial Arts Competition. Mr. Wu was the 1990 U.S. National Grand Champion in both Internal and External Styles. He is a rare and talented individual in our world today. He is sincere in his learning and has an earnest effort in his climb to the peak of Chinese martial arts and qigong. Mr. Wu has been teaching in the New England area for many years, helping other to excel and benefit from Chinese martial arts, Taijiquan, and qigong.

The cooperation of Mr. Liang and Mr. Wu, presenting and sharing their knowledge on qigong, will assist the readers in attaining the palace of health and longevity. This book is also assisted by the editorial input of Mr. Wu's wife, Denise Breiter-Wu. The combination of the Chinese and American talent by these aspirational individuals makes this book a remarkable work that will be both beneficial and enlightening to the readers.

Dr. Wu, Cheng-De
Fall 1996

Professor Emeritus — Shanghai Traditional Medicine and Herbology University
Committee Member — Shanghai Sports Medicine Association
Committee Member — Shanghai Rehabilitation Association
Advisor — Yangtze River Martial Arts and Physical Therapy Research Center
Committee Member — China Martial Arts Association
Vice Chairman — China Wushu and Medical Research Association

Preface:

by Liang, Shou-Yu

What is Qigong? Are humans really able to strengthen, heal, and prevent illness? Can humans really attain incredible strength, that is several times the strength of an average person, through qigong training? Can humans absorb the energy of the universe? Can humans really emit qi to heal others? How strong can humans emit qi and how far can it reach? Can qi penetrate solids? Do humans have auras? How can we see them? Can humans use their mind to control the physical body and other material? What is a Spiritual Connection? Can ... ? All these questions are the target of study for qigong practitioners and researchers.

Since ancient time, humans have been attempting to answer who we are, where we come from, and where we are going. The profound nature of qigong is also in search of the answers to the mystery of life, birth, aging, illness, and death; as well as, the mystery of the cosmos and that of the higher dimensional spaces. Through the millenniums, humans have used many different scientific approaches to train and to cultivate. Today, our technology is higher than ever. The space expeditions bring us increasingly closer to our understanding. Humans are always using many different approaches in search of the *Truth*.

In recent years, qigong has gotten more and more popular, and more and more training methods are surfacing. Unfortunately, along with the popularity of qigong are many real, as well as, faked extraordinary abilities. There are more and more methods to trick unsuspecting people. On the positive side, there have been hundreds of millions of people that have attained better health, prevented illness, and increased the quality of their lives through qigong training. The goal in qigong training includes attaining better health, strengthening the body, and preventing illness. Taking it one step further, qigong training is also a way to attain Great Wisdom, and to realize the true nature of human existence and its relation with the cosmos.

All the qigong methods in this volume are methods that I have personally practiced. Most of them are currently being taught as part of our schools' curriculum. There are other methods that we have not had my teachers' permission to present in this volume. We have, therefore, refrained from presenting them at this time. When my teachers grant me the permission, we will present them to interested individuals.

11

I began my martial arts qigong and martial arts training at age 6. Later I also studied many Daoist (Taoist), Buddhist, and Medical Qigong methods. I have many teachers and have taught many students. It is my goal to assist everyone in attaining the excitement, joy, calmness, and health benefits from qigong.

I believe, besides our teachers who have taught us directly, any individual that has provided us with knowledge through their books, tapes, newspaper and magazine articles, are also our teachers. Anything that helps us in the attainment of knowledge or provide us with a catalyst for our enlightenment are our teachers. "Even a piece of grass or a tree can be a teacher." In qigong cultivation the virtue of respecting one's teacher is held in very high esteem. In writing this book, we have included some essence of other qigong instructor's training philosophies. Therefore, all these people are also our teachers.

Every qigong method in this volume is the essence of the qigong masters of old. Anyone of these qigong methods can be beneficial to you. You can choose the ones that most suit you or you can practice them in order. However, don't attempt to practice too many methods at once. When you have attained a definite benefit and gain from one type then practice the other type. If you should feel that certain methods are not suitable for you, stop training that method and choose another one to practice. Some methods enable you to achieve extraordinary abilities, but don't search for them. Allow your ability to develop naturally. Everyone's foundation is different and everyone's development will be different. Extraordinary abilities should not be the goal of your training. When you have attained *Great Wisdom*, you will have it all.

In our schools, our qigong curriculum is divided into different courses. It is not necessary that everyone complete all the methods in this volume. If you should have questions regarding the training methods, please contact us. It is imperative that you understand the requirements of the training.

There are many things that can affect our health. These include heredity, living habits, nutrition, rest, emotion, character, etc. Therefore, we must pay attention to the overall effects. In the presentation of the methods in this volume, we have not deliberately made any mystery of the training methods. With continual practice anyone can achieve high attainment from their training.

We have presented many qigong methods in this volume. Many of the methods presented are not available in any other books. However, what we present in this volume is "like a drop of water in the wide, deep sea of qigong knowledge". It is only a *beginning*. When future conditions permit, we will introduce the qigong methods for next levels.

Thanks to Wen-Ching for his efforts in working with me in the presentation of this volume. Also, thanks to Denise for her efforts in editing our work. They have both done a tremendous amount of work to make this volume possible.

Preface:
by Wu, Wen-Ching

Qigong has been an integral part of Chinese culture since the beginning of its civilization. Learning qigong is not just for health, longevity, and spiritual development, it is also for learning about ancient Chinese culture and the wisdom inherent within the practice. As it is with all cultures that have lasted through the ages, the wisdom that we can learn from them are immeasurable.

Certain philosophical discussions in this volume may sound incredible for some people at their particular stage of development. Just because it sounds incredible, doesn't make it impossible. When the thought of impossibility is present, a huge obstacle has been placed on the path of growth. Higher learning and wisdom require an unrestricted, free, and open mind. If certain things sound incredible, take a step back. By removing ourselves from our preconceived ideology, and reevaluating the whole picture, we may be able to see the credibility in the incredible. By removing the limitations we have placed on our mind, we can set our mind *free* and enter into the infinite *reality* where there is no limit to growth.

There are many ways and many paths towards a greater consciousness. Each path may appear very different from the others. The ultimate objectives, however, are the same. Certain paths suit certain individuals better than others at that particular stage of one's growth; similar to the growth of an infant to adulthood, each has a different understanding and needs. In this volume, the views, training approaches, and emphasis in the Medical, Daoist, Buddhist, and Wushu Qigong differs and are presented under different books. However, it is important to note that the goals are similar. They all bring to mind the importance of self-awareness, self-reliance, and being responsible for our own physical and spiritual *well-being*.

As we continue to learn and take greater responsibility for our well-being, we are another step closer to our own spiritual understanding and goals. The understanding of ourselves and being responsible for our well-being is the path towards spiritual liberation. As we learn more about ourselves, we also become more aware of our surroundings and how our surroundings affect us. With this awareness, we can learn to live in harmony with our surroundings.

In our learning, we all need guidance from higher teachers and guides. Their teaching and guidance includes sharing with us their knowledge and help-

13

ing us develop self-reliance. However, they are not responsible for our growth, nor should we rely on them for our growth. Relying on our teachers for our growth does not help us develop our own being and self-reliance.

When teachers guide their students, they are fulfilling their responsibility to pass down their knowledge. Teachers realize that their knowledge does not belong to them or any particular group of people, it is universal and belongs to us all. Teachers not only guide and teach students, they also manifest their knowledge and experience in the way they live their lives. The greatest teaching a teacher can impart on their students, however, is not their knowledge; but by being a living example of great wisdom. The greatest teachers are the ones that are willing to guide wholeheartedly, and give students the liberty to excel without restriction.

In my learning, I have had the opportunity to study from three exceptional guides and mentors that are continuously guiding and inspiring me. They are Master Shou-Yu Liang, Professor Ju-Rong Wang, and Dr. Cheng-De Wu. They are not just experts in qigong, Taijiquan, and martial arts. They are also the most wonderful and wise people that I have had the good fortune of meeting and learning from.

Master Liang has been guiding me for the past 10 years. The opportunity to help present this book to the readers, is not just a privilege and honor, it is also one of the greatest opportunities I have had to learn and share this knowledge with my teacher. This book represents Master Liang's life long studies and accomplishments from age six to present. Few people in his age have accomplished as much as he has. I am very fortunate to have him as my teacher, guide, mentor, and inspiration. In the past 10 years, Master Liang has taught me more than qigong and martial arts. His *being* is a great inspiration which I admire and follow as a guide to my continuous learning.

Professor Wang is the leading authority on Chinese martial arts and a qigong expert. She inherited her father's (the late Grandmaster Wang Zi-Ping) lineage and has become a living legend of Chinese martial arts. It is a great honor and privilege to be able to study from such an admirable, wise, and knowledgeable teacher. Thank you Professor Wang.

Dr. Wu is both a highly skilled martial artist, qigong expert, and a doctor of Traditional Chinese Medicine. Dr. Wu's combined mastery in Chinese martial arts, qigong, and medicine gives him many insights and an understanding that only a few have been able to achieve. The opportunity to study from Dr. Wu is another great honor and privilege that I have. Thank you Dr. Wu. Also a heart felt thank you to Dr. Wu for writing the Foreword for this volume.

I am a very fortunate person with a wonderful family, inspirational teachers, and many wonderful friends that have helped me on my journey in this life. If it were not for all these wonderful people in my life, past and present, I would not be where I am today. Thank you to all my friends and students for their continuous support, which allows me to continue with my work, both as a teacher and writer. Words can't express my appreciation for all the wonderful people that have helped me, except to say it once again, thank you.

Learning and teaching are reciprocal, both the student and the teacher benefit from their interactions. By writing this book Master Liang and I have also furthered our own understanding on many levels. It is Master Liang and my hope that we are also making a positive contribution to your learning. For the people that we have the honor of meeting and sharing our life experiences, and to you our reader for honoring us by reading this book; we sincerely hope that with this volume, you will find whatever you may need to guide you toward your next stage of growth. It is also our hope that the exercises in this volume will not only bring you good health and longevity; but also a higher sense of awareness, leading us all to a greater consciousness of the human race.

Introduction

Qigong (Chi Kung) has been an integral part of Chinese culture since ancient China. High level qigong masters have always been respected and held in high esteem in Chinese society. They studied qigong not merely for the health and strength of the body, but as an attempt to understand human nature and its interactions with the environment and the universe as a whole. Realizing that humans are part of nature, any attempt to understand human physiology inevitably involves the study of the universe. These qigong masters were the pillars of Chinese society and included healers, philosophers, teachers, astrologers, scientists, martial artists, and government leaders. Their study resulted in the formation of the Yin-Yang and the Five Element Theories that have guided, and still guide the development and research of all fields of study, from medicine, to government, to the understanding of our greater existence.

Today, qigong is most often referred to as any set of breathing and qi circulation techniques that are capable of improving health, preventing illness, and strengthening the body. Generally speaking, *qi* is a Chinese term used to refer to all types of energy. It is the intrinsic substance or the *vital force* behind all things in the universe. It is the medium between and within all material substances. We are all immersed in it. The term *gong* refers to the power to produce an effect, an attainment of, or an accomplishment that is achieved with steady practice. Loosely, qigong can be translated as the *attainment of qi*. Healers and the medical society use qigong for healing and preventing illness. Martial artists use qigong for developing incredible strength and abilities. Others use qigong to attain a greater consciousness.

The practice of qigong aims at balancing and strengthening qi in the human body. In Medical Qigong, for example, the objective for healing illness is to build the patient's qi to counteract the pathogenic influences and to regulate the balance of yin-yang energy, thereby returning the body to a normal physiological state, thus regaining health. This way the energetic imbalance is rebalanced and the root cause of the illness is removed.

Traditional Chinese Medicine (TCM) stresses " To heal, look for the cause of the illness", and are strongly opposed to "treating only the head if the head hurts, and treating the foot if the foot hurts." They believe that the development of illness is due to the *battle* between qi in the human body and pathogenic influences. That is, the causes of illnesses are due to an energetic imbalance within the body. Therefore, to treat any illness, we will either need to eliminate the pathogenic influence, and/or balance and strengthen the qi in the body.

Under normal conditions, the human body is in an energetically balanced state that is capable of maintaining the physiological functions of the body and can adjust to changes in the environment. When the pathogenic influences are above and beyond the normal functioning of the body, and the body is unable to adjust; the normal physiological functioning of the body will be destroyed, creating obstructions, which results in illness. That is to say, the occurrence of illness is not only strongly related to the pathogenic influences that attack the human body, but it is also strongly dependent on the adaptability of the human body to the changing environment.

If qi in the human body is strong, then it will be difficult for the pathogenic influences to adversely affect the body. Even if the pathogenic influence does attack the body, the abundance of qi increases the immunity of the body and prevents disease from occurring. Only when the qi is weak or deficient will the pathogenic influences be able to cause irregularities in the physiological systems and result in diseases.

The TCM approach to treating illness includes the use of herbs, acupuncture, moxibustion, and massage to counteract the effects of pathogenic influences, thereby regaining health. Another approach would be to practice qigong and/or take herbs to strengthen the qi, thus improving the immunity of the body for fighting against the pathogenic influences.

One of the ways, doctors and healers can remove the physical manifestation of an illness is by balancing a patient's energy; and prescribing external assistance such as drugs, herbs, or nutritional supplements. In drastic cases, surgical removal of the manifestation of the illness. However, it is up to the individual to work on maintaining the balance of energy within the body to prevent the illness from remanifesting in a similar or other form. External assistance is not a permanent solution to problems associated with energetic imbalance. Once the external assistance is removed or stopped, the individual's body still may not have a natural response to prevent the illness. By practicing qigong, the natural response to establish balance within the body is achieved and strengthened, thus illness is prevented.

In Daoist (Taoist), Buddhist, and Wushu (martial arts) qigong training, the same approaches are also used to achieve a healthy mind and body. With a healthy mind and body, the higher levels of any achievement in any field can be accomplished because the foundation is strong enough to withstand the demands of continuous learning.

Qigong Training Approaches

There are four major approaches in qigong training: training the body, the breath, the voice, and the mind; with the training of the mind being of the highest importance. During training, the mind is placed on regulating the body, breathing, and vocalization. When you have gained control of your body, breathing, and vocalization, you will also have gained control of your mind through disciplining the other three. In this qigong volume, all four approaches will be presented

Body — Training the body includes sitting, standing still, and moving. In the still or meditation training, the body is positioned in a way that is best suited for energy circulation. In sitting meditation, for example, people often sit with their legs naturally crossed, Half Lotus, or Full Lotus. The hands are also placed in certain positions. The proper positioning of the body allows the energy in the body to flow smoother, as well as, becomes a better *receiver* to the energy of the cosmos. The moving aspect of qigong training is easier to comprehend. Each movement is designed to directly or indirectly stimulate specific areas of the body to increase qi circulation.

Breathing — Most qigong exercises are done very slowly. The slow movements allow the mind to register the movements throughout the body and to allow the body to be in a more relaxed state, than with fast paced exercise. This way the breathing can be slower and deeper; and the efficiency of the lungs to take in oxygen can be greatly increased. Many of the breathing exercises in qigong include body movements to assist with breathing. Breathing can also help with your concentration. By paying attention to your breathing, you will be able to reduce your scattered thoughts. When your mind is less busy, it will be easier for the body to perform its proper internal functions to keep you healthy — regulating qi flow and maintaining balance.

Sound — All material substances are in constant vibration. Molecules in our body are also constantly vibrating. Sound vibrations are capable of traveling through space and causing an avalanche. It can help you relax or give you a headache depending on the type of sound. In qigong training, specific sounds are used for specific purposes. For example, a *song* sound can help you relax, and a gentle *xu* sound can help calm the liver. Some sounds, chants, and mantras also have mystical connections with the cosmos.

Mind — The mind is the most important part of qigong training. The mind's potential is unlimited. In the training of the body, breathing, and voice, the mind is used to regulate them. When you are able to regulate your body, breathing, and voice, you will have also gained better control of your mind. When this conscious regulation becomes automatic, you will have attained a state of regulation without consciously regulating — a natural and automatic response to attain energetic harmony. Your mind will then be able to sense any potential problem and correct it before damage occurs. Our mind has amazing mental power. There is a saying in Buddhism, "All things are the result of the *heart* (mind)." The higher goals in qigong cultivation are to attain *Great Wisdom*, and realize the *Truth* of the cosmos.

Qigong Empowerment Contents

This volume of five books includes qigong practices from four of the major Chinese qigong societies — Medical, Daoist, Buddhist, and Wushu Qigong. Each book in this volume presents qigong practices with theoretical and philosophical discussions, and begins with the most basic to more advanced methods. Beginning through more experienced qigong practitioners, healthy or ill individuals, will find this volume to be a valuable reference and training guide for attaining a variety of goals; whether it be better health, healing, martial arts, or spiritual development. It is recommended that you read the first section of each book to have an over view of the different qigong methods, before you start practicing any of the methods.

Book 1 focuses on developing a strong foundation for qigong training. It consists of many Medical Qigong techniques for health, healing, and illness prevention. It is also a foundation for all other qigong training. Book 1 begins with an introduction to the energy concept in Traditional Chinese Medicine. It also includes relaxation techniques, Qi Permeating Technique, Health Maintenance Qigong, healing sounds, and suggested self-healing practices for specific illnesses.

Individuals that are new to qigong training should begin with Book 1 before engaging in other qigong training in this volume. People that have been training other qigong and have developed a strong foundation, may skip Book 1 and go on to the other training presented in this volume. Martial artists and other internal arts practitioners who are in good health and have a good energy foundation may also skip the training in Book 1 and go on to the Daoist, Buddhist, Absorbing, Emitting and Healing, or Wushu Qigong directly. However, it is a good idea to read the basic concepts presented in Book 1 before engaging in any other qigong training. It is always a good idea to practice the qigong methods in Book 1 to establish an even stronger foundation. The stronger your foundation, the higher you can achieve in your other qigong training.

Book 2 focuses on Daoist (Taoist) Qigong methods to further strengthen the body and attain longevity. Book 2 begins with a description of Daoist philosophy and qigong training concepts for health, longevity, and spiritual development. Section 2.2 includes methods for Fostering Jing into Qi, including the fundamentals of qi circulation, and Microcosmic and Macrocosmic Circulation. It also includes a supplemental qigong technique to assist individuals that may have difficulty in completing the Microcosmic or Macrocosmic Circulation. Section 2.3. and Section 2.4. include Level Two and Level Three Daoist Qigong. Individuals interested in the higher spiritual aspects will find Daoist Qigong techniques valuable tools in furthering their spiritual pursuits.

Book 3 focuses on Buddhist Qigong methods for health and developing an extraordinary potential. More specifically, Book 3 focuses on the Tantric Buddhist Qigong methods. It begins with a description of Buddhist philosophy and cultivation concepts; and continues with the basics for sitting meditation; and the cultivation of the Three Esoterics: Body, Speech, and Mind. This book also includes specific Buddhist breathing qigong, methods for protecting oneself from negative energies, and practices to unlock the inner potentials of the mind.

Book 4 focuses on methods for absorbing qi from nature and emitting qi, and exercises to develop your healing potential. It begin with a discussion on the human ability to emit qi; and continues with practices that unify the human and the cosmos; followed by qigong exercises to build and emit qi; and methods for absorbing qi from nature. Beginning and advanced qigong practitioners, and healers, will find this book very valuable for absorbing, building, and emitting their healing energy. Healers will find that being able to absorb energy from nature will make them feel even more energized and will allow them to help more people. Also, included are techniques to ward off negative energies which are especially useful for individuals that work in environments which are surrounded by negativity.

Book 5 focuses on Wushu Qigong. Wushu is the official name for Chinese martial arts. It begins with a discussion on Chinese martial arts training, followed by Iron Shirt Qigong and other Hard Qigong training for martial arts applications. Even though this book contains qigong specifically designed for martial artists, it is also useful for other athletes to build up strength in their body for other physical pursuits.

At the end of this volume you will find a set of Appendixes, which you may wish to refer to for additional information throughout your reading and practice, to help you better understand the material in the main text. In Appendix A, complete Acupuncture Charts are presented for your reference. However, most of the acupuncture points that you will need to know for your practice will also be shown along with the description of the qigong method.

Appendix B contains a set of exercises that can help relieve energetic stagnation from the stress of work or improper practice. In only rare occasions will you need to refer to this appendix. As long as you follow the procedures, keep an open mind, and respond naturally to the different sensations in your practice, you will not need to use this appendix. Nevertheless, it is a good idea to be familiar with this appendix and know where to find the information easily. You can refer to Appendix C for a glossary of terms used in this volume. Also, in the beginning of the glossary is a brief explanation about how the Chinese terms are romanized.

Today, we are thankful for the medical advances that can treat many life threatening illnesses. However, these medical advances alone cannot keep us healthy nor do they give us permission to relinquish our responsibility for our own well-being. We can rely on doctors for checkups and to give us suggestions for staying healthy, but we can't rely on them to keep us healthy. We are ultimately responsible for our own well-being. By taking an active role in acquiring better health, and with a consistent input of time and energy in your qigong practice, you will be able to gain the highest benefit from your qigong training.

Beside practicing qigong regularly, proper hygiene, diet, and maintaining a positive mental attitude, are all important to staying healthy. When we practice qigong, yet constantly abuse our body with unhealthy habits, we render the effectiveness of our qigong practice. The Daoist's view on personal well-being effectively summarizes this point:

> "People who know about healthy living, but not the means to attain health; know about death, but don't believe that there are ways to avoid death; know that proper diet can keep away illness, but still indulge excessively; and know that excessive sexual activity drains the vital essence, but still don't regulate sexual activities; though they may speak of the attainability of longevity, they can't achieve it."

Ignorance and lack of discipline are the main reasons for not being able to determine our own destiny. Life is hard to come by, therefore don't waste this opportunity.

Book 1:

Medical Qigong

1.1. The Energy Concept in Traditional Chinese Medicine

Medical Qigong is a compilation of effective preventive, healing, and strengthening exercises derived from a long history of the Chinese people's experiences as they struggled with nature. As early as the Shang Dynasty (1766-1123 B.C.) and the Zhou Dynasty (1122-249 B.C.), there have been drawings vividly representing the art similar to what we call qigong today. In the early part of the Spring-Autumn (722-480 B.C.) period, the *Yellow Emperor's Internal Classic*, the oldest Chinese medical text, was compiled and presented theories and methods for qigong training.

In Traditional Chinese Medicine (TCM), the human body is treated as an integral system of interrelated networks with different physiological functions. This integral system uses the energy pathways to link the organs and other human systems into an unified whole, making the communication and interaction between parts of the body possible. The energy that flows in the energy pathways is called qi. It extends internally to the organs and externally throughout the body, completing an interrelated system of networks.

The energy meridians were accurately charted by Dr. Wang Wei-Yi (987-1067 A.D.). He was a distinguished acupuncturist in the Northern Dynasty. Dr. Wang was responsible for casting the two life-size bronze acupuncture figures,

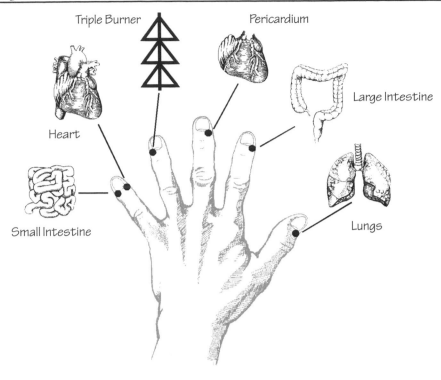

Drawing 1-1

and was in charge of compiling the *Manual of the Illustrated Points for Acupuncture and Moxibustion*. The bronze figures and the manual facilitated the research, development, and teaching of acupuncture.

Energy Meridians

The qi pathways in the human body include 12 *channels*, 8 extraordinary *vessels*, 15 *main branches*, and *collaterals*. In this book, channels refer to energy pathways that connect to the organs internally and extend to the limbs externally, and have accessible acupuncture points on the surface of the body. *Vessels* are energy pathways that connect to the channels, but without a direct connection to the organs, and have no accessible acupuncture points of its own, except for the *Conception* and *Governing Vessels*. The 15 main branches are branches of the 12 channels plus one from the Conception Vessel, one from the Governing Vessel, and an additional one from the Spleen Channel. The smaller netlike energy pathways, branching out of the energy pathways are called *collaterals*. These energy pathways are the connectors between the organs and the limbs, link to the upper and lower body, the regulator and the balancer for the entire body; making the human body an *integrated whole* (Drawings 1-1 and 1-2).

The 12 qi channels are connected to 6 viscera and 6 bowels. The 8 qi vessels that do not have a direct connection with the organs, supplement the 12 qi

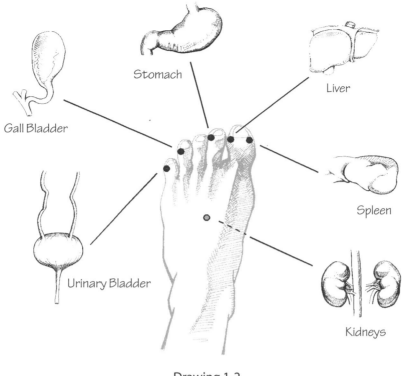

Drawing 1-2

channels. Sometimes the combination of the 12 qi channels, and the Conception and Governing Vessels are lumped together and called the *14 Channels and Vessels*. They are lumped together because they all can be accessed externally through the *acupuncture points*.

Acupuncture points or qi cavities are locations on the surface of the skin which connect to the channels or vessels. These locations either have a greater accumulation of qi, are points for draining or nourishing qi, or are important passages for the energy pathways. Since these points connect with the energy pathways which in turn connect directly or indirectly to the organs, they can affect the flow of qi through and from the organs. Through the stimulation of these points with acupuncture, massage, moxibustion, or qigong exercises, a person who is ill can regulate and balance their qi to maintain or regain health.

When the energy pathways are not able to function and regulate the qi properly, pathogenic influences can follow the energy pathways into the organs. Similarly, when the organs are diseased, the body will manifest signs of illness externally through the energy pathways.

There are two primary functions for the energy pathways. First, they conduct regular patterns of physiological activities when the body is functioning in a normal state. Secondly, they systematically reflect symptoms of disease when the body is ill. A TCM doctor can decipher the irregular manifestations in the physical body, in order to help with their treatment of the disease.

When the human body is ill or injured, the symptoms which appear will depend upon the condition of qi in the body. During illness, qi generally manifests in two ways: *qi-deficiency* or *qi-stagnation*. *Qi-deficiency* refers to a weakness in the functioning of the body or the organ systems. *Qi-stagnation* refers to a restricted flow of qi in the body. Qi flows throughout the human body. It is suppose to flow unrestricted. If any part of the body is injured, or is ill, a restriction of qi and blood has occurred.

Jing, Qi, Shen

TCM uses the terms *jing (essence-of-life)*, *qi (energy)*, and *shen (spirit)* to theorize and explain the human physiological system. It is believed that these *three treasures* (jing, qi, and shen) are the fundamentals for all facets of life and its many variations. Deficiency in any of the three will influence the others and can result in illness if not replenished or corrected.

Jing or *essence-of-life* is the fundamental material that makes up the human body, the material foundation of life. It is further classified under two categories, *innate-jing* and *acquired-jing*. *Innate-jing* is that which we inherit from our parents. *Acquired-jing* is from food and water converted by the *stomach* and *spleen*, with the excess stored in the *kidneys* along with *innate-jing*. Therefore, what you eat can significantly affect the *jing* in your body which in turn affects your qi and vitality. *Innate-jing* and *acquired-jing* are not separate parts *stored* in the kidneys. They mutually utilize and promote each other. When we are born, *innate-jing* already exists, providing the foundation for *acquired-jing*. After birth, *acquired-jing* is continually nurtured by the *innate-jing* to maintain and develop it functions.

Innate-jing includes reproductive essence or semen — the original substance needed for the construction of the human body. The *jing* stored in the kidneys is also closely related to reproduction and sexual function. *Acquired-jing* from food and water, is the essential substance needed for all human bodily activities and metabolism. *Jing* is continually being used and is also continually being replenished with food and water. Under normal conditions the surplus of *jing* is stored in the kidneys. When *jing* is abundant, then your vitality will be strong and your adaptability to environmental changes will be adequate, to prevent illness. When *jing* is deficient, then your vitality will be weak and immunity to illness will be impaired.

Qi, generally speaking, is the intrinsic substance that makes up the cosmos, and produces all things through its movements and variations. The physiological definition of qi in TCM is the *intrinsic substance* that flows in the human body and is the impelling force for all activities. Qi includes the energy derived from the air, food, and water, as well as, the innate energy source we inherit from our parents. The existence of qi is felt indirectly and manifested as a result of the body's interactions within its integral parts and with its surroundings.

Qi in the human body is classified according to the source of the qi. *Innate-qi* comes from our parents. It is the energy source that we inherit from our parents when we are born. It is converted from *innate-jing*. *Acquired-qi* is converted from food, water, and air. The combination of *innate-qi* with *acquired-qi* is further classified as *genuine-qi*, serving as the dynamic force of all vital human functions. Because qi distributes in different parts of the body, it is further classified into different categories to explain the function of qi in different areas of the body.

The general term for these different types of qi, whether it is from *innate-qi* and/or *acquired-qi* sources, is called *vital-qi*. It is the cumulative term describing the human ability to defend against *pathogenic influences* that cause dis-ease. That is, the ability of the human body to ward off diseases depends on the abundance or lack of *vital-qi* in the body. The basic premise of qigong training is to remove stagnation and balance qi, and to build and strengthen *vital-qi*.

Qi is not visible to the untrained eye. Many gifted individuals and qigong practitioners are able to see a manifestation of qi as an aura. Even though most people are unable to see the qi, everyone can feel the qi. Qi can be felt as warmth, coolness, tingling, and magnetic repulsion sensations.

Shen, loosely translates as *spirit*, is explained in TCM as mental faculties; and the expression of one's *vitality of spirit*. It is closely related to the function of the *heart*. It is the individual's expression of consciousness and living activities. Shen is derived from *innate-jing*, and relies on *acquired-jing* and qi for nourishment to maintain its function. It is the most important component of the human system. When shen is abundant, then the body will be strong, and all the human systems will function harmoniously. When shen is scattered, then all the human functions will be debilitated. Shen is the cumulative term for the expression of one's vitality, as well as, the reflection or manifestation of the functions within the human body.

The condition of one's *vitality of spirit*, is also an expression of one's emotional state. Emotional disturbances can in turn cause energetic changes in the human body. One's vitality of spirit is an important factor that can influence one's health, recovery from disease, or can impede body functions. A stable emotional state and positive state of mind can maintain health and speed recovery. Whereas a low vitality of spirit and a constant bombardment of emotional disturbances will cause a scattering or stagnation of energy. Constant prolonged emotional disturbances manifest itself as physical dis-eases.

Causes of Illnesses

TCM believes that the vitality of spirit is influenced by 7 emotions — joy, anger, pensiveness, worry, sorrow, shock, and fear. Since emotions are closely related to the energetics and functions of the organs, any prolonged excessive emotional state can cause disease in the organ systems. It is stated in the *Yellow Emperor's Internal Classic* that "excessive anger damages the liver, excessive joy damages the heart, excessive pensiveness damages the spleen, excessive sorrow damages the lungs, and excessive fear damages the kidneys." Also, "excessive anger causes qi to rise, excessive joy causes qi to retard, excessive sorrow cause qi to diminish, excessive fear cause qi to fall, excessive shock cause qi to scatter, and excessive pensiveness causes qi to stagnate." In TCM, the emphasis is placed more on the various physiological functions of an organ, rather than on its anatomical structure, because one of the main causes of disease is that of emotional trauma, which results in a malfunctioning of the internal organs.

Emotional trauma is considered an internal cause of disease. It falls under one of the three categories of the causes of disease: the exogenous (external), the endogenous (internal), and those that are neither exogenous nor endogenous. The exogenous causes of disease refer mainly to excessive atmospheric influences; namely the wind, cold, summer heat, dampness, dryness, and fire. That is, if our body can't effectively adapt to the changing seasons, our body's energy flow will be unbalanced and illness can result. The endogenous causes of disease refer mainly to excessive emotional trauma; namely the excesses of joy, anger, pensiveness, worry, sorrow, fear, and shock. The third cause of disease refers to diseases that are from neither external nor internal influences, such as overworking, excessive drinking, overeating, and unregulated sexual activities. Excesses of any of the pathogens can influence the circulation of qi and blood to the internal organs and can cause disease.

The Yin-Yang and Five Element Theories

In an attempt to understand and describe the phenomenon of the universe, ancient Chinese philosophers, astrologers, and doctors, used the Yin-Yang and Five Element Theories to describe everything in the cosmos. The Yin-Yang and Five Element Theories have been the basic reasoning behind all ancient Chinese natural science. Ancient Chinese believed that the production, the development, and the changes of everything in the cosmos were the result of the interaction of yin-qi and yang-qi. The interaction of yin-qi and yang-qi is also used in the description of the interactions within the fundamental elements. These five symbolic elements are Wood, Fire, Earth, Metal, and Water which make up the universe. Table 1-1 shows the classifications of the human body and nature in the Five Elements.

The basic theory behind the five elements can be summed up by two normal and three adverse interactions. Mutual Nourishment (interpromoting) and Mutual Restraint (interacting), are normal cyclic patterns. Mutual Over-Restraint (encroachment), Reverse-Restraint (violating), and Mutual Burdening are the adverse conditions. By understanding the cyclic patterns in the human

FIVE ELEMENTS		WOOD	FIRE	EARTH	METAL	WATER
HUMAN BODY	**Emotions**	Anger	Joy	Pensiveness	Sorrow	Fear
	Anatomy	Tendons	Blood Vessels	Muscles	Skin & Hair	Bones
	Specific Openings	Eyes	Tongue	Mouth	Nose	Ears
	Bowels	Gall Bladder	Small Intestine	Stomach	Large Intestine	Urinary Bladder
	Viscera	Liver	Heart	Spleen	Lungs	Kidneys
NATURE	**Directions**	East	South	Center	West	North
	Seasons	Spring	Summer	Late Summer	Autumn	Winter
	Weather	Wind	Hot	Wet	Dry	Cold
	Develop-Ments	Production	Growth	Transforma-tion	Harvest	Storage
	Colors	Green	Red	Yellow	White	Black
	Tastes	Sour	Bitter	Sweet	Spicy	Salty

Table 1-1

organs (elements) and the possible adverse conditions, the illness of one organ can also indicate problems in the corresponding organs.

Mutual Nourishment refers to the cyclic enhancement or interpromoting pattern of the Five Elements. In this normal cycle, each element gives and receives nourishment in the cyclic pattern. Mutual Restraint refers to the cyclic neutralizing of the elements in order to keep each other in check and balance. Mutual Nourishment and Restraint cycles are not independent cycles. They interact with each other and are closely related. Drawing 1-3 is a typical representation of the normal cyclic interactions of the Five Elements.

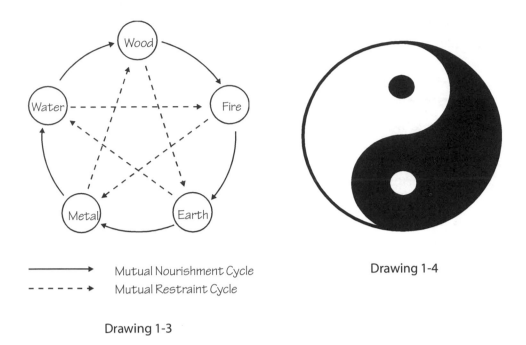

Mutual Nourishment Cycle
Mutual Restraint Cycle

Drawing 1-4

Drawing 1-3

Everything in the great cosmos contains many linkages. Any object that has any type of interaction with another object, and within itself, has an opposing, yet interdependent nature. This opposing, yet interdependent nature, is due to the interaction of *yin* and *yang*. The Yin-Yang philosophy is a means to understand and grasp the laws of nature. It is the empirical reasoning for the production, development, and perishing of all things in the great cosmos.

Drawing 1-4 is the most commonly used symbol to represent the yin-yang philosophy. This symbol is known as *Taiji* — the grand ultimate. The big enclosed circle symbolizes the *whole* universe. The curvature within the circle symbolizes the opposing, yet interdependent nature of yin and yang. The black (yin) and the white (yang) tear drop shapes symbolize the decreasing and increasing of yin and yang, as well as, the transformation of yin and yang. At the highest concentration of yang there is a black dot, and at the highest concentration of yin, there is a white dot. The dots symbolize that yin and yang are not absolute. They are not only interdependent, but there are subdivisions of yin and yang within yin and within yang.

The Yin-Yang Theory is primarily used to describe the opposing, interdependent, waxing and waning, and transformational nature of all things in the cosmos. The Five Element Theory is primarily used to explain characteristics, classifications, and the law of mutual nourishment and mutual restraint. In the practical applications of Yin-Yang and the Five Elements, they are used in conjunction with one another.

Human physiology, and the causes and development of diseases are also within the Yin-Yang and Five Element Theories. In the Spring-Autumn and Warring Kingdom periods in China (8th-3rd Century B.C.), the Yin-Yang and Five Element philosophy was appended into Chinese medicine to describe human physiology, illness, herbal characteristics, and the relationship between humans and nature. This effectively guided the diagnostic and healing processes and became an important component of Chinese medicine.

In TCM, yin-yang also refers to the various antitheses in the human body which occur in the anatomy, physiology, pathology, diagnosis and treatment. For example, the material aspect of the body is yin, and the functional aspect of the body is yang. The five elements are used in TCM to expound on the unity of the human body and the environment, and the physiological and pathological relationship between the human internal organs.

Contents in Book 1

Qigong methods for self-healing involve the training of an individual's qi and/or receiving external qi, to regulate unbalanced qi or to strengthen qi. Medical Qigong methods target at balancing yin-yang, smoothing out the qi pathways, harmonizing qi and blood, regulating the organ functions, and strengthening *vital-qi* to prevent pathogenic influences from affecting the body's energetic balance.

Book 1, begins with an introduction of relaxation methods in Section 1.2. It is followed by Qi Permeating Technique in Section 1.3., which work on absorbing the *pure essence* of the universe into the body and discharging all the impurities from the body. In Section 1.4., we will present Medical Qigong practices to maintain, heal, and rejuvenate the functions of the organs. This section also includes Healing Sounds for Life Nourishing; and Lying Down and Walking Qigong. Section 1.5. includes a list of suggested qigong practices for healing specific illnesses.

1.2. Learn to Relax

In our daily lives, during leisure, study, or work, our mind is constantly receiving new signals that require processing and reprocessing. These signals can result in different levels of tension or stress that is stored in different parts of our body, especially our head. Our body also goes through different types of physical stress and strain that may lead to the stiffness of muscles. The relaxation required in qigong practice is an active relaxation of the mind and body, not limpness or lifelessness.

Mental relaxation requires that the mind reach a *calm abiding state* of being. That is, to reduce the constant bombardment of thoughts flooding our mind. This requires a high level of mental control that can only be attained through practice. To attain mental control, we can indirectly train our mind, by regulating our body and breathing with our mind. This will take our mind away from distracting thoughts, while gaining better control of our mind.

It does not matter whether you are practicing qigong, Taijiquan (Tai Chi Chuan), or any other internal healing art, it is imperative that you first learn how to *relax*. The better you are at relaxing, the greater benefits you will attain from your practice. In our relaxation training, you will need to coordinate the positioning of your body and breathing, with your mind. The body must also be natural to attain relaxation. If your body posture is awkward, then it will be difficult to attain total relaxation.

1. BASIC RELAXATION TECHNIQUE

The Basic Relaxation Technique *(Fangsong Gong)* is especially effective for helping people with *deficient-yin accompanied with excess-fire*, and people with high blood pressure. It is also helpful for relaxing nervous tension from the pressure of work, and to regain a vitality of spirit. Fangsong Gong will also set a foundation for your other qigong training.

We will be using exhalations to assist our mental and physical relaxation. During inhalation, the body is in a *condensing* mode. This makes it difficult for the body to relax. During exhalation, the body is in an *expanding* mode. This makes it easier for the body to relax. Also, physiologically speaking, during an inhalation, the intercostal muscles and diaphragm must contract to raise the ribs. During an exhalation, the intercostal muscles and the diaphragm naturally relax and return to the uncontracted position, making it easier for the body to relax.

Preparation:

Posture: Sit comfortably on a chair with your hands placed naturally on your knees (Figure 1-1), or with your hands overlapping and thumbs touching each other (Figure 1-2). Men should have their left hand on top and women should have their right hand on top.

Visualization:

Step 1. With your eyes closed, sit for about three minutes. While exhaling direct the mind to relax the entire body, one section at a time. Begin from your head (eyes, ears, nose, mouth, ...) and pay special attention to your eye bridge area (*Yintang*). Relax your hands, your chest, your abdomen, your thighs, and down to the top of your feet.

Figure 1-1   Figure 1-2

Then relax the back of your head, relax your back, relax your waist, relax your hips, relax the back of your thighs, and relax the bottom of your feet. Repeat the exercise a few more times until you feel light, relaxed, and comfortable.

Step 2. Next simply think of the word *song*, or pronounce the word *song* softly as you exhale and spread *song* all over your body. Feel your body and energy channels, immersing and melting into a tranquil comfortable state.

The word *song*, literally means loose. It is pronounced, first with your teeth gently touching each other and with your tongue pressing gently on your teeth as you release the air in your lungs from your mouth, making a *sssss...* sound. Then separate your teeth and allow the air to exit from both your mouth and nose making a *ong...* sound that resonates like a bell.

Key Points:

A. If you should find that some areas are not easy to relax, don't be overly concerned, go on to the next area. With practice you will gradually be able to relax your entire body.

B. If you should feel that some areas of your body are tingling, itching, are warm, or your muscles contract slightly, or you see flashing lights during the training, don't worry. These are natural qi reactions called *qigan* — qi sensations.

C. Usually after this qigong training, you will have a peaceful, relaxing sleep. Some people, however, when they first begin their training, are energized and can't fall asleep. If this should happen to you, lay down on your bed and do this Relaxation Technique. This should help you fall asleep.

D. If your eye lids should twitch and they are unable to stop moving, you should open your eyes for a while, then close your eyes halfway and continue the training.

E. If you should feel any discomfort during training, check your posture and make any necessary adjustments until you feel comfortable. Make sure that you are not leaning, your waist is relaxed, your shoulders are down, and your hands are placed comfortably in place.

2. RELAXING THE BODY AND CALMING THE MIND

Relaxing the Body and Calming the Mind Technique *(Song Jing Jianshen Gong)* is a more advanced relaxation technique that relaxes the body by mentally relaxing the acupuncture points. It is especially beneficial if practiced before the Stomach and Spleen Qigong, and Liver Qigong in Section 1.4. This technique is also a way to calm the mind by lowering unsteady and scattered energy.

Preparation:

Posture: This technique can be trained while sitting, standing, or lying down. In a sitting position, place your feet flat on the floor with your palms resting on the inside corner of your knees without touching. The *laogong* points on your palms should be on top of your *xuehai* point.

In a standing position, allow your arms to hang naturally at your sides. In a reclined position, lay on your back with your arms at your sides and palms facing down.

Visualization:

Step 1. Use Drawing 1-5 to locate the points. Mentally relax the points and areas by focusing on the word *song*, starting from your *baihui*, to *Yintang*, to both *jianjing*, to *shanzhong*, to *dantian*, to *huiyin*, to *yinlingquan*, to *sanyinjiao*, to *yongquan*, to your big toe, to your second toe, to your third toe, to your fourth toe, and to your small toe.

Then continue in the same direction around your feet and bring your mind back to your *yongquan* points. Imagine that you are standing on top of two wells, one foot on each well, with your *yongquan* points touching the top of the water.

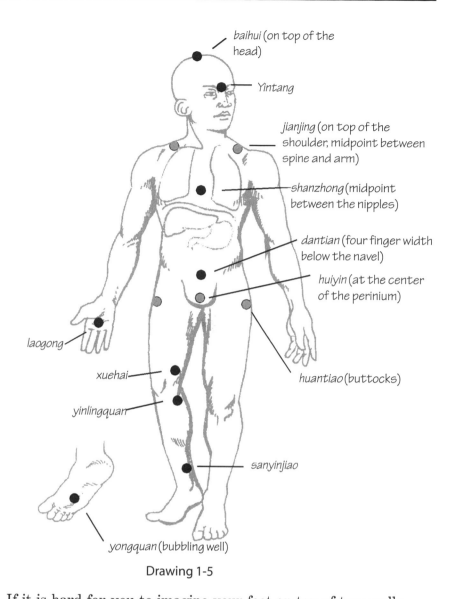

baihui (on top of the head)

Yintang

jianjing (on top of the shoulder, midpoint between spine and arm)

shanzhong (midpoint between the nipples)

dantian (four finger width below the navel)

huiyin (at the center of the perinium)

laogong

xuehai

yinlingquan

huantiao (buttocks)

sanyinjiao

yongquan (bubbling well)

Drawing 1-5

Step 2. If it is hard for you to imagine your feet on top of two wells, bring your mind up from your *yongquan* points along the inside of your legs, up to *yinlingquan*, to *huantiao*, to *huiyin*, to *mingmen*, to your *dantian*. Then follow the previous path down to your *huiyin*, to *yinlingquan*, to *sanyinjiao*, to *yongquan*, to your big toe, to your second toe, to your third toe, to your fourth toe, to your small toe. Then circle along the edges of your feet and bring your mind back to your *yongquan* points.

Then imagine that you are standing on top of two wells, one foot on each well, with your *yongquan* points touching the top of the water. If you are still unable to focus your mind on this imagery, repeat Step 2 a few more times.

1.3. Qi Permeating Technique

Qi Permeating Technique *(Guanqifa)* utilizes the movements of the arms to assist in leading the qi throughout the body. Its goal is to achieve a harmonious relationship between mind, body, and qi. The movements of the arms are used to assist the mind in directing the circulation of qi. The intent is to channel the *pure essence* of the universe into the body through the *baihui* point, and to drain out the *impurities* from the body. Many older people often have energy pathways with qi that are scattered and unbalanced. Their *Upper Burner* is too stuffy and has stagnating qi; and their *Lower Burner* is deficient in *vital-qi*. The first stage of qigong training is to reverse this condition. That is, to raise the *vital-qi* and to eliminate the stagnate qi. This will correct scattered energy and make it circulate smoothly in the body. Qi Permeating Technique is an excellent way for the beginner to attain smoother energy. Once the qi in the body is flowing smoothly, you will have a solid foundation for furthering your qigong training.

When training Qi Permeating Technique, your sensations of qi will be heightened. Sensations such as tingling, heat, slight sweating, or qi movements along the specific pathways, may be felt. Most people will feel a warm or heat sensation. Some people may have a cool sensation. When you lead the qi down, you may also feel the bottom of your feet, the *yongquan (bubbling well)* points, have a sensation of heat or coolness. These are all good sensations and are normal.

Qi Permeating Technique is capable of smoothing out the channels in the entire body. The goal is to have all the energy pathways flowing smoothly. Once this is accomplished, all illnesses can be eliminated. It can be trained while standing, sitting, or lying down. The arms need not move during practice. Simply use your mind to lead the qi as described. Your breathing should be natural.

Before learning this exercise, familiarize yourself with the areas involved in this exercise. They are: *baihui*, on the top of your head; *dantian*, slightly below your navel; *huiyin*, at the perineum — the area in front of your anus; *yongquan (bubbling well)*, two-thirds of the way up the center line of the foot from your heel; *mingmen*, on your back directly behind your belly button; *huantiao*, around the middle of your buttocks; and *laogong*, on your palm where your middle finger touches when holding a fist. Once you have located these areas don't be overly concerned with pinpointing them exactly, during the qigong exercise. What is important is to *sense* these areas with your mind.

Preparation and Movements:

Preparation: Stand with your feet shoulder width apart. Grip the ground gently with your big toe and your second toe. Place your palms naturally at your sides. Bend your knees slightly. Keep your

| Figure 1-3 | Figure 1-4 | Figure 1-5 |

body erect. Your *baihui*, *huiyin* points and the midpoint between your *mingmen* points should all line up in a vertical line.

Your nose and your navel should also be vertically aligned. Relax your body, especially the *huiyin* point. Close your eyes slightly, leaving only a small gap. Stand like this and breathe naturally, until your mind is calm and your breathing is steady (Figure 1-3).

Movements: Raise both hands over your head, with your *laogong* points pointing at your *baihui* point (Figure 1-4). Lower your palms in front of your body slowly (Figure 1-5). Continue lowering your palms until they are next to your sides as in Figure 1-3. As you do the visualization described below, move your arms slightly ahead of the points or path of your visualization.

Visualization:

Step 1. Front Path (Drawing 1-6): Use your mind to lead the qi down from your *baihui*, imagine that the *pure essence* of the universe is filling your body. Divide into two paths, down past your ears and meet at your throat. Again, divide into two paths, down past your collar bones, to your nipples and meet at your navel.

Continue down to your *dantian* and then to your *huiyin*. Then separate into two paths, down the inside of your legs; imagining that all your stress and tension are being led down through your *bubbling wells*, and three feet into the ground.

When your arms are hanging down naturally at your sides, relax completely from your head down to your toes (Relax your

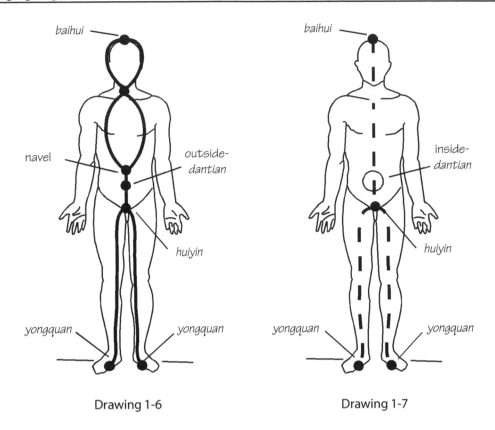

Drawing 1-6   Drawing 1-7

hair, forehead, back of your head, ears, nose, mouth, chin, neck, shoulder, chest, back, stomach, waist, thighs, knees, calves, heels, feet, toes, shoulders, arms, wrists, palms, fingers, and your organs). Swallow your saliva and hold for 5-10 seconds in this relaxed state.

Repeat Step 1, two more times.

Step 2. Middle Path (Drawing 1-7): Use your mind to lead the qi down from your *baihui*, imagine that the *pure essence* of the universe is filling your body. Lead the qi through your head, down the middle of your body, through your organs and *dantian* until your *huiyin*.

Then separate into two paths down through the bone marrows of your legs; imagining that all your stress and tension are being led down through your *bubbling wells*, and three feet into the ground.

When your arms are hanging down naturally at your sides, relax completely from your head down to your toes (Relax your hair, forehead, back of your head, ears, nose, mouth, chin, neck,

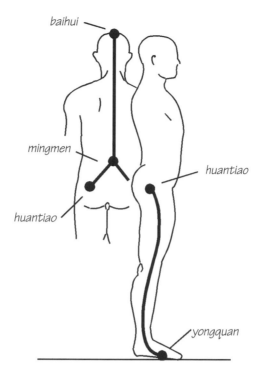

baihui

mingmen

huantiao

huantiao

yongquan

Drawing 1-8

shoulder, chest, back, stomach, waist, thighs, knees, calves, heels, feet, toes, shoulders, arms, wrists, palms, fingers, and your organs). Swallow your saliva and hold for 5-10 seconds in this relaxed state.

Repeat Step 2, two more times.

Step 3. Back Path (Drawing 1-8): Use your mind to lead the qi down from your *baihui*, imagine that the *pure essence* of the universe is filling your body. Lead the qi down the back of your head to your neck, down along your spine, until your *mingmen*.

Then separate into two paths across your *huantiao*; imagining that all your stress and tension are being led down along the sides of your legs through your *bubbling wells*, and three feet into the ground.

When your arms are hanging down naturally at your sides. Relax completely from your head down to your toes (Relax your hair, forehead, back of your head, ears, nose, mouth, chin, neck, shoulder, chest, back, stomach, waist, thighs, knees, calves, heels, feet, toes, shoulders, arms, wrists, palms, fingers, and your organs). Swallow your saliva and hold for 5-10 seconds in this relaxed state.

Repeat Step 3, two more times.

Key Points:

A. People who have high blood pressure shouldn't raise their hands too slowly over their head, but should lower their hands as slowly as possible. People with low blood pressure should raise their hands slower, but lower their hands a little quicker.

People with normal blood pressure, should follow a comfortable pace. As a general guide, the pace of your arm movement, should be comfortable and slow enough to be able to *sense* the points with your mind.

B. As an alternative, beginners may wish to simplify the visualization process into two stages in the following way:

1. Use your mind to lead the qi down from your *baihui*, down the Front, Middle, or Back path.

2. Next, relax completely from your head down to your toes, and imagine the *pure essence* of the universe is permeating throughout your body. Then imagine all the impurities are draining out of your legs through your *bubbling wells*, and three feet into the ground.

C. Breath naturally; don't be concerned with abdominal breathing. You may keep your eyes closed, open, or half closed during this practice.

D. Each time, practice nine qi permeating cycles of one path. When you are smooth with all three paths individually, you can practice all three paths together for a total of nine times, three times with each path.

E. You can practice as often as you wish, morning or evening. The morning, however, is the best time to practice.

F. Don't practice when you are too hungry, too full, or too tired. People with low blood pressure or people who are too hungry, may feel dizzy during practice. If this happens, stop training, sit down for a while, and drink some warm water.

G. After completing nine cycles, raise your heels off the floor, drop them down, stomping the floor. This will provide a gentle vibration throughout your body.

H. When you hold for 5-10 seconds in a relaxed state, breath naturally. As an alternative, you may place your mind on an area of your body that is ill to enhance its healing.

1.4. Health Maintenance Qigong

Health Maintenance Qigong *(Baojian Qigong)* is also known as Medical Restorative Qigong *(Yiliao Qigong)*. Health Maintenance Qigong can maintain health for healthy individuals and prevent illness. It is also capable of helping ill individuals to regain health. The following exercises are all traditional techniques with only slight modifications. The effectiveness of Health Maintenance Qigong has been well documented by many qigong masters, qigong centers, and health organizations in China. These techniques are relatively simple. Once you learn them, you can teach your family and friends so that everyone can benefit. Many of the exercises are described from a standing position. By following the same basic training guidelines, you may sit on a chair to do the exercises and attain the same benefits.

The Qigong techniques in this section require a general knowledge of the acupuncture chart and points. We have provided reference drawings in the description. The more familiar you are with the charts and points, the easier it will be to learn the technique. However, it is not necessary to be very specific on locating the energy pathways or points. A general location will suffice. You may also refer to Appendix A for a complete set of charts and points.

1. LUNG QIGONG

According to TCM, the lungs are not only responsible for respiration, they are also responsible for maintaining normal water metabolism. Normal water circulation, especially that of the urinary bladder is made possible by the downward drive of qi from the lungs. The lungs are also responsible for supplying the skin with nutrients and superficial resistance to pathogenic influences. Diseases of the lungs make people perspire spontaneously and more vulnerable to colds. The lungs have their specific opening in the nose.

Since the skin and hair are the outer most layer of your body, they are the protective layers to fend against pathogenic influences of the environment. When the *lung-qi* is abundant, then the *guardian-qi* will also be abundant, which in turn can protect against pathogenic influences of the environment, and improve the body's immunity.

Most of the energy generated from metabolism is used up during our daily routines, with only a small portion of the energy stored for emergencies. If the storage of energy is not kept up, the balance of *yin-yang* in the human body can easily be disrupted when the individual is overtired, injured, or attacked by pathogenic influences.

An average person only uses a fraction of their lung cells in regular breathing. With the practice of Lung Qigong, you will increase the usage of your lungs, increase your oxygen intake, thus increasing your energy intake from breathing. When the intake of energy is more than what is needed to maintain normal daily functions, the excess will be stored in your *dantian* to nourish your *original-qi*. When your *original-qi* is full, *yin-yang* will gradually return to a balance and illness can be corrected.

Part 1. Cleansing the Lungs

This Qigong technique is used for healing emphysema, asthma, gastroptosis, and a prolapse of the uterus.

Movement and Intention:

Step 1. Stand with your feet shoulder width apart, head and body upright, eyes look straight ahead, and arms placed naturally at your sides. Then overlap both hands on top of your *dantian* (Figure 1-6).

Men, keep your left hand on your *dantian*, with your right hand on top of your left hand. Women, keep your right hand on your *dantian*, with your left hand on top of your right hand.

Step 2. Press gently on your *dantian* as you exhale and draw your abdomen in. As you exhale, bend your upper body forward. Use your mind to imagine that you are touching your abdomen to your back (Figure 1-7). Then straighten your body and breathe in naturally. Repeat 3 times.

Step 3. From an upright position, lean back slightly as you extend both arms slightly back while inhaling (Figure 1-8). When extending your arms back, expand your lungs as much as possible, then hold your breath for as long as you can. Then return to the upright position as you exhale all the impurities from your mouth.

Key Points:

A. In Step 2, your intent is placed on exhalation only, inhale naturally. Physically, the bending movement is directly stimulating the diaphragm to improve its *elasticity*. If you have poor balance, you should do this exercise sitting down.

B. In Step 3, the abdomen draws in during inhalation, where as, in Step 1, the abdomen draws in during exhalation.

C. In Step 3, hold up your *huiyin* area slightly as you inhale, but do not sink your qi to your *dantian*. Push up with your head slightly. Inhale from your nose and exhale through your mouth. Physically, this

Figure 1-6

Figure 1-7

Figure 1-8

exercise stimulates the lungs to an elevated state. It trains you to use more of your lungs.

D. Don't overextend your body when leaning back. Only lean to the point that you do not tense up or lose your balance.

Part 2. Strengthening the Lungs

This technique is for strengthening the respiratory and cardiovascular systems, increasing the efficiency of the lungs, moisturizing the skin, preventing colds, and smoothing bowel movements. It can also strengthen the abdominal muscles which in turn, would allow the blood circulation of your lower body to smoothly return to your heart and increase your heart's pumping effectiveness, and help prevent varicose veins.

After training for a while, your saliva generation will increase. When you feel saliva filling your mouth, swallow it as if you were swallowing food down to your stomach. Then use your mind to lead your qi to your *dantian*. Often times you will feel your stomach growling, sensations of heat flowing down your legs, and a very comfortable feeling in your chest. This will increase *original-qi* significantly.

Movement and Intention:

Step 1. Sit comfortably on a chair. Gently press your index and middle fingers of your right hand on the pulse area of your left wrist (Figure 1-9 or 1-10). Gently press your tongue to the roof of your mouth and relax your chest. Breathe in deeply through your nose until your abdomen is raised, then hold your breath and count your pulse for 20 to 40 times (the number of times depends on your condition).

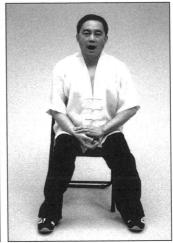

Figure 1-9   Figure 1-10

Then lower your tongue and make a round shape with your mouth and exhale. As you exhale through your mouth, draw your stomach in, and focus on or say the word *song*. After exhaling all you can, inhale again and repeat the exercise. Each time, train only 3 to 5 breathing cycles. Do this exercise once in the morning and once in the evening. After three months of training, go on to the next exercise.

Step 2. After training Step 1 for a period of time, you should feel that your breathing pattern is getting smoother and that you are able to do ordinary exercise or work without a shortness of breath. If so, then you can start training Step 2.

From the same sitting and hand position as in Step 1, inhale until your abdomen is raised, then inhale a little more by raising your chest (abdomen and chest breathing). After inhaling to the maximum, hold your breath and count your pulse. After a period of training, you will be able to hold your breath for 100 to 140 pulses or more.

When you can no longer hold your breath, open your mouth wide and make a soft *ha* sound as you exhale all the impurities from your mouth. After exhaling all you can, repeat the exercise. Do three breathing cycles each time you train. Train once in the morning and once in the evening.

44

Key Points:

A. People with cardiovascular problems, and people that are weak and old, should not practice holding the breath right away. These individuals should first practice deep inhalation and slow exhalation breathing. Deep inhalation and slow exhalation is accomplished by first calming your mind and bringing your attention to your *dantian* area. Then breathe in and out slowly. Find out the rate of your breathing. An average person breaths about 18 to 20 cycles per minute.

B. Train 3 to 5 minutes each time. With the practice of deep inhalations and slow exhalations, you can gradually decrease the rate of your breathing down to 6 to 12 cycles per minute. When you can reduce your breathing rate to between 6 to 12 cycles per minute and feel comfortable doing it, then gradually include short periods of holding your breath. In about 3 months, you should be ready to do Step 1.

Part 3. Si Sound for Nourishing the Lungs

Movement and Intention:

Step 1. Use Drawing 1-9 as a reference. Stand (or sit) with your feet shoulder width apart, and arms to your sides (Figure 1-11). Pay attention to your exhalation three times, to remove the impurities from your lungs.

Then take a deep breath. When you take a deep breath, use your mind to lead the qi from the universe into your body and down to the *lidui* point on the lateral side of the tip of your second toe. This is also the last point on the Stomach Channel.

Step 2. Hold your breath. Raise your hands up in front of your body, with your hands facing up, and the fingers pointing toward each other. As your hands reach your *shanzhong* point, midway between your nipples (Figure 1-12), rotate your palms until they are facing out.

As you raise your hands, use your mind to lead the qi from your second toe up the Liver Channel, starting from *dadun*, to *taichong*, along the inside of your legs, to *jimai*, to *zhangmen*, to *qimen*, and then enter into your lungs.

Step 3. Exhale, and begin making the *Si (Sssssss)* sound. At the same time, push your arms to the sides as you hold up your *huiyin* area and bring your abdomen in (Figure 1-13).

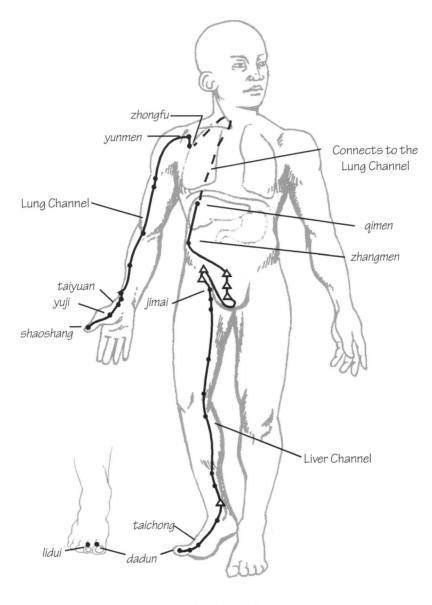

Drawing 1-9

As you make the *Si* sound, lead the impurities out of your lungs through your mouth and the Lung Channel passing *zhongfu, yunmen,* along your arms, to *taiyuan,* to *yuji,* and out of your *shaoshang* point on the medial corner of your thumbnail.

Repeat Steps 1 to 3, 6 times.

Figure 1-11

Figure 1-12

Figure 1-13

2. KIDNEY QIGONG

According to TCM, the kidneys are in charge of growth, development, reproduction, urinary functions, and store the *essence-of-life (jing)*. The kidneys not only have a leading role in maintaining the fluid balance of the body, but are also responsible for the condition of the bone and marrow, activities of the brain, and hearing. This is based on the belief that bones are nourished by *jing* which is derived from the kidneys. The kidneys are the foundation of one's innate constitution and physiologically relate to one's memory and will.

Normal kidney function can also be affected by excess fear. The kidneys have their specific opening in the ears. Therefore, healthy kidneys can ensure good hearing. Kidneys also have their specific openings in the urinogenital orifice and the anus. Therefore, chronic diarrhea, urinary problems, and premature ejaculations are also related to the condition of the kidneys. A darkening of one's complexion is usually seen in severe and chronic cases of blood stasis, accompanied by chills, and lowered vital functioning of the kidneys.

TCM also states that if either the kidneys, lungs, or spleen are deficient in *vital-qi*, then the *guardian-qi* (energy field on the surface of the body) will also be deficient. The body's immunity will be reduced and begin to affect other organs. About 400 years ago, during the Ming Dynasty (1368-1644 A.D.), medical expert, Dr. Qi Shi said, "Curing a deficiency starts from the three roots: kidneys, lungs, and spleen." A deficiency in *kidney-jing* will affect your growth and the development of your body. A deficiency in *kidney-qi* will also affect your hearing and cause a shortness of energy. The improper regulation of sexual activities will deplete your *jing* and cause eventual loss of sexual organ function and frequent urination will occur. If you are deficient in *kidney-yin*, your vision will deteriorate; and dizziness, ringing in the ears, weight loss, sweating during sleep, and/or nocturnal emission will occur.

Figure 1-14   Figure 1-15

If you are deficient in *kidney-yang*, then your *life-fire* will be deficient. Your vitality of spirit will be low, you'll tire easily. Your limbs may get cold and you may be afraid of cold. There may be pain and coldness in your waist area. Men may not be able to get an erection. Women may feel coldness in their womb. Practicing Elevating the Kidneys and Strengthening the Kidneys can help cure many kidney related illnesses.

Part 1. Elevating the Kidneys

This technique is especially good for curing an inflammation of the urinary bladder, kidney stones, urine containing blood, womb bleeding, frequent urination, and nocturnal emission.

Preparation and Movements:

Step 1. Sit straight with your feet touching the floor about a shoulder width apart. Sit with only one-third of your hips on the chair. Don't lean back on the chair with your back. Place your hands naturally on top of your knees (Figure 1-14).

As an alternative, you may stand with your feet shoulder width apart and with your hands overlapping on your dantian (Figure 1-15)

Step 2. Place your mind at your *huiyin* area. Exhale slowly, draw in and hold up your *huiyin* area slightly. Inhale slowly and release the *huiyin* area as you push your stomach out.

Key Points:

A. The *huiyin* area refers to the testicles, vas deferens, penis and the anus muscles for men; the vulva, vagina, clitoris, and the anus muscles for women.

B. This technique can be trained at any time. However, do not train more than 20 circles at a time. After each set, rest for a while before repeating the training. Too many circles at one time, may cause dizziness for some people.

C. People with high blood pressure should rest after every 5 circles, before resuming the training again.

D. People that have a hard time falling asleep should avoid training this technique at night.

Part 2. Strengthening the Kidneys

This technique takes in the *pure essence* of the universe; and supplements the innate essence in your kidneys. This solidifies the foundation of life and strengthens your *jing*.

Movements and Intention:

Step 1. Sit straight with your feet touching the floor about a shoulder width apart. Sit with only one-third of your hips on the chair. Don't lean back on the chair. Place your hands naturally on top of your knees as in Figure 1-14.

Step 2. Breathe naturally until your *dantian* is full of qi. Exhale slowly, draw in your abdomen and *hold up* the *huiyin* area slightly. At the same time, lead the qi from your *dantian* to your coccyx and up to your *mingmen* point, then separate into two paths around your waist and meet at your navel.

Inhale slowly and release the *huiyin* area as you push your stomach out. At the same time, lead the qi from your navel to your *dantian*.

Key Points:

The same key points as in Elevating the Kidneys technique.

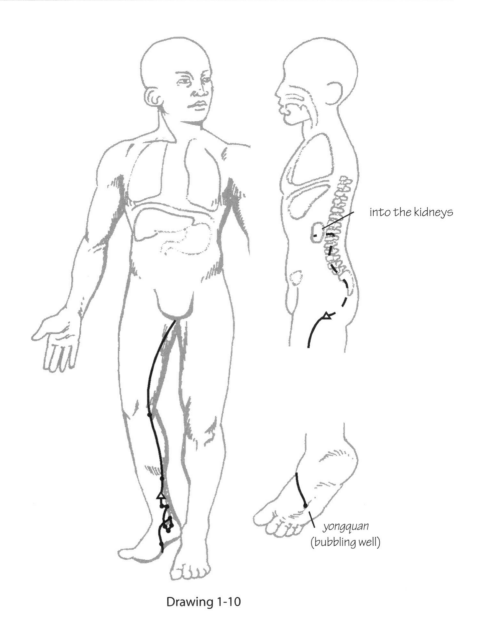

into the kidneys

yongquan
(bubbling well)

Drawing 1-10

Part 3. Chui Sound to Ensure Kidney Health

Movement and Intention:

Step 1. Use Drawing 1-10 as a reference. Stand or sit with your feet shoulder width apart, and arms to your sides (Figure 1-16). Inhale, begin raising your hands up towards your lower back with the back of your hands facing your body (Figure 1-17).

As your hands reach kidney level, bring both hands forward towards your belly button with your fingers pointing down. As

Figure 1-16

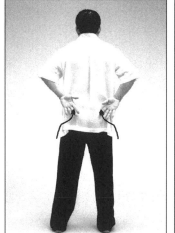

Figure 1-17

Figure 1-18

Figure 1-19

Figure 1-20

you raise your hands, lead the qi up from your *yongquan* points on the bottom of your feet, up along the Kidney Channel on the inside of your legs, into the tailbone, up along the lower part of your spine, and into your kidneys.

Continue the arm movements and bring your arms up in front of your chest (along the Kidney Channel) until they are right below your collar bone and turn your palms to face each other (Figures 1-18 and 1-19).

Step 2. Exhale, make the *Chui* sound by opening your mouth slightly with your tongue drawn in, and the corner of your mouth pulled slightly to the sides. At the same time, squeeze in with your hands as though you were holding a ball, and squat down (Figure 1-20).

Keep your upper body as straight as you can, hold up your *huiyin* area, and pull your abdomen in. As you exhale and make the *Chui* sound, use your mind to lead all the impurities from your kidney channel and kidneys out of your mouth.

After completing Step 2, stand up slowly and repeat Step 1 and 2, a total of 6 times.

3. LIVER QIGONG

According to TCM, the liver is not only responsible for storing blood and regulating the distribution of blood, it also controls the function of the tendons. The bluish discoloration of one's complexion is usually caused by the stagnation and obstruction of blood and qi, indicating the presence of coldness, pain, blood stasis, convulsion or illness of the liver. "The eyes are the specific opening of the liver." Normal eyesight relies on the proper functioning of the liver. "The liver stores one's soul." Patients with liver diseases tend to have dreadful dreams, restlessness, and irritability.

Premature whitening of the hair is also allegedly to be due to insufficient blood stored in the liver and the decreased function of the kidneys. Since blood is made up of food essence and nutrients produced in the spleen and stomach, combined with the *innate-jing* stored in the kidneys, this links the liver and kidneys together. Therefore, the deficiency of either one can affect the other.

Part 1. Easing the Liver

Movements and Intention:

Step 1. Stand (or sit) with your feet shoulder width apart, knees slightly bent, and your hands at your sides. Eyes gently closed, focus your mind, and regulate your breathing . Then overlap your palms on top of your *dantian.* Inhale from your nose and exhale from your mouth, while letting out the *xu* sound as your mind concentrates on your *dantian* (Figure 1-21).

Step 2. Use Drawing 1-11 as a reference. Hold your hands as if you were holding a ball in front of your abdomen (Figure 1-22). Raise your palms up until they are over your *baihui* and imagine that pure energy is entering your body from your *baihui* (Figure 1-23).

Lower your palms in front of your body, passing your eyes, passing your *quepen* point on the Stomach Channel, until your *qimen* point on the Liver Channel (Figure 1-24).

Figure 1-21

Figure 1-22

Figure 1-23

Figure 1-24

Figure 1-25

Figure 1-26

Step 3. Next with your palms on top of your *qimen* points, massage 6 circles in each direction. Press your palms on top of your *qimen* points and bend your body from left to right, 4 times on each side (Figure 1-25).

Step 4. Slide your palms down to your *zhangmen* point and massage 6 circles in each direction (Figure 1-26). Overlap both palms on top of your *dantian*. Then bend your body forward and back, 4 times (Figures 1-27 and 1-28).

Step 5. Then separate your palms and begin moving down along the inside of your legs, on the Liver Channel. Exhale as you bend your body and lower your palms. Your palms should pass your *ququan*, your *taichong*, and your *xingjian* points, and end with

Figure 1-27

Figure 1-28

Figure 1-29

Figure 1-30

your middle finger pointing at your *dadun* point without touching (Figure 1-29 and 1-30). Stay there for a few seconds, then bend your knees slightly, stand up.

Repeat Steps 2 to 5, 3 to 10 times.

Key Points:

A. During training, imagine that your qi is flowing smoothly up and down, your liver is very relaxed, and all discomfort is disappearing.

B. Stay away from frightening or infuriating situations, keep away from alcohol, drink a lot of water, and balance work with rest.

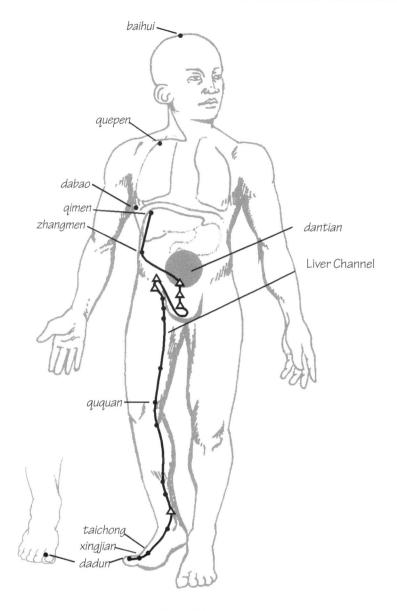

baihui

quepen

dabao

qimen

zhangmen

dantian

Liver Channel

ququan

taichong
xingjian
dadun

Drawing 1-11

Part 2. Xu Sound to Calm the Liver

Movement and Intention:

Step 1. Stand naturally, overlap your hands on top of your abdomen. Men place your left *laogong* point on top of your *dantian*, women with right hand on top of your *dantian*, as in Figure 1-21.

Step 2. Use Drawing 1-11 as a reference. Inhale, use your mind to lead qi from the *dadun* point, on your Liver Channel, along the inside

Figure 1-31

of your thighs, past the reproductive organs, and up to *zhangmen*, then to *qimen*.

Step 3. Exhale, open your eyes wide, but mentally look into your liver, and let out the *Xu (Shuuu...yiii...)* sound as you lean forward slightly (Figure 1-31). At the same time, hold up your *huiyin* area and draw your abdomen in to *squeeze* out the impurities from your liver. Repeat 6 inhalations and exhalations.

4. LYING DOWN AND WALKING QIGONG

This section includes Lying Down and Walking techniques. The Laying Down technique is described in the Chinese medical diagnostic text, *Zhubingyuan Houlun*, written in the Western Jin Dynasty (265-317 A.D.). It is especially beneficial for individuals that can't quench their thirst and have problems urinating. At the completion of the Lying Down technique, the medical text suggests walking after practice, so we have included the traditional Carefree Walking technique in this training.

The Lying Down and Walking Qigong is especially good training for the waist, chest, neck, limbs, muscles, bones, and ligaments. It is also good for strengthening the heart functions, regulating blood circulation, reducing blood pressure, preventing heart diseases, improving digestion, preventing constipation, and assisting in weight loss. The combined training of the Lying Down and Waking Qigong can also effectively prevent diabetes.

In many qigong centers in China, the Lying Down technique and the Carefree Walking techniques have been shown to be very effective for improving the health and strength of individuals that are physically weak. From our experience, the combined practice of the Lying down and the Carefree Walking

Figure 1-32   Figure 1-33

techniques can give a participant even greater benefits. We will present two different types of walking qigong. You can choose the one you like to practice.

Part 1. Lying Down Qigong

Movement and Intention:

Step 1. Loosen your clothing and lie on your back, allow your waist to rise off the bed. Place your arms naturally at your sides, eyes closed, and tongue gently touching the palate of your mouth.

Step 2. Inhale and exhale through your nose with deep, long, fine, and even breaths, 5 times. When you inhale, allow your abdomen to expand.

Step 3. Then circle your tongue between your lips and teeth, 9 circles in each direction. Next, gargle your saliva 18 times and swallow your saliva in a few gulps. Use your mind to lead the *feeling* of the saliva, down to your *dantian*. Remain in the reclined down position for 5 minutes, then stand up and do the next exercise.

Part 2. Walking Qigong - 1

Movement:

When you walk, start by lifting your back heel up and push down gently with your big toe (Figure 1-32). When you step, touch down with your heel first and your toes pointing up, then roll down to the inside edge of your foot, and keep your knees slightly bent (Figure 1-33).

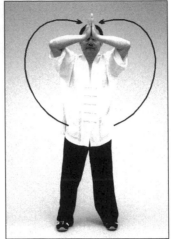

Figure 1-34   Figure 1-35

When walking, use your shoulders movements to move your neck, chest, waist, hips, and arms. Allow your head to sway in the direction of your step. Fingers should be naturally coiled in, rotate your wrist slightly, but keep your *laogong* points facing each other (Figure 1-34).

Intention:

Step 1. Inhale naturally without intention. Exhale, focus on the word *song*, and use your mind to follow your breath down to your *dantian*. Once you are able to control your intention easily, proceed to Step 2, otherwise skip Step 2 and proceed to the *Closing*.

Step 2. Inhale, bring your mind from your *huiyin*, past your *mingmen*, to your *dantian*. Exhale, bring your mind back to your *huiyin*.

Closing:

Step 1. After you have walked for at least 10 minutes, begin doing deep inhalations and exhalations, 24 times. When you exhale, use your mind to lead the qi in your body out of your skin to the farthest reaches of the cosmos. Inhale naturally. Then walk for 4-5 minutes without thinking of breathing or intention.

Step 2. After coming to a stop, stand with your feet about shoulder width apart. Then circle both hands out to your sides and in to your *Yintang* (Figure 1-35). Repeat the arm movements, 3 times.

Step 3. Next rub your hands together until you feel warmth and gently massage your face for about 10 seconds.

Key Points:

A. During training, the mind and body should be free from worry and comfortable. Stay away from fatty foods, excessive sweets, excessive oily foods, and stale food. This way, the benefits of this training can be more effectively attained.

Part 3. Walking Qigong - 2

Movement:

When you walk, sway your arms from one side of your body to the other, coordinating with your step. Sway your arms to your left when you step forward with your left foot. Sway your arms to your right when you step forward with your right foot. Your palms should face down naturally at an angle. This exercise should be done outdoors where the air is fresh. Dress warm.

Intention:

Step 1. Left side: Take two small inhalations as you step forward with your left foot. Exhale once as you step forward with your right foot. Walk for 20 minutes.

Step 2. Right side: Take two small inhalations as you step forward with your right foot. Exhale once as you step forward with your left foot. Walk for 20 minutes.

5. HEART QIGONG

According to TCM, the heart not only controls blood circulation, but it also controls mental activities, including consciousness and thought. Dysfunctions of the heart can cause heart diseases such as insomnia, amnesia, impairment of consciousness, and psychosis. Also, the heart controls the *fire*, and the kidneys control the *water*. Under normal conditions, the fire of the heart comes down to warm the kidneys, and the water of the kidneys rises to cool the heart. If an imbalance occurs, serious fire symptoms of the heart such as fidgeting, palpitation, and insomnia can occur.

"The heart has its outward manifestation in one's complexion." The tongue is the specific opening of the heart. TCM doctors can tell the condition of a patient's heart by the color of their tongues. A dark purple tongue indicates

Figure 1-36   Figure 1-37

blood stasis of the heart, a pale white tongue indicates a blood deficiency of the heart, and an ulcer on the tongue indicates excessive fire of the heart.

Heart Qigong practice can increase the efficiency of the oxygen supply from your heart, increase the adaptability of your heart's pumping requirements, and reduce or slow down the illnesses associated with your heart. The heart corresponds to the element of Fire and the season of Summer. In the summer months, your *heart-fire* may rise and may manifest as excessive swallowing, sores in your mouth, sores on your tongue, and you may become upset easily. These symptoms are generally due to the scorching heat of the summer. If your heart contains excess fire, the symptoms may be a dry throat, thirst, swelling of the chest and rib cage, yellow urine, pangs in the heart region, and pain in the arm pits. If your heart is deficient in *vital-qi*, the symptoms may be heart palpitation, insomnia, night sweats, neurasthenia, and feeling panicky.

Part 1. Ke Sound To Ease the Heart Fire

The traditional Ke Sound Qigong is capable of balancing heart fire. It is especially effective in treating and healing heart diseases.

Movement and Intention:

Step 1. Use Drawing 1-12 as a reference. Inhale naturally and hold your breath. Raise both arms up from your sides, palms face down. Relax your shoulders; keep your wrists and elbows, naturally bent and relaxed (Figure 1-36).

When your arms are even with your shoulders, rotate your palms until they are facing in and circle them towards your chest. Then rotate your palms until the fingers of both hands

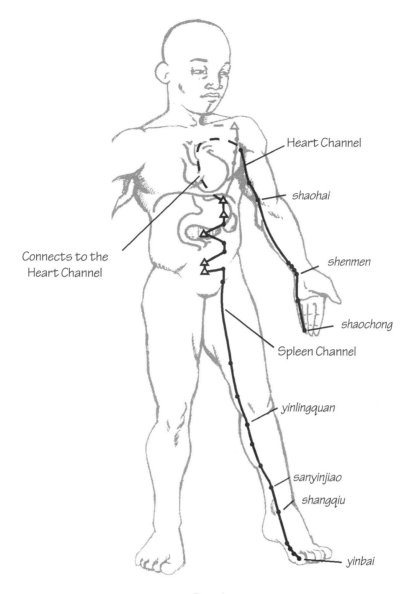

Heart Channel

shaohai

shenmen

shaochong

Connects to the
Heart Channel

Spleen Channel

yinlingquan

sanyinjiao

shangqiu

yinbai

Drawing 1-12

are pointing at each other, without touching, and palms face down (Figure 1-37).

While holding your breath, use your mind to lead qi up from your *yinbai* point on the Spleen Channel, passing through your *shangqiu*, your *sanyinjiao*, and your *yinlingquan* points. Then lead the qi up the inside of your thighs and into your abdomen. Continue up into your Heart Channel.

Step 2. Exhale and vocalize the sound *Ke*, with your mouth half open, tongue touching the bottom of your mouth, and exerting a slight pressure with your jaw. At the same time, lower both palms down until your abdomen level. Hold up your anus area and draw your abdomen in.

During exhalation, lead qi from your Heart Channel through your *shaohai* point, to your *shenmen* point, and out through your *shaochong* point at the tip of your little finger. Exhale out all the impurities in your Heart Channel.

Repeat Steps 1 and 2, 6 times. This completes a set. Do three sets.

Part 2. Strengthening the Lungs Qigong

Refer to the Lung Qigong description.

Part 3. Lying Down and Waking Qigong

Refer to the Lying Down and Walking Qigong description.

6. STOMACH AND SPLEEN QIGONG

The stomach and spleen both provide the material basis for human survival. According to TCM, the stomach receives and digests food, and the spleen transports the food essence. Therefore, they are often lumped together in discussion. After preliminary digestion, the stomach sends the chyme down to the small intestine. Therefore, *stomach-qi* is smooth when flowing downward. If it is not functioning properly, vomiting may occur.

The spleen is known as the foundation of *acquired-jing* because its function includes transporting *acquired-jing* throughout the body. The spleen also transports *acquired-jing* to the lungs. The lungs then in turn, distribute the *acquired-jing* to other organs. The spleen is also responsible for nourishing the flesh and the limbs. Therefore, the problems associated with the spleen may manifest itself as weakness in the limbs. A sallow complexion is usually caused by a dysfunction of the spleen, indicating the presence of *dampness* and *heat*.

Part 1. Massage the Abdomen to Strengthen the Stomach and Spleen

This technique is designed to strengthen the muscles around the intestines and stomach, to improve blood circulation, thus providing the abdominal muscles and organs in that area with more nutrients; and to strengthen the diaphragm. The stimulation of the nerves in the abdomen can also help with the production of digestive juices in the stomach, intestines, and liver; improving

Figure 1-38

Figure 1-39

Figure 1-40

the movements of the intestines, and strengthening the stomach and spleen. This technique can be done while standing or sitting.

Movement:

Step 1. Use Drawing 1-13 as a reference. Place the three middle fingers of each hand on top of your solar plexus and massage clockwise, towards your left , 21 circles (Figure 1-38). Next massage down towards your pubic bone. Then separate the hands and circle back to your solar plexus (Figures 1-39 and 1-40).

Next push down gently with both hands from your solar plexus to your pubic bone, 21 times (Figure 1-41). Relax your left hand and place your right hand on your navel, and massage clockwise, 21 circles (Figure 1-42). Next, relax your right hand and place your left hand on your navel, and massage counterclockwise, 21 circles (Figure 1-43).

Step 2. Place your right hand on the left side of your chest and your left hand on the edge of your ribs. Gently squeeze and tug with your left hand on your waist (Figure 1-44).

Massage your right hand down towards the inside of your left leg, passing your *biguan* point; and down towards the outside of your leg, passing your *zusanli* point, brush across the top of your feet until the back of your heel (Figures 1-45 to 1-48). Repeat 9 to 21 times.

Step 3. Next bend your knees slightly and stand up. Repeat Step 2 on the other side by placing your right hand on the edge of your right ribs and gently squeeze and tug. Then place your left hand

Figure 1-41

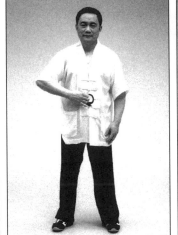

Figure 1-42

Figure 1-43

Figure 1-44

Figure 1-45

Figure 1-46

under your right nipple and slide down towards the inside of your left leg, passing your *biguan* point; and down towards the outside of your leg, passing your *zusanli* point, until the back of your heel . Repeat 9 to 21 times.

Step 4. Repeat the entire exercise, Steps 1 through 3, for 7 sets. The above movements should be done slowly and with your mind focused on what you are doing. When first learning the above exercise, 3 sets are enough. Gradually increase to 7 sets as you get more comfortable doing this exercise. After completing, proceed to the next step.

Step 5. Sit with your legs crossed (or sit on a chair), place your hands on top of your knees in a loose fist, and coil your toes in slightly (Figure 1-49). Rotate your chest from left to right, 21 times; then from right to left, 21 times.

Figure 1-47

Figure 1-48

Figure 1-49

Do not overextend your body when rotating, and don't move too fast or with too much force. Allow the body to move as naturally as possible. Proceed to the next step.

Step 6. Extend your legs and gently hit the *zusanli* points on each leg with your knuckles, a 100 times on each side (Figure 1-50). The *zusanli* point is located about four fingers widths down from your knee cap, on lateral side of your tibia.

Key Points:

A. When doing the above exercise, your mind should be focused, and your breathing should be natural. If possible place your hands directly on your skin when practicing. All movements should be done slowly and gently. Don't use too much force.

B. Women should not do this technique while pregnant. During menstruation, women should train more gently, than at other times.

C. Don't train when you are too full or are too hungry.

D. Make sure you use the toilet before practice.

Part 2. Hu Sound to Strengthen the Stomach and Spleen

Movement:

Stand naturally upright. Inhale and bring your hands next to your *shanzhong* point, with your palms facing up and fingers pointing at each other (Figure 1-51). Exhale and rotate your

Figure 1-50   Figure 1-51   Figure 1-52

right palm out and up, and rotate your left palm in and down; then extend both hands up and down (Figure 1-52).

Then inhale and bring both hands down facing each other at your *shanzhong* point. Next rotate your left palm out and up, and rotate your right palm in and down. Then extend both palms up and down and exhale as you did on the other side. Repeat a total of 6 inhalations and exhalations.

Intention:

Use Drawing 1-13 as a reference. During inhalation, use your mind to lead the qi from your *yinbai* point on your big toe, the beginning of the Spleen Channel, to *dadu*, to *gongsun*, to *sanyijiao*, to *xuehai*, to *jimen*, along the inside of your leg, and up to your spleen.

When exhaling, use your mind to lead the impurities from your spleen out, passing your *zhourong* point towards your *daboa* point. When exhaling make a *Hu* sound; while drawing your stomach in and holding up your *huiyin* area, *squeeze* out the impurities from your spleen.

Key Points:

A. This technique is also effective without using your intention, provided that you hold up your *huiyin* area and draw in your abdomen to *squeeze* out the impurities from your spleen.

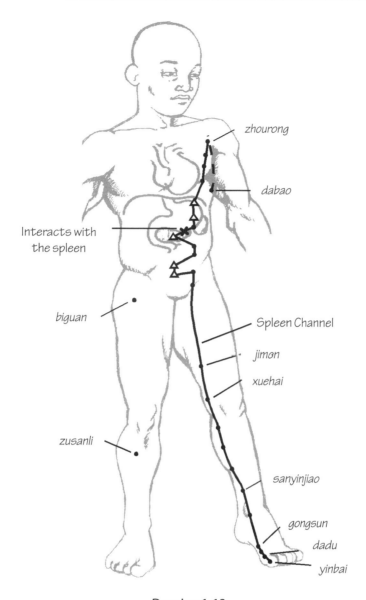

zhourong

dabao

Interacts with
the spleen

biguan

Spleen Channel

jimen

xuehai

zusanli

sanyinjiao

gongsun

dadu

yinbai

Drawing 1-13

7. TRIPLE BURNER ADMINISTERING QIGONG

The Triple Burner includes the Upper Burner, the Middle Burner, and the Lower Burner. The Upper Burner refers to the area of the torso above the diaphragm. It contains the heart and the lungs. The Middle Burner refers to the area of the torso between the diaphragm and the belly button. It contains the spleen and the stomach. The Lower Burner refers to the area in the lower portion of the torso. It contains the kidneys, urinary bladder, small intestine, large intestine, and the liver. According to ancient Chinese physicians, "The Triple Burner has a name but is without a physical shape."

Figure 1-53   Figure 1-54

The Upper Burner is responsible for taking in air and functions as a *sprayer* by distributing nutrients and qi throughout the body, through the functions of the lungs and heart. The Middle Burner is responsible for digesting food and transforming it into nutrients through the *fermentation* process of the stomach and the spleen. The Lower Burner is responsible for eliminating waste through the *filter passages* of the kidneys, urinary bladder, and large intestine.

Part 1. Xi Sound to Regulate the Triple Burner

Movement and Intention:

Step 1. Use Drawing 1-14 as a reference. Stand with your feet shoulder width apart, and arms naturally down at your sides. Inhale, bring both arms up along the front of your body with your hands facing up and the fingers of both hands pointing toward each other (Figure 1-53). As your hands reach your *shanzhong* point, rotate your hands until they are facing up.

Use your mind to lead the qi up from your *qiaoyin* point on the Gall Bladder Channel, passing *quixu, xiyangguan, huantiao,* and into the Triple Burner.

Step 2. Exhale, and make the *Xi (Seeeeee)* sound. The sound is made with your upper and lower teeth close, but not touching, and your tongue gently pointing down. As you make the sound, extend your arms up above your head, hold up your *huiyin* area, and pull your abdomen in, as you exhale all the impurities from your body (Figure 1-54).

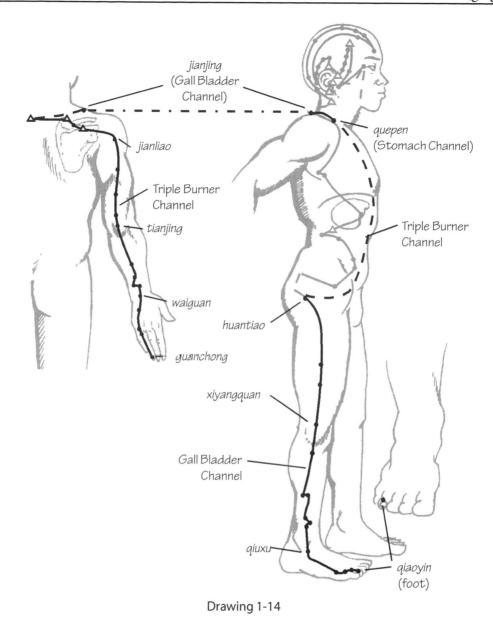

jianjing
(Gall Bladder
Channel)

jianliao

Triple Burner
Channel

tianjing

waiguan

guanchong

quepen
(Stomach Channel)

Triple Burner
Channel

huantiao

xiyangquan

Gall Bladder
Channel

qiuxu

qiaoyin
(foot)

Drawing 1-14

Use your mind to lead the impurities out of your Triple Burner, passing *quepe*n on the Stomach Channel and *jianjing* on the Gall Bladder Channel. Continue along the Triple Burner Channel, passing *jianliao*, *tianjing*, *waiguan*, and *guanchong* on the lateral side of your fourth finger.

Step 3. After completing your exhalation, rotate your hands until they are facing in with your fingers pointing up, and lower them slowly in front of your body. When your hands pass your *shanzhong* point, point your fingers down, while continuing to lower your hands down until they are at your sides. Inhale and exhale naturally. Bring your mind back to your *qiaoyin* point on the Gall Bladder Channel on your fourth toe. Repeat Steps 1 to 3, 6 times.

Part 2. Hu Sound to Strengthen the Stomach and Spleen

Refer to the Stomach and Spleen Qigong description.

8. SIX HEALING SOUNDS FOR NOURISHING LIFE

The practice of the Six Healing Sounds for Nourishing Life has a long history. As early as the Qin Dynasty (221-207 B.C.) there has been a record of healing sound practices. During the Sui Dynasty (590-618 A.D.), a Tiantai Buddhist high priest, Zhi Zhuan, pointed out the healing potential of the Six Healing Sounds. The Six Healing Sounds were recorded as Chui, Hu, Xi, Ke, Xu, and Si. Table 1-2 shows the sounds and their relations.

In the Tang Dynasty (618-906 A.D.) a medical expert and doctor of TCM, Sun Si-Miao, wrote in the *Song of Hygiene* about the Six Healing Sounds and can be paraphrased as follows:

> The Liver and Spring are classified as Wood elements; the Xu sound in the Spring will brighten the eyes and relieve liver stagnation. The Heart and Summer are classified as Fire elements; the Ke sound in the Summer will relieve fire in the heart. The Lungs and Fall are classified as Metal elements; the Si sound in the Fall will nourish the lungs. The Kidneys and Winter are classified as Water elements; the Chui sound in the Winter will keep the kidneys at ease. The Xi sound will regulate the Triple Burner and eliminate annoying heat. The Hu sound during the four seasons will assist the assimilation of food by the spleen. It is not necessary to make any noise when you practice. The benefit is greater than miraculous pills.

Master Liang's mother, Ms. Huang Zhe-Xi, was very sickly in her youth. She went to Huang Mountain to learn the Six Healing Sounds. Later, she also studied from the well-known qigong master, Master Ma Li-Tang. From then on, her health got better and better and filled her with energy.

The practice of the Six Healing Sounds is very flexible. You can practice all six sounds in order or only practice specific sounds to treat specific conditions in the body. You can also practice the sounds according to the seasons of the year. If you practice all six healing sounds, you should practice them in this order: Xu, Ke, Hu, Si, Chui, and Xi.

We have already presented the training methods for this, in the other qigong techniques in this section. In the Lung Qigong, we have included the *Si*

Sounds Relations	XU	KE	HU	SI	CHUI	XI
Organs	Liver	Heart	Spleen	Lungs	Kidneys	Triple Burner
Seasons	Spring	Summer	Late Summer	Fall	Winter	---
Elements	Wood	Fire	Earth	Metal	Water	---
Specific Openings	Eyes	Tongue	Mouth	Nose	Ears	---

Table 1-2

sound; in the Kidney Qigong, we have included the *Chui* sound; in the Liver Qigong, we have included the *Xu* sound; in the Heart Qigong, we have included the *Ke* sound; in the Stomach and Spleen Qigong, we have included the *Hu* sound; in the Triple Burner Administering Qigong we have included the *Xi* sound. We will not repeat them here.

1.5. Qigong for Healing Specific Illnesses

Qigong for Healing Specific Illnesses is intended to be used as a supplemental self-healing practice along with the assistance of doctors, acupuncturists, prescribed medications, herbs, etc. This will greatly improve and increase your chance of a speedy recovery.

1. HEART DISEASE

Proper qigong training for people with heart disease can increase the heart's oxygen supplying potential, improve the adaptability of the heart to a regular amount of activity, and reduce symptoms associated with heart disease.

Suggested Practices:

Step 1. Basic Relaxation Technique

Step 2. Lying Down and Walking Qigong

2. TUBERCULOSIS

Tuberculosis is a chronic illness. Besides treating it with drugs and herbs, practicing qigong aggressively is also very important.

Suggested Practices:

Step 1. Sit or lie down, focus your mind on your *dantian* for 20 minutes.

Step 2. Practice Walking Qigong for 10-20 minutes.

Step 3. Practice Cleansing the Lungs from Lung Qigong.

Step 4. Push and press on your *neiguan* point (Pericardium Channel) on both arms for two minutes on each side. Rub up and down on your *yinlingquan* points (Spleen Channel) on both legs 200 times. Then massage your chest with your palms a 100 times, clockwise.

> *Neiguan* is on the inner side of your forearm. It is located two thumb widths above the wrist line, on the center line of your forearm. *Yinlingquan* is below the knee, and on the medial side of the tibia, around the indentation between the top of the tibia and the calf muscles.

3. KIDNEY AILMENTS

Suggested Practices:

Step 1. Do the Basic Relaxation Technique. Then sit on a chair and focus your mind at your lower *dantian* for 10 minutes.

Step 2. Do Kidney Qigong.

Step 3. Massage your abdomen, your waist, and your *mingmen* point (opposite to your belly button on your back), a 100 times. Then rub up and down on both *sanyinjiao* points (Spleen Channel), 200 times. Your *mingmen* is located on the back, opposite to your navel. *Sanyinjiao* is located about four finger widths above the ankle, on the medial side of the leg.

4. STOMACH AND DUODENAL ULCER

Suggested Practices:

Step 1. Do the Basic Relaxation Technique. Then sit on a chair and focus your mind on your *lower-dantian* for 10 minutes.

Step 2. Press and push on your *zhongwan* point on the Conception Vessel for 1-3 minutes. *Zhongwan* is located above the navel about the width of the entire palm.

Step 3. Keep a regular eating schedule, limit what you eat to a set amount, and take the prescribed medications and herbs.

5. LIVER AILMENTS

Suggested Practices:

Step 1. Qi Permeating Technique

Step 2. Easing the Liver technique from Liver Qigong

Step 3. Massage both *zusanli* points (Stomach Channel), a 100 times on each side. Then massage from both of your *xingjian* points to your *taichong* points (Liver Channel), a 100 times.

> *Zusanli* is located four finger widths below the knee cap, on the lateral side of the tibia. *Xingjian* and *taichong* are located on top of the foot, between the first and second metatarsals (the bones connecting to the big toe and the second toe).

6. HIGH BLOOD PRESSURE

Suggested Practices:

Step 1. Basic Relaxation Technique and Qi Permeating Technique.

Step 2. Lying Down and Walking Qigong

Step 3. Press on both *Taiyang* (temple) points for one minute. Squeeze both *fengchi* points (Gall Bladder Channel) for one minute. Massage your *quze* point (Pericardium Channel) for one minute on each side. Press and massage on both *renying* points (Stomach Channel) for one minute. Massage both *yongquan* points, a 100 times.

> *Taiyang* is the equivalent of your temple. *Fengche* is on the back of your head, on either side of the first cervical vertebra. *Quze* is located in the middle on the inside of the elbow. *Renyin* is located on the pulse area of your neck, midway between your head and shoulder.

7. DIABETES

Suggested Practices:

Step 1. Lying Down and Waking Qigong

Step 2. Sit or stand. Focus on your lower *dantian* 10 to 30 minutes.

Step 3. Massage both *zusanli* points (Stomach Channel), a 100 times. Massage both *sanyinjiao* points (Spleen Channel), a 100 times.

Massage up and down on your lower back, on both sides, around your waist, 200 times.

Sanyinjao is located about four finger widths above the ankle, on the medial side of the leg. *Zusanli* is located four finger widths below the knee cap, on the lateral side of the tibia.

8. ASTHMA

Suggested Practices:

Step 1. Sit, stand, or lie down. Focus on your *Zhichuan* points (located on either side of the spine, between the seventh cervical and the first thoracic vertebrae) for 20-30 minutes. *Zhichuan* means *asthma healing*.

Step 2. Cleansing the Lungs Technique from Lung Qigong.

Step 3. Massage your *tiantu* point (Conception Vessel). Massage down the Lung Channel until it is hot. *Tiantu* point is located at the bottom of the throat, right above the collar bones.

9. LOWER BACK PAIN

Suggested Practices:

Step 1. Sit or lie down. Focus your mind on your *yaoyangguan* point (Governing Vessel) for 10-20 minutes. *Yaoyangguan* is located right below the fourth lumbar vertebra.

Step 2. Use your middle finger to press on both *shenshu* points (Urinary Bladder), 24 times. Then massage them for 10 minutes. The *shenshu* points are located on either side of the second lumbar vertebra.

Step 3. Massage up and down your *mingmen* point to your coccyx for 5 minutes.

Step 4. This step is for men with lower back problems associated with a kidney deficiency.

Hold on to your genitals including the testes with your right hand, and place your left hand on your solar plexus. Exhale, lower your left hand down towards your pubic bone and pull your genitals gently up with your right hand. Inhale, return your hands to the starting position. Repeat 81 times.

10. CHOLECYSTITIS AND GALL STONES

Suggested Practices:

Step 1. Do the Six Healing Sounds for Nourishing Life: *Xu, Ke, Hu, Si, Chui, Xi.*

Step 2. Emphasize more on the Xu sound. Even though the Liver and Gall Bladder have different physiological functions, they are closely interconnected energetically. The Xu sound can ease the liver and it can also cleanse the gall bladder.

Step 3. Inhale and exhale slowly and naturally, while massaging both *riyue* points (Gall Bladder) for 10 to 30 minutes. The *riyue* points are located below either nipple, between the seventh and the eighth rib bones.

11. RHINITIS AND LARYNGITIS

Suggested Practices:

Step 1. Do the Six Healing Sounds for Nourishing Life: *Xu, Ke, Hu, Si, Chui, Xi.*

Step 2. Emphasize more on the *Si* Sound for Nourishing the Lungs. The specific opening of the lungs is the nose. By strengthening the lungs, you will be able correct the problems associated with your nose.

Step 3. Massage the sides of your nose with your fingers. Then massage both *yingxiang* points (Large Intestine Channel), 64 times. Repeat three times a day. The *yingxiang* points are located on the corners of the nose.

   The nose and the throat are interconnected. The Six Healing Sounds can nourish the five viscera. When the five viscera are strengthened, the bodily fluids will be sufficient to nourish the throat.

Step 4. Turn your head left and right, to exercise your neck and increase the flow of qi and blood to the area.

Step 5. Take your prescribed medication and/or herbs.

Book 2:

Daoist (Taoist) Qigong

2.1. Daoist Philosophy and Training Concepts

Aside from Medical Qigong, other Chinese societies have also made important contributions to the development of qigong. The most widely acclaimed high level qigong achievers are among the Daoist (Taoist), Buddhist, and Wushu (martial arts) societies. In Book 2, we will focus on Daoist Qigong methods. We will be discussing both the longevity training, as well as, the higher spiritual purposes of their training. However, our training focus will be on health, healing, and longevity. Since a healthy body is the stepping stone towards higher spiritual development, individuals interested in pursuing higher spiritual goals will find the qigong training in Book 2 very helpful.

Traditional Chinese Medicine (TCM) and Daoism mutually inherited, influenced, and further developed qigong from each other, both in theory and in practice. The oldest and most influential Chinese medical text, the *Yellow Emperor's Internal Classic*, is also one of the most important Daoist Cannons. They both believe in the unity of *human* (Small Cosmos) and *heaven* (Great Cosmos), the Five Element Theory, the Yin-Yang Theory, the qi meridians, and the physiological functions of the organs. These are just some of the many common values between TCM and Daoism. Many of the basic concepts on healing and health are the same. However, due to the differences in their objectives, many of the commonly used terms have different implications.

After thousands of years of searching for longevity and immortality, Daoist masters developed many healing, life prolonging, and spiritual cultivation methods. Their effective, profound, and esoteric cultivation resulted in many qigong techniques that can be used for health, healing, and longevity exercises for the lay person; and enlightenment training for individuals in search of higher spiritual realization.

Dao (Tao) was a term used by all the *schools of thought* in China before the Later Han Dynasty (25-220 A.D.). It is a philosophy and science resulting from human's primordial need to find their place in the Great Cosmos. Dao was used as the universal term to describe the philosophy and theory of all schools of thought. Dao was also used to teach their philosophy and theory. It is loosely translated in the English language as the *Way*.

Daoism refers to both the Daoist School of Thought and the Daoist Religion. The term for *teach* in Chinese is *jiao*, which is the same character used for *religion*. Before the Later Han Dynasty, *daojiao* literally meant *use the Dao to teach*, not Daoist Religion. After the Later Han Dynasty, the teachings of the Daoist School of Thought were combined with ancient Chinese religion and became Daoist Religion.

Daoist School of Thought

Daoist School of Thought included everything from philosophy, to government, to science, to technology. It is a way of life and a path towards the ultimate *Truth*. It has lasted the test of time and continues to be treasured by its followers. The fundamental texts used in the Daoist School of Thought and Daoist religious teachings are based on the legendary *Four Classics of the Yellow Emperor, Daodejing (Tao Teh Ching)*, and *Zhuangzi (Chuang Tzu)*.

The Four Classics of the Yellow Emperor are the legendary work of the Yellow Emperor (2697-2597 B.C.), the father of Chinese civilization. Today little is known about the *Four Classics of the Yellow Emperor*, with only fragmented evidence indicating its existence in ancient China. Legend has it that the Yellow Emperor and some other talented people of his time invented clothing, crowns, palaces, boats, bow and arrows, compasses, astrology, calendars, musical notations, etc. According to Chinese *Historical Records*, the Yellow Emperor was a superhuman. He accomplished many incredible tasks; he went everywhere to search for immortals and the Dao, for the proper ways to govern his kingdom. At the end of his physical life, he "rode the dragon to the heavens" and became an immortal. Similar to many other Chinese social or religious groups, whether or not the Yellow Emperor had any direct influence on the Daoist School of Thought, they give credit to the Yellow Emperor as the founder, to honor the father of Chinese civilization.

The **Daodejing** is a philosophical text written by Laozi (Lao Tzu). It is regarded as one of the most influential books ever written in the history of human civilization. According to Chinese *Historical Records*, Laozi was born during the Spring-Autumn (722-480 B.C.) period in China. Laozi is the honorary name given to Li Er. Lao literally means old. Zi in this case means a person of high virtue and accomplishment. That is, Laozi is more than just a name for Li Er. It is a title given to one of the most respected people in Chinese history.

The popular versions of the *Daodejing* today are presented in two sections. The first section introduces *Dao*; the second section introduces *De*. Therefore, Laozi's book was later named *Daodejing*; with Jing meaning a classic or cannon. Many of the teachings in the *Daodejing* are used as the theoretical foundation for attaining longevity and immortality.

The essence of the *Daodejing* is about being natural. Because of this, the *Daodejing* has also been referred to as the *philosophy of being natural*. Being natural refers to letting the course of events happen, as it would, without any added external human influence. The profound nature of the *Daodejing* immortalized Laozi. This immortalization gradually led to the formation of the Daoist Religion in the Later Han Dynasty, by combining the philosophy of the Daoist School of Thought with ancient Chinese religious beliefs.

Zhuangzi is the title of a book written by Zhuan Zhou. It is also the honorary name given to Zhuan Zhou. Zhuang Zhou was a follower of Laozi's philosophy and a prominent representative of the Daoist School of Thought. He lived during the Warring Kingdom (403-221 B.C.) period in China. The book *Zhuangzi* is a sequel to the *Daodejing*. There are many stories in this book about the Dao, the Yellow Emperor, Laozi, and the cultivation of longevity. This book is a work about the *wisdom of being natural*.

Zhuangzi believed, "humans need to be aware that their own existence is an integral part of limitless time and the universe. They are constantly interacting. Humans must use nature to observe everything. Don't use other's standards as a standard for yourself, don't use the past and future as a division for the present, don't use death as a division for life, and don't use infinity as a division for finites. This way humans will be able to go beyond their bondage and attain freedom". Zhuangzi realized, "the root of human problems stem from their lack of freedom. Humans are not free because of their overdependency. Humans depend too much on materials, emotions, knowledge, art, spiritual leaders, gods, ... for their well-being and daily life. These dependencies sink humans into a self-created pit of bondage. To gain liberation, humans will have to clear away their dependency."

Zhuangzi's philosophy is the *philosophy of freedom*. It is a philosophy that places life in infinite time and space to gain experience. People today tend to *dissect the frog* to understand its body and functions, where as, Zhuangzi wanted to experience the living quality of the frog. Many people like the shape and color of a flower; where as, Zhuangzi liked the life of the flower itself. Zhuanzi wrote, "The human life span is limited. Knowledge is unlimited. It is very dangerous to use a limited life span to seek limitless knowledge. It is even more dangerous when you know that it is dangerous, yet still think that knowledge makes you smart."

Daoist Religion

During the Later Han Dynasty (947-950 A.D.), Zhang Dao-Ling, founded Five Unit of Rice Dao, the first religious organization that used the *Daodejing* as the theoretical foundation for their beliefs. The name, Five Unit of Rice Dao, was derived from the requirement set forth for becoming a member of this organization. Each member was required to contribute five *dou* (a unit of grain equals about 10 pints) of rice. Followers of Zhang Dao-Ling referred to Zhang as the Heavenly Teacher. Therefore, this early Daoist religious organization was also known as the Dao of Heavenly Teachings. This Daoist group used the *Daodejing* as their main study text, and they regarded Laozi as their symbolic leader. When the term *daojiao* (meaning use Dao to teach) also became the popular term referring to the Daoist religion, other schools of thought in China, gradually stopped using this term to refer to their teachings.

Daoist Philosophy

Daoists believe that the Dao is the *Origin*, the *Source* of the Great Cosmos. Dao is that which is beyond what our languages can explain and beyond what our mind can comprehend. Dao is a conceptual term for the principle governing all that we know and don't know, and all that we can see and can't see. Dao has no shape and can't be fully felt with our limited senses. Dao is unobjective, yet encompasses all. Dao is within and beyond space and time.

Dao should not be opposed. Opposition will only result in disaster. In the describing the Dao, terms such as *Void*, *Emptiness*, and *Undefinable* are often used. Dao is unlimited. The term Dao, itself, is reluctantly used as a reference to satisfy the human need to classify people and things into different categories. Since Dao is the origin, the root of everything in the Great Cosmos, it can't be fully explained with the language we know. Because when it is explained as *A* it is differentiated from *B*; when it is explained as *B*, then it differentiated from *A*. We need to use our heart and spirit to feel and experience its essence, to know what it is.

When Dao is limited by our perceptions and classifications, then it can't be the origin of the Great Cosmos. If our mind were to concretely figure out what Dao is, then Dao will have lost its totality. This is like the mind bogging example of, going half the distance each time, from point A to point B. One can never get to point B, if one only intellectualizes and uses *human created* rules to reach their destination. Dao, however, will continuously reveal many insights accompanied by unfolding realizations for its seekers.

To use our limited language to set a definition for the Dao would only lead to erroneous conclusions. Dao is beyond the limitation of linear time and three dimensional space. It therefore can't be proven by conscious thinking, with everyday language, and man made scientific reasoning. That was why the first verse in the *Daodejing* states that, "Dao that can be explained is not the complete Dao". To realize Dao one needs to understand from proper cultivation and experience.

The Dao has been explained with the term *Void*, implying that which transcends duality and the comprehension of the ordinary, limited mind. It is *Undefinable*. *Void* in this case does not mean nothingness. It simply implies that which was in the beginning. Daoist philosophy begins from the view that the Great Cosmos is an integrated whole. They believe that the Dao of the Great Cosmos and the Dao of life all comprise the same patterns and principles of nature.

The profound nature of the Dao gives its seekers different insights as they think, approach, and continue with their own unique stages of realization. Philosophers use Dao, government uses Dao, military forces use Dao, martial artists use Dao, and astrologers use Dao. Everyone uses Dao. Dao encompasses all and is unlimited. The famous Chinese poet, Su Dong-Po (1036-1101 A.D.) wrote this about Dao:

> "A man born into this earth blind, has never seen the sun. He asked people what the sun looked like. One person told him that the sun is shaped like a gong. One day he heard the sound of a gong and he thought that it was the sound of the sun. Another told him, the light from the sun is like the light from a candle. He then touched a candle stick to know its shape. Later he touched a short section of a flute and he though it was the sun".

Su Dong-Po's poem reminds his readers that all things are part of the Dao, but not the complete Dao.

Referring to the Dao, Laozi had this to say, "Great scholars work unceasingly when they hear of the Dao. Mediocre scholar are bewildered when they hear of the Dao. Ordinary scholar burst into laughter when they hear of the Dao."

Here Dao refers to the universal *Truth*. It is everywhere. Whether or not an individual is able to comprehend the Dao depends on one's current experience and understanding. Great scholars realized how little they knew compared to the greatness of the Dao. They cultivated unceasingly to experience it. When the mediocre scholars heard of the Dao, they were uncertain and couldn't decide whether to believe the Dao, or not, due to their insufficient experience and knowledge. They however, knew enough not to dismiss it totally. When the ordinary scholars heard of the Dao, they burst into laughter and thought of it as nonsense. They laughed because of their lack of experience and understanding. It is because they laughed that showed the extensive nature of the Dao. If they had not laughed, it would not have shown the profoundness of the Dao.

The *Daodejing* contains the foundation and the outline of Daoist philosophy. Even though its content is broad and extensive, it can be boiled down to two words Dao and De (Virtue). To take it one step further, it can be boiled down to just the word Dao. When one has attained complete realization, all the ritualistic formalities are discarded. Everything becomes simple and clear. Because everything in the cosmos is of the Dao, and Dao encompasses all things. When one has attained the Dao, one will have mastered the true nature of all things.

The characteristics of Dao are natural, complete, basic, untainted, simple, uncontrived, flexible, yielding, not contending, etc. When expressed in human action it is called De (Virtue). Therefore the book by Laozi is referred to as the *Daodejing*. The highest form of Virtue is natural and invisible. It is from within, silent, and expressed without mental processing. Whatever the characteristics of the Dao are, will also be the characteristics of Virtue.

We have not fully realized and attained the Dao, therefore, we must speak of Virtue and its cultivation. The continual cultivation of Virtue assists us in realizing and attaining the Dao. When we have achieved Dao, it is no longer necessary to speak of Virtue, because everything will already be in unity with the Dao. Without Virtue, one will not be able to realize and attain the Dao.

It is imperative that one understand the meaning of Virtue, the relationship between the Dao and Virtue, as well as the relationship between Virtue and cultivation. If one doesn't understand Virtue, doesn't value Virtue, doesn't cultivate Virtue, and doesn't maintain the integrity of Virtue, one will only remain in a state of qi, and be unable to continue the evolution of the spirit to attain the union of the spirit and the Dao.

The inherent nature of Virtue is true goodness, with a *heart* that is filled with loyalty, filial piety, kindness, compassion, equality, universal love, passion to enlighten others, honesty, consideration, graciousness, patience, courage, forgiveness, etc. "One must not speak, if it is disrespectful; not listen, if it is disrespectful; not look, if it is disrespectful; and not act, if it is disrespectful." When Virtue is complete, the *heart* will be calm. With a calm and pure *heart*, Dao will be attainable.

Virtue is often categorized as Genuine Virtue, Mystical Virtue, Yin Virtue, and Apparent Virtue. Genuine Virtue is natural and uncontrived, without any formulated mental process. It is a genuine and natural expression of the harmony of Dao and De.

Mystical Virtue is the expression of Virtue by cultivators in the process of nurturing the spirit. They are knowingly and unknowingly helping others and society by healing the sick, helping people in trouble, protecting the balance of nature, etc. They are able to do good deeds without people knowing.

82

Yin Virtue must rely on the physical body to express. Do kind deeds without expecting rewards. Do kind deeds without leaving names. Even though Yin Virtue is not completely in accordance with nature, it is the foundation of a true cultivator. It is important to continuously work on Yin Virtue to cross over to Mystical Virtue.

Apparent Virtue is one that is visible to others, and rewarded with material and/or verbal gratitude. Apparent Virtue is an even exchange of energy, there is no accumulation of Virtue for the cultivator. People that only donate money and do kind deeds when they can gain prestige and fame don't accumulate Virtue. If one does good deeds and expects to be rewarded, it is no longer a Virtue.

The cultivation of Virtue is not without rewards. Its "reward is in the heavens" and in the Dao. It is reward without shape or form. It is important to note that the high level of achievement in one's qigong cultivation is not totally dependent on practicing qigong, it is also dependent on the cultivation of Virtue.

With each kind deed, one's *heart* becomes purer and the activities of the spirit increases. The gap between the subjective thinking and the spirit will be reduced. People that cultivate Virtue and the Dao will develop a strong presence that attracts help from everywhere.

Almost all the religions in the world today, along with researchers of spiritual phenomenon, hypnotists, etc., all value the importance of accumulating Virtue. They use prayers to request for help and protection, and repent to purify one's spirit. Prayers and repentance can assist in one's cultivation. In Daoism, before one engages in high level training, one must also pray, communicate and pledge to one's teacher that they repent for all the wrong they have done and promise to engage in accumulating Virtue.

Chapter 33 of the *Daodejing* effectively summarized the Daoist philosophy of nourishing life and attaining the Dao. This Chapter emphasized self-awareness, self-control, contentment, and aspiration:

"Knowing others can only be considered being intelligent; knowing one's own character is to attain true clarity of being." This verse states, to understand others we need to have the ability to distinguish different behaviors. To distinguish behaviors we need to be intelligent. To understand ourselves, we need to gain the ability to reflect internally. To reflect internally, we need to regulate our emotions, restrain our desires, control ourselves, and be generous.

We can see far into the distance, yet we can't see our own eyebrows. We can see the small errors of others, yet we can't see our own faults. The more time we spend criticizing others, the more we lose, because we have less time to reflect internally. The more time spent learning about ourselves, the more we can cultivate our character and attain higher realization. Ancient Chinese compare *intelligence* to a candle, and *clarity of being* to a mirror. As a candle burns, it become shorter; on the other hand, as a mirror is being polished, it becomes clearer. That is why Laozi did not value intelligence and holds *clarity of being* in high esteem.

"Winning over others is strong; winning over oneself is true power." We all have different degrees of selfishness and different degrees of lust. It does not matter how strong we are compared to others, we can't use this strength to conquer our own selfishness and lust. The only way to remove our selfishness and lust, is through introspection and removing our undesirable traits. Because this is difficult to do, people that are able to remove undesirable traits are considered to have true power.

"Being content is being wealthy." As people attain more wealth, people tend to want even more. This is the discontentment that causes unhappiness. Here contentment simply implies not being greedy and constantly desiring more. When one has attained contentment, one will always be wealthy, because one is happy with what one has.

"To persist is to have inspiration." It is important to realize the profound nature of the Dao; it is even more important to actively engage in the attainment of the Dao. The higher the goal, the more obstacles will be encountered on the path. If we give up because of obstacles, we will lose all the effort we put forth. It is necessary to continually work on the attainment of the Dao. It is through this persistence that one will achieve the goal, and this persistence is one's true inspiration.

"Not deviating from the Dao is everlasting." All things in the Great Cosmos came from the Dao. Humans live in an oxygen rich environment; if we lose oxygen, we will die. Fishes born in water need water; if they leave water, they will die. Trees grow on earth; if you pull them away from the ground, they will die. Because we live in the natural patterns of the Dao, we must adhere to the principles of the Dao to survive. Deviating from the Dao will result in premature deterioration.

"Death without perishing is longevity." True longevity is the continuation of the spirit after the physical body has died. We live and we die, this is the norm. Don't be sad or worry. What is important is to establish the true value of existence — the continuation of the spirit. Only the spirit that has united with the Dao is everlasting.

Daoist View of the Cosmos and Spirit — Food for Thought

There are controversial and superstitious beliefs in Daoism, just as there are in other philosophies in the world today. It is unwise to accept any philosophy blindly. It is just as unwise to dismiss any belief just because we do not understand it and modern science is unable to verify it yet. We should maintain an earnest effort to repeatedly experience and verify what we know and that which we are unfamiliar with.

Daoists believe the cosmos includes Three Planes: the Lower, Middle, and Upper Planes. The Lower Plane consists of 6 levels, and is also referred to as the Six Physical Levels. These levels are visible to the human eye, consists of all physical forms, desires, senses, emotions, yin and yang are interacting, and humans are reborn. The Middle Plane consists of 18 levels, and is also referred to as the Eighteen Sensory Levels. The Middle Plane is visible to the human eye; consists of senses but no desire; no yin and yang interaction; and spirit is able to evolve. The Upper Plane consists of 4 levels, and is also referred to as the Four Mental Levels. These levels are not visible to the human eye and there is no physical forms or senses, only pure mentality.

Within the Three Planes, there are a total of 28 levels. Beyond the Three Planes there are Four Enlightened Levels and Four Infinite Levels. The Four Infinite Levels are what is referred to as the Grand Purity Level, the Great Grand Purity Level, the Jade Purity Level, and the Final Level. There are a combined total of 36 levels that the spirit needs to evolve, before it is reunited with the Dao.

The Dao is the regulator of all levels. The Upper Plane also regulates the Middle and the Lower Planes, and the Middle Plane regulates the Lower Plane. The evolution of the spirit differs in different planes. Qualitative evolution must be completed before the spirit is able to move up to the higher planes.

There are other philosophies and religions that have similar beliefs. Buddhism is one of them. Daoists and Buddhists have mutually influenced each other over the millenniums. Therefore there are many similarities in their philosophies. Buddhist philosophy also views the cosmos to have the Physical, Sensory, and Mental Planes. In Buddhism, the Sensory Plane alone consists of 33 levels, and the Mental Plane consists of 18 levels. Also, within each of the levels are many sublevels. They also believe that there are an infinite amount of cosmos, planes, and levels.

Yet, another philosophy views the cosmos as consisting of 7 planes. They are the Physical Plane, the Lower Astral Plane, the Upper Astral Plane, the Causal Plane, the Mental Plane, the Buddhic Plane, and the Dao. Within each one of these Planes are 7 levels. The Physical Plane includes all material substances, organic and inorganic. Everything that is visible to the human eye is in the Physical Plane. This includes all living and nonliving matters in the cosmos. The Lower Astral Plane includes spirits traveling to it from the Physical Plane, usually during meditation or in a dream state. It is also inhabited by those spirits that are between bodies, and spirits that are trying to complete their final karma without being reborn in the physical body. It also includes spirits that are partially reunited with each other as the spirits evolve and are closer to the Dao, they unite with other spirits as they work towards the ultimate unification with the Dao.

Where did the Daoist and Buddhist and other spiritual beliefs derive their philosophy? Modern science is still unable to verify these beliefs. However, the similarity between their believes are striking. There are many books written in the English language on this subject. These books include the research and records of hypnotic healing, out of body experiences, research on unidentified flying objects, and the space exploration of astronauts and satellites. Many of these beliefs and observations are not yet verified by modern science, but they coincide with ancient Daoist and Buddhist beliefs.

Daoism believes the human spirit consist of two components, the Original Spirit and the Personality (Post-Birth Spirit). Prior to the birth of a baby, a Spiritual Luminance enters the womb. The Combination of the Spiritual Luminance, the *innate-qi*, and *innate-jing* results in the Original Spirit. The Original Spirit contains knowledge learned from numerous other lifetimes about the *Truth* of the cosmos, and higher potentials. It is stored in the deep consciousness. Original Spirit appears as light, and has multiple colors. The Personality includes the learning and experience in this lifetime. It has an overshadowing and suppressing effect on the Original Spirit.

Our Original Spirit contains information from numerous past lifetimes. Our Personality only contains information we learned in this lifetime. Original Spirit is hundreds of thousands of times wiser than our Personality. Through training we will allow the Original Spirit to emerge. Our Original Spirit can enter the astral planes (fourth and higher dimensions). When Original Spirit enters the astral planes, it can receive the teachings and help from Spiritual Guides and attain higher wisdom.

Both Daoists and Traditional Chinese Medicine believe that humans consist of *three finer spirits* and *seven baser spirits*, together they animate the human body. The *three finer spirits* are classified as yang and the seven *baser spirits* are classified as yin. The cultivation of the spirit in Daoist training is to cultivate the three *finer spirits* to become Yang Spirit and the seven *baser spirits* to become Yin Spirit. The combination of the Yin Spirit and the Yang Spirit is the Original Spirit. Further cultivation combines the Original Spirit with the Dao.

The astral travels of the Original Spirit is not the same as an out of body experience. Most out of body experience are usually that of the Yin Spirit leaving the body when individuals are sleeping, are ill and weak, and sometimes during early stages of qigong training. The Yin Spirit can easily be affected and attacked by ghosts on the lower astral planes, as well as, one's own negative Personality. The astral travels of the Yin Spirit are usually confined to the lower astral planes. When the Yang Spirit astral travels, it travels up to the higher astral planes. It does not float around.

When the Original Spirit astral travels, it leaves the body through the *baihui* point, belly button, and other spiritual connection points on the body. Its travels are far and extensive, as it receives the guidance and teachings of the Spiritual Guides, to attain Great Wisdom, and continue the evolution of the spirit. When the Original Spirit is no longer regulated by yin-yang and the Five Elements of the Lower Plane, it will be able to achieve swift and enormous evolution. The wisdom and pure essence brought back to the physical body by the Original Spirit are also beneficial to the body, and sets a solid foundation for immortality. This type of spirit evolution process is much greater than going through countless reincarnations.

In the cultivation to become one with the Dao, high level qigong achievers also attain many extraordinary abilities or Spiritual Connections. These abilities include clairvoyance, clairaudience, telepathy, precognition/regression, teleportation, and immortality. Spiritual Connections are either a by product of one's spiritual evolution or channeled. Throughout the many dynasties in China, many highly accomplished Daoist masters were known to have attained longevity and were able to do extraordinary and mystical tasks. Their Spiritual Connections were a prelude to attaining the Dao.

Spiritual Connections are innate within humans and animals. The question is whether or not, one is able to bring about this potential with proper cultivation. It is easier to bring about this potential when one is young and before one's Personality completely overshadows their Original Spirit. From ancient times until today, there have been many sages, religious leaders, preachers, and psychics who all have a very strong potential and extraordinary abilities. Their abilities are the by-product of the evolution of their spirit, not the goal they sought. Throughout history, the masters of old cautioned students not to seek these extraordinary abilities. When one has evolved to have these abilities, one must use them with caution, use them sparsely, and best not to use them at all. They are not to be used for demonstrations.

The only way to continue to evolve to higher levels is to continue cultivating one's spirit. The extraordinary abilities of gifted young people that are not derived from cultivation, are usually unstable. If they don't train their body, qi, and cultivate their spirit, they will deplete their *innate-jing* and *innate-qi*. Without the support of these vital substances, their abilities will gradually decrease and vanish.

Some individuals are able to channel Spiritual Connections. These individuals have achieved a definite qigong foundation. They can use specific channeling methods to acquire the assistance of Spiritual Guides. They use symbols, incantations, mantras, and/or prayers to procure the assistance of Spiritual Guides to produce miraculous effects. Daoist priests often use channeling to attain Spiritual Connections for eliminating misfortune, to bring good luck and fortune, and to heal the sick. They also help others to release pent-up grief, to accumulate Virtue, and cultivate the Dao.

Similar to many other channels in different parts of the world, Daoist priests also ask Spiritual Guides to manifest in their body, to help them resolve problems. If, however, the invited Spiritual Guide is not a highly evolved spirit, the extraordinary abilities will not be able to occur. This is especially apparent when channeling is done in temples, churches, or in the presence of priests and individuals with a very strong potential and spirit evolution themselves. The leader of a nation, head of a religion, high priests, high lamas, highly achieved qigong cultivator, and individuals that steadily walk on the righteous path all have a very strong inner potential. Their inner potential can also prevent bad influences from affecting them.

Their is a famous saying, "High level Daoists cultivate the spirit, middle level Daoists cultivate the qi, and lower level Daoists cultivate the jing." Jing and qi are the material foundation for the spirit. They are also the activation force for the spirit. They are like the fuel in your car, if you drive recklessly and waste fuel with bad driving habits, your gas mileage will be reduced and you will not be able to go as far. Wastefulness will prevent your spirit from reaching the next, more wonderful destination.

Daoist Cultivation and Training Concepts

Daoists *value life* and *enjoy life*, and believe that this life is not only precious, but also hard to come by. Since *life* is *precious*, one must seek ways to live a *good, healthy, long* life. Not valuing life, one will not take good care of life, one will not be healthy. When the body is unhealthy, illness will surround the body. Therefore, they cultivate their life to keep it healthy, so as to attain a solid foundation for furthering their spiritual development. Individuals interested in higher spiritual aspects will find the techniques in Daoist Qigong, not only to be health, healing, and longevity exercises, but also an important foundation for furthering their spiritual pursuits.

Daoists are interested in figuring out the mystery of life and its relationship with nature, to discover life nourishing techniques, so as to attain the highest possible goal of existence — being one with the Dao. In their cultivation, they strove to understand the integrated system, not just the parts. It is not possible to understand the complete human phenomenon by isolating ourselves from nature. We can only attain full realization of ourselves through the understanding the interrelations between nature and us. Because of this integral study; Daoists have not only contributed in the development of health, healing, and longevity methods; they also have made valuable contributions to our civilization, such as the development of fire powder, medical advances, astrology, chemistry, etc.

Daoist cultivation training views the human body as a *Small Cosmos*, and views the Great Cosmos as a *Big Human Body*. The human body follows the same principles and contains the same energy as the Great Cosmos, because

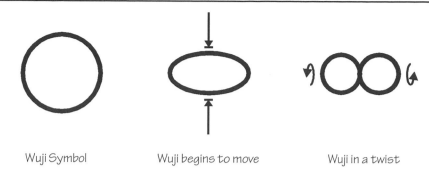

Wuji Symbol   Wuji begins to move   Wuji in a twist

Drawing 2-1

the Great Cosmos and the human body are from the same origin; they were originally one. Everything in the Great Cosmos came from the *Void* and all things are in constant change, some vary at a fast pace, some at an extremely slow pace relative to the human life span. Not one thing in the Great Cosmos is everlasting. Even the stars and the earth have their limits. The only eternity is Dao. Therefore, to attain immortality and to be the controller of one's own destiny, it is imperative that one return to the Dao.

Daoism utilizes yin and yang to generalize all things in the cosmos. Everything has yin and yang. This includes *space*. Everything in the visible first three dimensions is classified as yang. What we can't see with the ordinary eye in the fourth dimension and up are classified as yin. Within yin, there is yang and within yang, there is yin. Yin, by itself, cannot produce and yang, by itself, cannot grow. When yin grows, yang diminishes; and when yang waxes, yin wanes. Yin and yang are always in dynamic equilibrium.

In a Taiji Symbol, one side is yang the other is yin, and the curvature in the middle is the Taiji Cord. Taiji is derived from Wuji, the original nature of the Dao. If we compress a Wuji Symbol (a circle) then twist the compressed symbol (oval) it becomes a Wuji Twist (Wuji in a twist). Overlap the Wuji Symbol with the Wuji Twist and it becomes a representation of the Taiji Symbol (Drawing 2-1). The ability to reverse the twist and return it to its *original nature* is the way to the Dao.

The human body is like a Taiji Symbol. The channel in the middle of the body (Thrusting Vessel) is the Taiji Cord, the Governing Vessel is the arc on the yang side of the symbol, and the Conception Vessel is the arc on the yin side of the symbol. The channel in the middle is the path to which the Original Spirit enters and leaves the body, and the Governing Vessel is the governor of the physical body.

Daoists believe that yin and yang are products of the Dao. There are over three thousand, six hundred traditional Daoist schools, each with their unique cultivation methods. Philosophically, the highest cultivation of all the schools is to achieve the ability to reverse the *twist* in the Taiji Cord, thereby returning to Wuji. The major obstacle in high level qigong, and the attainment of immortality, and the eventual unification with the Dao, lies in whether or not one is able to break through the Taiji Cord.

Daoists don't view life as misery, but rather a trial and tribulation experience. One must hold on to this life to contribute to the world and accumulate Virtue, the required step towards spiritual evolution. The physical body is like a laboratory for experiments. Daoists are always in search of methods to attain longevity, methods to break through the Taiji Cord and unite with the Dao.

Daoism views the existence of the Small Cosmos (human body) through this process "Void changes into Spirit, Spirit changes into Pure Energy, Pure Energy changes into Pure Essence, and Pure Essence produces the physical body". Based on this belief, in order for humans to reunite with the Dao, humans will have to reverse this process to become free from this physical existence and achieve immortality. Thus, the process of cultivation will start from training the physical body, training *jing* (essence), training *qi* (energy), training the *shen* (spirit), and finally returning back to the *Void* and uniting with the Dao.

The **jing, qi,** and **shen,** correspond to Pure Essence, Pure Energy and Spirit respectively. Through the perfection of *jing, qi,* and *shen;* longevity, immortality, and unification with the Dao can be attained. It is, therefore, not surprising that the stages of Daoist training include the cultivation of *jing, qi, and shen.*

Generally speaking, *jing* is the essence of the body. It is a life activating and nurturing substance. *Qi* is the life activating force. It is the energy that gives rise to life and performs all its activities. *Shen* is the spirit that controls and regulates life. It is that which gives rise to higher realization.

As we get older *jing* and *qi* deplete faster and faster. The consumption of *jing* also accelerates as we get older. To attain good health and longevity, we must assure an abundance of *jing*. Therefore, Daoist qigong training also targets at refilling depleted *jing*. Daoists believe that "*Qi* is like the root and *jing* is like the trunk of the tree. If the root is not deep, it can easily be pulled; and if the trunk is not strong, then it will fall. When one is able to firmly store *qi* and guard *jing*, one will be able to attain longevity."

Through training, cultivators condense their *heart*, nourish the qi, gain the ability to regulate their Personality, and remove post-birth characteristics. This will allow the Original Spirit to emerge, to be nurtured, and go out into the astral planes to absorb the pure essence, and accept the teachings of the Spiritual Guides. In the cultivation of the Original Spirit, there are three important requirements. They are: 1. Value and cultivate Virtue. 2. Understand the principles and the methods of cultivation. 3. Have the guidance of higher teachers, especially the guidance of Spiritual Guides.

The uniqueness of Daoist training is in its emphasis on both the physical body and the spirit. The connection between spirit and the physical body is like the relationship of humans with their homes. When the home is damaged and beyond repair, humans then leave the house, and look for a new home. Some religious philosophies believe this life is filled with misery and there is nothing in this life to keep them here. These religious philosophies also put hope in the afterlife and place their hope on the salvation of the spirit after death. Daoist philosophy, on the other hand, believes that this life is hard to come by. One must hold on to this life and cultivate unceasingly. Once the spirit has left the physical body, a rare opportunity to significantly improve the quality of the spirit has been lost.

The simultaneous cultivation of the spirit and the physical body is a very profound study. It is said, "Spirit is realized by oneself, methods to train the body are taught by teachers." Teachers can only show you the proper methods, explain the principles, and guide you according to your evolution. They can help you train your physical body and attain good health. The improvement of the spirit, however, depends on your own *realization* and effort.

By taking care of this physical body, and allowing the spirit to cultivate and evolve while in this physical body, one will be able to achieve true liberation. By following proper cultivation methods with dedication and focus, the physical body can become immortal; or the spirit can leave the physical body and become independent. Since life is hard to come by, one should not waste this opportunity. One should not rely on the next life or wait until death to ascend to *heaven*.

To return to the Dao one must first have an abundance of energy and a strong, healthy body to attain longevity. Daoism values life. To attain longevity one needs to actively work on their training. They do not believe that life is completely determined by fate. They believe that, "My life depends on me; and it is not predetermined." They also believe that old age and sickness can be avoided, and immortality can be attained, provided one continually cultivates and engages in learning about and living harmoniously with nature. Ignorance and lack of discipline are the reasons for not being able to master one's life and determine one's destiny.

Daoist Training Approaches and Steps

Daoists cultivation methods are classified into Lower, Middle, and High Attainment Approaches. The Lower Attainment Approach focuses on developing one's mental power by repeated recitation of mantras, prayers, or symbolic drawings to accumulate one's potential for specific tasks. This method can only achieve a low level of attainment. The Middle Attainment approach focuses on the cultivation of qi. The High Attainment Approach is the cultivation of the Original Spirit.

Generally speaking the cultivation process is divided into several steps. The process includes: Use Movements to Purify Jing (Foundation Stage), Foster Jing into Qi, Foster Qi into Shen, Foster Shen into Void, and Return the Void Back to the Dao (Shatter the Void). Each of these steps include training that is either Low, Middle, High, or a combination of the three Attainment Approaches.

Use Movement to Purify Jing includes training to discipline the mind and repair physical damage. The disciplining of the mind includes regulating the mind, condensing scattered thoughts to develop one's mental efficiency to a higher level, and attaining the ability to remain in a calm abiding state.

Most exercises are capable of purifying *jing*, through its movements to strengthen the body. Martial artists are mostly in the stage of cultivating jing. Internal Style martial artists and beginning qigong practitioners are in the early stage of cultivating qi. Most qigong teachers, qigong healers, people that emit and absorb qi, are cultivating qi. Qi cultivators are attempting to foster qi into Original Spirit (Foster Qi into Shen). The next stage is to Foster Shen into the Void — the cultivation of the Original Spirit. The final completion of the Daoist cultivation is to Return the Void Back to the Dao or Shatter the Void, implying that at the conclusion of the last stage, even the concept of the Void must also be given up to attain the unification with the Dao.

All training methods start by actively engaging in the training, until it is no longer necessary to follow the ritualistic methods. One must have the insights of the most subtle to understand the profound. Teachers can only guide you based on the principles. The mystical nature cannot be thoroughly explained. Teachers are also not to overly verbalize the depth and profound scenery, otherwise students may be restricted by preconceptions and have difficulty breaking through and developing their Original Spirit. Teachers sometimes use story telling to provide some examples to enlighten you, without you knowing. Whether or not you are able to realize the insights, depends on you.

The cultivation of the spirit and the physical body is equally important. Younger individuals and healthy middle age people may begin cultivating the spirit, then begin the training of the physical. Older people and weak people should begin with the training of the physical body. It is imperative that one first strengthen their health.

Repairing damage to the body can't be overly emphasized. If one is ill, one should heal the illness by using health rejuvenating qigong, herbs, acupuncture, and/or the assistance of doctors or healers. If the body is weak, jing and qi are deficient, then one must also take nourishing, energy building foods and herbs to strengthen the body.

There are people only interested in cultivating the spirit. Many people became physically weak, lose their strength to do even the minute everyday tasks. They only cultivate the spirit and ignore the physical body. Conversely, there are people that only train the physical body and ignore the cultivation of the spirit. They become physically strong, but are unable to attain the Dao. It is important that both the physical and the spirit be cultivated.

Cultivating the spirit is for improving the quality of the spirit, and training the physical is to protect the *house*. Daoists believe, "My life depends on me; and it is not predetermined." So they place their emphasis on never ending cultivation. They are not pessimistic and do not give in to fate. They work to understand the principle and the variations of yin and yang, one step at a time, to become one with the Dao.

The ideals of Daoism were not limited to their search for health, longevity, and immortality. Daoists were also concerned with establishing a peaceful society and equality for all. Daoists wished for humans to live in peace; respect and love each other; were against the strong taking advantage of the weak; were against one people oppressing another; and were against people that exploited other people.

Daoism was able to continue for thousands of years because of the extensive and profound nature of its teachings, which accommodated the needs of people in all walks of life. Daoism is a religion for those people that practice it as a religion. It is a philosophy of life for those that choose to lead a life following the Dao. It is a science for those that attempt not only to understand themselves, but also understand the Great Cosmos. Dao is everything that we can conceive and can't conceive with our limited mind. It is everything definable and undefinable. It is both physical and nonphysical. It has to be understood through introspection and realization of a greater consciousness.

Contents in Book 2

The focus in Book 1 was on developing a healthy foundation. The training in Book 2 will begin with fundamental drills to prepare you for Microcosmic and Macrocosmic Circulation — the training of Fostering Jing into Qi. After you have successfully completed the Microcosmic and Macrocosmic Circulation and attained a definite result, you can then proceed to the subsequent sections.

2.2. Level One

Qi in the human body circulates throughout the body in a cyclic pattern similar to the changing seasons, which occurs due to the rotation of the earth on its orbit around the sun. An effective method for fostering jing into qi is the *Microcosmic Circulation Qigong*. This qigong emphasizes improving the connection of the two energy vessels in the human body, the Conception and the Governing Vessels (Drawing 2-2). During Microcosmic Circulation, *innate-qi* is combined with *acquired-qi* resulting in *original-qi* that follows the movement of your mind. All other energy channels will also be activated as your mind and qi combine in the Microcosmic Circulation.

The Conception and Governing Vessels are known as the paths of *energy essence* in Daoist training. They are the *sea* of human *yin-yang*. When qi circulates without obstruction in these two vessels, the flow of all other channels will also be enhanced and flow smoothly without restriction. The Conception Vessel is located in the front of the body; and is known as the Red Route. Its path is next to the heart, therefore, *heart-qi* also circulates in it. The heart is classified as a *Fire* element in the Five Element Theory and has the characteristic of rising. It is necessary to lower the *fire-qi* to cool the heart and warm the kidneys below. The Governing Vessel is known as the Black Route. Its path is next to the kidneys, therefore, *kidney-qi* also circulates in it. The kidneys are classified as a *Water* element in the Five Element Theory and has the characteristic of *sinking*. Therefore, it is necessary to raise the *water-qi* to keep it in balance.

There are three areas on the path of the Governing Vessel that tend to restrict the flow of qi during the practice of Microcosmic Circulation. The initial training of Microcosmic Circulation is to overcome these three restrictions known as the *Three Check Points* or *Three Gates* (Drawing 2-3). The first obstacle is at the *Tailbone Gate*. The second obstacle is at the *Dorsal Gate* located between the shoulder blades and behind the heart. The third obstacle is at the *Jade Pillow Gate* at the back of the head. One needs an abundance of qi to pass through these gates.

When you practice circulating qi through the Three Gates on the Governing Vessel, the pace of qi movements are like a *goat pace*, *deer pace*, and *ox pace*. A goat moves slowly, implying that when qi circulates through the Tailbone Gate, your intention should be gentle to allow qi to accumulate. A deer is very agile, implying that when qi circulates through the Dorsal Gate, qi should circulate through smoothly with little effort. An ox moves slowly, but is strong and determined, implying the obstacles that one will encounter, combined with the slow pace of qi circulating at the Jade Pillow Gate, will require a stronger intention to lead qi through this gate.

Qi is naturally circulating in the Conception and Governing Vessels. The attempt of Microcosmic Circulation Qigong is to enhance this circulation. In

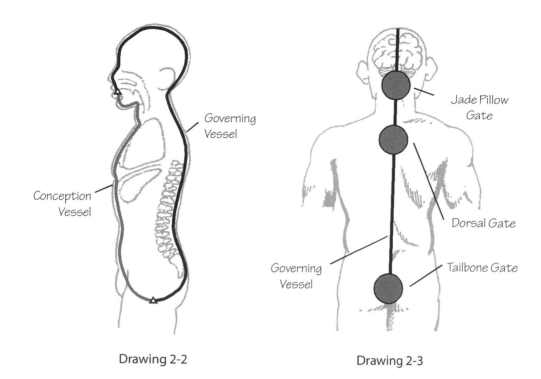

Drawing 2-2   Drawing 2-3

the human body, yin and yang energy accumulates at different areas on the path of the Conception and the Governing Vessels. Generally speaking, extreme yang occurs around noon time, between 11 A.M. to 1 P.M. Extreme yin occurs around midnight, between 11 P.M. to 1 A.M (Drawing 2-4). Following the *yin-yang* theory, when *yin* is at an extreme, *yang* is born. Since *yang-qi* begins above the *huiyin*, around the location of the male sexual organ, in a healthy male, the sexual organ will naturally be effected by the rising *yang* energy.

In a healthy individual, the body will have biological signs indicating the rising of *yang* energy. In men, this is indicated by the stiffening of the sexual organ at the end of extreme *yin* energy and beginning of rising *yang* energy. When an erection occurs naturally in a healthy male without sexual thoughts, it is known as the *biological midnight* of a person. The best time to practice Microcosmic Circulation Qigong is during your biological midnight.

Your biological midnight changes as you get older. It is believed that every ten years after a man reaches full sexual maturity, their biological midnight moves back about two hours. This is a very general reference. It also depends on the health condition of the individual. Healthy individuals will have less of a change compared to an individual who is unhealthy.

Even though the best time to practice Microcosmic Circulation is around a person's biological midnight, it does not mean that one can not practice during other times. When one can attain a calm abiding state, and create an ideal condition for Microcosmic Circulation, one will be in the state known as the *cre-*

Drawing 2-4

ative midnight. The training of Microcosmic Circulation can be done anytime, however, the best time is at your biological midnight.

In this section, we will introduce both the Microcosmic and Macrocosmic Circulation Qigong training methods to complement each other and provide a more complete Fostering Jing into Qi training. This section also consists of the Fundamentals of Qi Circulation that develop the harmony and integration of breathing, body movements, and mind. They are basic drills that prepare your body's automatic response for energy circulation. When you have achieved an automatic response from the basic drills, then training qi circulation will be much easier. We have also included the technique for Absorbing Qi for individuals who have difficulty in building enough energy to complete the Microcosmic and the Macrocosmic Circulation. At the end of this section, is the Nourishing Qi Method for nourishing your qi.

1. FUNDAMENTALS OF QI CIRCULATION

Part 1. Smooth the Qi Flow in the Front of the Body

Movement and Intention:

Movement: Stand comfortably with your tongue gently touching the palate of your mouth. Inhale, as you begin raising your arms

Figure 2-1

Figure 2-2

over your head (Figure 2-1). Exhale and begin lowering your arms down until your sides (Figure 2-2). Repeat 21 times.

Intention: Breath naturally during the inhalation. During the exhalation, lead qi from your *baihui* down to your cheeks, to the palate of your mouth, to the root of your tongue, down your Conception Vessel, to your *dantian*, to your *huiyin*, down the Yin-Activation Vessel (inside of your legs), then to *yongquan* on the bottom of your feet (Drawing 2-5).

Part 2. Smooth the Qi Flow in the Back of the Body

Movement and Intention:

Movement: The same movement as in Smooth the Qi in the Front of the Body, but without touching your tongue on the palate of your mouth. Repeat 21 times.

Intention: Breath naturally during the inhalation. During the exhalation, lead qi from your *baihui* down the back of your head, down your Governing Vessel, to your *huiyin*, down the Yin-Activation Vessel, then to your *yongquan* (Drawing 2-6).

Part 3. Expanding and Contracting Abdomen

Movement and Intention:

Movement: Stand comfortably. Place your hands in front of your abdomen with your palms facing each other, fingers naturally apart, relax your shoulders and elbows (Figure 2-3).

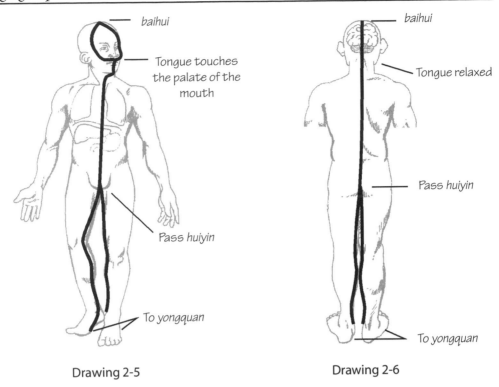

Drawing 2-5   Drawing 2-6

Inhale as you draw your abdomen in, touch the tip of your tongue gently on the palate of your mouth, and gradually pull your palms away form each other. Exhale as you push your abdomen out slightly, press your tongue gently on the bottom of your mouth, and gradually return your palms to the starting position (Figure 2-4 and Drawing 2-7). Repeat 21 times.

Part 4. Small Circle Breathing

Movement and Intention:

Movement: Interlock your fingers in front of your abdomen with the tip of your thumbs touching each other. Inhale, draw your stomach in, bring your arms up to your solar plexus level, in a forward arc. Exhale, push your abdomen out slightly, and continue the circular movement of your hands and return to the starting position (Figure 2-5). Repeat 21 times.

Intention: During the inhalation, use your mind to lead the qi from your *huiyin* to your *mingmen*. During the exhalation, use your mind to lead the qi from your *mingmen* through your *inside-dantian* to your *outside-dantian (quanyuan)* (Drawing 2-8).

| Figure 2-3 | Figure 2-4 | Figure 2-5 |

Part 5. Large Circle Breathing

Movements and Intention:

Movement: Stand comfortably. Inhale through your nose and exhale through your mouth, seven times. Pay more attention to your exhalation than your inhalation. Then do the same arm movements as in Parts 1 and 2.

Then inhale through your nose, touch your tongue gently on the palate of your mouth, draw your stomach in, hold up your *huiyin* area, and raise your arms over your head. Exhale through your nose, lower your arms, tongue presses down gently on the bottom of your mouth, swallow saliva, push your stomach out slightly, and relax your *huiyin*. Repeat 21 times.

Intention: During the inhalation and as you hold up your *huiyin* area, use your mind to lead qi from your *huiyin* up along the Governing Vessel, past your sacrum, past your *Dorsal Gate*, past your *Jade Pillow Gate*, to your *baihui*.

During the exhalation, use your mind to lead the qi down two paths on either side of your eyes, to the tip of your mouth (at this time, gently press your tongue down on the bottom of your mouth and swallow the qi, as if you were swallowing food). Continue to use your mind to lead the qi down the Conception Vessel to your *dantian*, and back to your *huiyin* as you complete your exhalation (Drawing 2-9).

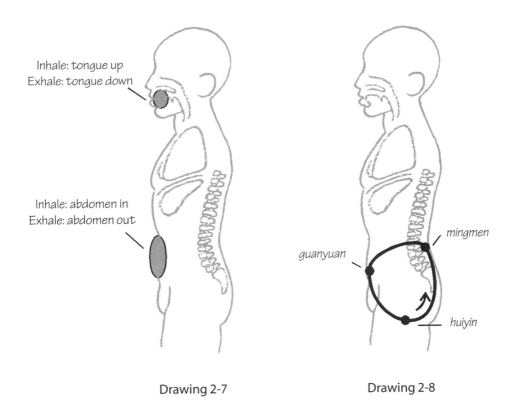

Inhale: tongue up
Exhale: tongue down

Inhale: abdomen in
Exhale: abdomen out

guanyuan

mingmen

huiyin

Drawing 2-7   Drawing 2-8

Parts 1 through 5 are preparation techniques for qi circulation training. You must train them regularly to build up natural reflexes, to assist your qi circulation training. After completing the above five parts, gently inhale and exhale seven times, paying more attention to your exhalations than your inhalations. This will help bring your qi back to your *dantian*.

Part 6. Concluding Massage

Movement:

Step 1. *Massage your nose, face, and head*: Rub your hands together until they are warm. Use your palms, especially your middle fingers, to rub your nose and face. Starting from the base of your nose up to your eye brows, circle out and down your face, 7 - 9 times. Then reverse directions, 7 - 9 times.

Next rub your palms on your head. Starting from your chin, up to the top of your head, back down along the back of your head, and down to the back of your neck. Repeat the head massage, 7 - 9 times.

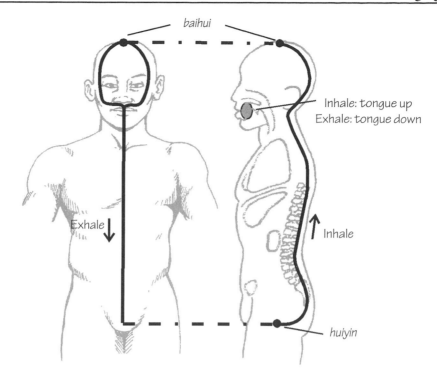

Drawing 2-9

Step 2. *Massage your dantian*: Place your palms over your *dantian* area and massage in a circular pattern from right to left, 36 times; then from left to right, 36 times.

Step 3. *Massage the Conception Vessel*: Place your fingers on the center line of your chest with your palms resting on your chest. Press and push your palms down your Conception Vessel from your throat to your pubic bone - fingers massage your Conception Vessel, and palms massage your chest and abdomen. Repeat 7 - 9 times.

Step 4. *Gently hit the Governing Vessel*: Ask a partner to use his or her palm to hit your back from your sacrum up along your Governing Vessel to your *baihui*. Repeat 7 - 9 times. If you do not have a partner, use one hand to hit the lower part of your back, then use the other hand to hit the upper part of your back up to your *baihui*.

2. MICROCOSMIC CIRCULATION

Microcosmic Circulation should be practiced in a step by step manner. After completing one stage, then go on to the next stage. Don't rush your training. When the qi reaches your head, don't focus too hard on leading the qi. You should not forget about the qi, yet, you should not help it either. That is, your mind is aware of it, but not forcing it to move, by pulling it or by pushing it. Be as natural as possible.

Microcosmic Circulation can be practiced while standing or sitting in a comfortable position. During your training you should maintain a calm, relaxed, and worry-free state of mind. Your eyes are slightly closed and your teeth gently touching each other. There are five stages of training in this Microcosmic Circulation training. For the best results, it is best trained along with the Fundamentals of Qi Circulation techniques listed below. The 5 stages are as follow:

Stage 1.

Movement and Intention:

Step 1. Do Parts 1 through 3 of the Fundamentals of Qi Circulation standing.

Step 2. Sitting: Inhale and exhale, 3 times. Pay more attention to your exhalations, than your inhalations. Next, inhale, place your intent on your *mingmen*. Exhale and place your intent on your navel (Drawing 2-10). Practice 20 minutes or more each session.

> After practicing for a period of time, you will feel the flow of qi from your navel moving down to your *yongquan* during the exhalation; and you will feel a flow of qi up your legs to your *mingmen* during your inhalation. When you are able to feel this regularly, the first gate of the Microcosmic Circulation, the Tailbone Gate, will have opened.

Step 3. Do Part 6 of the Fundamentals of Qi Circulation.

Stage 2.

Movement and Intention:

Step 1. Do Parts 1 through 4 of the Fundamentals of Qi Circulation standing.

Step 2. Sitting: Inhale, place your intent on your *Dorsal Gate*. Exhale, place your intent on your navel (Drawing 2-11). Practice for 20

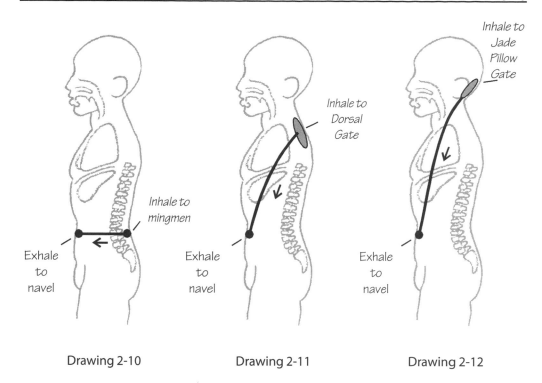

Drawing 2-10   Drawing 2-11   Drawing 2-12

minutes or more each session. After practicing for a period of time, you will begin to feel tingling, swelling, and heat sensations at your *Dorsal Gate*.

Later you will begin to feel qi flowing from your *mingmen* filling up to your *Dorsal Gate*. This sensation will become stronger and stronger. When you feel a sensation of qi at your Dorsal Gate area that is about the dimension of your palm; the second gate of the Microcosmic Circulation, will have opened.

Step 3. Do Part 6 of the Fundamentals of Qi Circulation.

Stage 3.

Movement and Intention:

Step 1. Do Parts 1 through 5 of the Fundamentals of Qi Circulation.

Step 2. Sitting: Inhale, place your intent on your *Jade Pillow Gate*. Exhale, place your intent on your navel (Drawing 2-12). Practice 20 minutes or more each session.

After practicing for a period of time, when you feel a sensation of qi at your *Jade Pillow Gate* area that is about the dimension of your palm, the third gate of the Microcosmic Circulation, will have opened.

Step 3. Do Part 6 of the Fundamentals of Qi Circulation.

Stage 4.

Movement and Intention:

Step 1. Do Parts 1 through 5 of the Fundamentals of Qi Circulation.

Step 2. Sitting: Gently touch the tip of your tongue on the palate of your mouth. After opening the three gates of the Microcosmic Circulation and when you feel qi accumulate at your *Jade Pillow Gate* area, use your mind to lead the qi up to your *baihui*.

This is accomplished by mentally using your eyes to look up and back at the *Jade Pillow Gate*, then bring the qi up to your *baihui*. Then lead the qi from your *baihui* down to your forehead. At this time, you will feel a comfortable, cool, moist sensation. Your entire body should feel very comfortable. Then press your tongue gently on the bottom of your mouth.

Don't use too strong an intent to lead the qi, be natural. Qi will naturally flow down your Conception Vessel back to your *dantian*. Practice for 10 minutes, rest for a while, then practice for another 10 minutes.

Step 3. Do Part 6 of the Fundamentals of Qi Circulation.

Stage 5. The Completed Microcosmic Circulation

When you have overcome the three restrictions in the first 4 Stages of the Microcosmic Circulation training, you are now ready to do the Microcosmic Circulation. The training method is as follows:

Posture and Intention:

Posture: Sit on a comfortable chair with about 1/3 of your hips on the chair. Your thighs should be horizontal to the floor, your knees bent at about 90 degrees, your knees about shoulder width apart, and your feet parallel. Place your palms face down on top of your knees.

Your *baihui* and your *huiyin* should be in a vertical line. Tuck your chin in slightly. Relax your shoulders and keep your back straight without straining it. Relax your entire body, eyes half closed, teeth gently touching. Eliminate scattered thoughts, keep your mind calm and carefree (Figure 2-6).

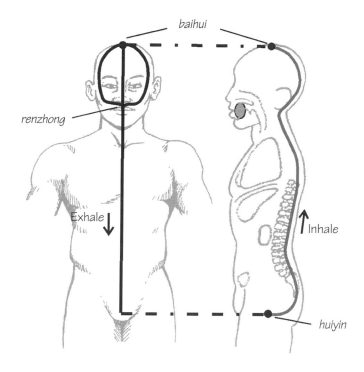

Drawing 2-13

Intention: Inhale and exhale 7 times, paying more attention to your exhalations, than your inhalations. Gently press your tongue on the palate of your mouth. Inhale through your nose and begin drawing in your abdomen, at the same time hold up your anus. Lead the qi from your *huiyin* up along the Governing Vessel, passing your sacrum, *Dorsal Gate, Jade Pillow Gate*, and up to your *baihui*.

Next, exhale, push your abdomen out slightly and relax your anus. At this time, allow the qi to flow down three paths: from your *baihui* down your nose to your *renzhong*, and from each side of your face between your eyes and ears, to your mouth. At this time, lower your tongue and gently press down on the bottom of your mouth. Qi will naturally flow down your Conception Vessel, to your *dantian (guanyuan)*, and back to your *huiyin*. Complete your exhalation (Drawing 2-13).

This completes one cycle of the Microcosmic Circulation. Practice 20 to 30 minutes each session.

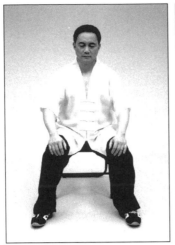

Figure 2-6   Figure 2-7

Figure 2-8

3. MACROCOSMIC CIRCULATION

The training principle of the Macrocosmic Circulation is the same as the Microcosmic Circulation. From the foundation you built in the Microcosmic Circulation, you are now prepared to extend the qi down to your legs and compete the Macrocosmic Circulation, taking your qigong training to another level.

Posture and Intention:

Posture: Sit as you did in Microcosmic Circulation, or stand comfortably (Figure 2-7), or lie down comfortably on your right side — your heart is located slightly to the left of your chest, so by lying down on your right side, you prevent your heart from being put under undue pressure (Figure 2-8). Use the other posture requirements from the Microcosmic Circulation.

Intention: Exhale, tongue touches the bottom of your mouth, bring your qi and intent down to your *dantian*. Completely exhale as

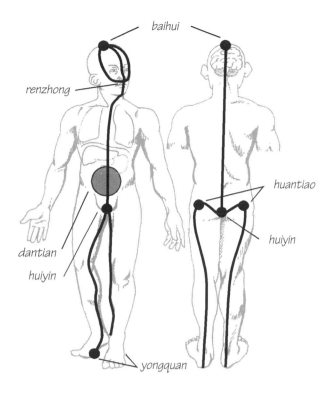

Drawing 2-14

you bring your qi and intent down to your *huiyin*, along the inside of your thighs and legs to your *yongquan*.

Inhale, begin drawing your abdomen in, and change your tongue so it touches the palate of your mouth. As you inhale, use your mind to lead the qi up from your *yongquan*, to the back of your heels, up along the back of your legs and thighs, to *huantiao* (buttocks), and meet at your *huiyin*. Hold up your anus, and lead the qi up your Governing Vessel, through the Three Gates of the Microcosmic Circulation, up to your *baihui*.

Allow the qi to flow down three paths: one from your *baihui* down your nose to *renzhong*, and one on each side of your face between your eyes and ears. The three paths converge at the tip of your tongue. At the same time, exhale, touch your tongue to the bottom of your mouth. Qi will naturally flow down your Conception Vessel, to your *dantian (guanyuan)* (Drawing 2-14). This completes one cycle of the Macrocosmic Circulation.

To continue the cycle, lead the qi down to your *yongquan* as you complete your exhalation. Practice 20 to 30 minutes each session.

This circulation is also known as the Macrocosmic Yin-Yang Circulation. Its purpose is to increase the interaction between the Conception Vessel, the Governing Vessel, and the three yang channels of the legs, and the three yin channels of the legs. The three yang channels of the legs are, the Stomach Channel, the Urinary Bladder Channel, and the Gall Bladder Channel. The three yin channels of the legs are, the Spleen Channel, the Kidney Channel, and the Liver Channel. Build a good habit of practicing Macrocosmic Circulation and Taijiquan regularly to assist in healing many chronic illnesses.

4. ABSORBING QI TO MAKE UP FOR THE LEAKAGE

This method was passed down by Zhang Zhi-Yang from Sichuan, China about 200 years ago. It is a method targeted for individuals that are unable to complete the Microcosmic Circulation due to deficient *jing*. The Chinese have a common saying, "There are many who want to learn the Dao and attain the goals, but there are only a few who are successful." One of the main reasons for men not being able to complete the Microcosmic Circulation is due to excessive sexual activities. All the benefits that come from the training are often lost, for this reason. It is like one is spending more than one is saving. You can figure out the consequences — you will be running on empty, when your reserve runs out.

It is not that one should not have sex. It is simply a cautious reminder to regulate one's sexual activities. This is especially important for men over forty. You are the judge of what is excessive. Your body will tell you if you pay attention to it. Some of the common symptoms are: chronic lower back pain, pain at your *mingmen*, pain at your sacrum, low energy level, dizziness, and ringing in the ears.

It is very important to regulate sexual activities. With proper training, you can strengthen your kidneys. This will also improve your sex life. There are methods that teach ways to improve the functioning of the sexual organs for the needs of some individuals. However, this is not the intent of this book. The purpose of this method is to maintain and strengthen your body. This technique absorbs energy from the universe to make up for loss, due to any kind of leakage.

This technique is especially valuable for individuals that are weak, old, deficient in both *yin* and *yang*, are unable to attain normal results from their training, are deficient in *jing*, or are unable to build up enough qi to complete the Microcosmic Circulation and Macrocosmic Circulation. With perseverance and continual practice, this method will allow your qi flow to become smoother and invigorate your life. Just practicing this method alone, can also help maintain your health and attain longevity.

Movement and Intention:

Step 1. *Intent at Your Yintang*: Sit comfortably on a chair, crossed legs, or lying on your right side. Relax your mind and body, and let go of all worries. Close your eyes halfway and place your attention on your *Yintang* — pay more attention to your inhalations, than your exhalations.

Stay in this state until your breathing become regular and smooth, so that not even the stimulation of feather on your nose will bother you.

Step 2. *Fill the Yintang*: Stay in the same sitting position. Visualize the qi that has gathered at your *Yintang* is now being led into your forehead — pay more attention to your inhalations, than your exhalations. Stay in this state until you are *full*. That is, when you feel tired and sleepy, like a contented baby after a meal.

Step 3. *Distributing Qi*: Lie down on your right side as in Figure 2-8. Use your mind to lead the qi that you have been absorbing, to your entire body. After the qi has been distributed to the rest of your body, you will feel cool, comfortable, energized, have a shining complexion, and a lifted spirit. You will feel the most wonderful sensations.

Notes:

After training Steps 1 through 3 for a period of time, replace Stage 2 by: inhaling, leading the qi from the tip of your nose to your *Yintang* to make up the leakage and for storage. Exhale, lead the qi down to your *mingmen* and sacrum area to solidify your *life-qi* and strengthen your *kidney-yang*. This will stabilizing your *mingmen* qi

Kidney-yang is also called *kan-water*, it is externally yin and internally yang. The most important aspect is the *internal-yang*. *Internal-yang* is responsible for the rising of qi. It is often weakened by poor life habits. This technique is for strengthening the *kidney-qi* and strengthening the *kidney-yang* which in turn assists in the rising of qi. The more you train, the more qi will be stored. Only when enough qi has been stored, will your body have enough potential for raising qi. Besides helping to raise qi and to circulate energy, this training can also help strengthen the body, providing you with higher energy, health, and longevity.

5. NOURISHING QI METHOD

Nourishing Qi Method, as the name implies, is for nourishing your qi. If we don't nourish our qi, then our *genuine-qi* will be deficient and our attainment will be low. With constant nourishment you will be able to attain a higher potential. By practicing Nourishing Qi Methods regularly you will develop an even strong foundation and attainment potential for all the qi circulation methods.

Posture and Intention:

Posture: Stand, sit or lie down. Relax your body, breathe naturally.

Intention: Pay attention to your *dantian* (Women during their period should pay attention to the *shanzhong* area, the midpoint between the nipples). However, don't use too strong a focus. Gently overlap your palms on top of your abdomen, men with their left hand inside, women with their right hand inside. Practice as long as you wish during each session.

After a long period of regular practice, *genuine-qi* will accumulate in your *dantian* and become a qi ball, qi elixir. As an alternative, you can simply relax your entire body and not pay attention to any particular spot. You can practice anytime, while standing or sitting, by placing your palms on top of your abdomen. By practicing this method in a relaxed state, some illnesses can also be eliminated. It is necessary to practice with perseverance to build an even stronger foundation for other qigong training.

2.3. Level Two

From the foundation you have achieved through the Microcosmic and Macrocosmic Circulation, you are now ready for the next level of Daoist Qigong training. This section consists of: Nine Rotations to Bring Back the Spiritual Elixir, Eight Extraordinary Vessel Circulation, 14 Meridian Circulation, and Sunrise and Sunset Circulation. You can select one or more of the four qigong methods to practice.

We have also included an Accumulating Qi Method and Golden Light Method that can assist you in attaining an even stronger foundation for your continual training. We will introduce these two methods first.

1. ACCUMULATING QI METHOD

This method can accumulate qi quickly, allowing the *genuine-qi* to fill up in your *dantian* and provide a stronger potential to pass through the paths of qi circulation. It is also trained as a foundation for other qigong methods.

Movement and Visualization:

Step 1. Visualize, "I am immersed in qi, qi is within me, I am unified with the cosmos, and qi is available for me to use." Relax your entire body and immerse your body in the etheric qi field.

Step 2. Draw a circle in a spiral pattern above your *dantian* (don't touch your body) with your right palm, men circle clockwise, women circle counterclockwise. Gradually increase the size of the circle over your body as big as your hand can reach.

Then gradually decrease the size of the circle and back to *dantian*. Repeat as many times as you wish. When drawing the spiral, visualize qi and the light of the cosmos are being absorbed into your body towards your abdomen.

Notes:

Under normal conditions, the *genuine-qi* in the body is in a state of calm and balance. When your hand spirals over your body, the *genuine-qi* begins to circulate. A centripetal force is generated and pulls the *genuine-qi* towards the center of the spiral and gradually fills up the entire body.

Even after you have stopped spiraling, the genuine-qi will still condense towards the center for a period of time. It is like swirling water in a bucket. With the combination of spiraling the hand and your mind, *genuine-qi* can be gathered and fill your entire body in a short period of time.

2. GOLDEN LIGHT METHOD

The Golden Light Method is for cultivating the body, regulating the spirit, guarding against negative energies, increasing your energy field, increasing your Yang-Qi and refining your Yin-Qi. It is especially advantageous in the protection of the cultivators' *heart* and body. Wandering Daoists of the past used this method to bring good luck and prevent misfortune, increase their precognition ability; and prevent the distractions of society and that of the lower astral planes. When one is able to sustain the Golden Light, one will be able to prevent external negative influences from affecting one's cultivation. You will be able to realize the mystical potential after a long period of practice. We can only point you in that direction.

Part 1. Preparation

Movement and Intention:

Step 1. Before beginning this training, rinse your mouth and wash your hands.

Step 2. Sit with your back straight on a chair or sit cross leg or on a mat. Overlap your hands on top of each other with your thumbs gently touching each other, men with their left hand on top, women with their right hand on top. Place your hands in front of your abdomen without touching your abdomen. Your armpits should be open.

Step 3. This is a high level Daoist Qigong method. While cultivating this method, one asks and hopes for assistance from the astral planes. Like a religious prayer, you must ask your God, Creator, Buddha, and/or Entity that you pray to for assistance. You must also thank the teacher that taught you this method, and thank your teacher's teachers.

You must also promise to cultivate with perseverance, promise to have a compassionate heart, promise to help other people, promise to forgive others, promise to have universal love. Then, you must repent all wrong that you have done and set your cultivation goals.

Step 4. Relax your mind, relax your emotions. Don't think of external thoughts, don't look at external scenery, and don't listen to external sounds. Relax your body. Relax your hair, skin, muscles, tendons, blood vessels, nervous system, bones, and organs. Your entire body should be relaxed.

Step 5. Calm your *heart* in a peaceful environment.

Step 6. Breathe naturally and allow the body to be in a natural state. Be natural and release the restriction of your Personality (Post-Birth Spirit).

Part 2. Golden Light Hand Seal

Movement and Visualization:

Step 1. Change your hand posture to the Golden Light Hand Seal in front of you (Figure 2-9).

Figure 2-9

The Golden Light Hand Seal is accomplished by coiling your middle and fourth fingers in and placing your thumb gently on top of them. Then gently press the index and small fingers of both hands towards each other.

Step 2. Close your eyes or half close your eyes. Visualize a white full moon in front of you, illuminating your entire body. After a few moments, visualize that the full moon enters your Heavenly Eye (Third Eye) into your head, and up to the top of your head *(baihui)*. Then down to your *shanzhong* point and enters into your heart.

Step 3. Visualize and look *internally* at your heart. Your heart is illuminating a golden radiance from small to large. This golden radiance becomes the rising reddish sun (radiating golden radiance) and illuminating the organs in your chest. Remain in this state of visualization for 3 to 5 minutes. If you should feel that the energy is too great, then start with only 1 or 2 minutes. Gradually increase the time after a period of practice.

Step 4. Next, lead the reddish sun to your *shanzhong* point. Pause there for 30 seconds to one minute. Then lower the reddish sun with the golden radiance down the center line of your chest to the middle of your lower abdomen, *inside-dantian*. Visualize that the golden radiance from the reddish sun is increasing in size and fills your body from the inside, out to every pore and every strand of hair.

Continue to expand the golden radiance in a spherical pattern until it covers the size of the room you are practicing in or 10 to 20 feet around you. Be as clear with your visualization as possible.

Figure 2-10   Figure 2-11

Part 3. Closing

Movements and Visualization

Step 1. Raise your arms over your head with your palms facing each other as though you are holding a ball (Figure 2-10). As you inhale deeply, lower your hands slowly down as you bring your hands together in front of your chest (Figure 2-11). At the same time, visualize that the golden light quickly shrinks back down to your *inside-dantian* becoming a reddish elixir pill illuminating a red radiance.

Repeat Step 1, 3 times to condense all the illuminating qi into your *lower-dantian*.

Step 2. Next, warm up your palms by rubbing them together and massage your face, your ears, the back of your neck, and your arms.

Notes:

1. Practice 1 or 2 times daily. Generally, it will take about 15 to 20 minutes per session. If you should feel too hot, reduce the time of your practice for each session.

2. Some people will feel their body expanding suddenly during practice. Don't be afraid or get nervous. Let the sensations occur naturally and pay attention to the sensations to realize this amazing state.

3. During the Closing, some people will feel their body shrinking. This is also normal.

4. This training can be practiced with any other qigong method. With time and practice, a purple radiance will appear around the golden light. Individuals with a good qigong foundation may be able to see auras. Negative energies will not be able to hurt you. At the very least, you will be able to receive signals and the *pure essence* of the cosmos.

5. There is a Golden Light Mantra that is practiced with this method. When you have a chance, ask your teacher to teach you and recite it with you.

3. NINE ROTATIONS TO BRING BACK THE SPIRITUAL ELIXIR

Posture and Intention:

Posture: Sit, stand, or lie down. Rotate your tongue in your mouth three times. Swallow your saliva and lead your qi down to your pubic bone. When you feel a qi sensation at your pubic area, then do the following exercise (Use Drawing 2-15 as a reference).

Intention: Exhale and lead qi to your big toe then to your heels. Inhale and lead qi up to your *weizhong*, your *huantiao*, to your *huiyin*, past your anus, to your *changqiang*, and to your *jiaji*.

Exhale and lead qi to your *jiquan*, to your *zhongchong* on the tip of your middle finger. Inhale and lead qi back to your *jianjing*, to the *Dorsal Gate*, then to the *Jade Pillow Gate*.

Exhale and lead qi to the bottom of your ears, to the top of your ears, circle three times around your ears, back to the *Jade Pillow Gate*. Inhale and *use your eyes* to bring qi from the Jade Pillow Gate to your *baihui*.

Exhale and lead qi to your *renzhong*, to the tip of your tongue, down your Conception Vessel, and back to your pubic bone. Continue down to your big toe and repeat the cycle.

The above path is also called the Macrocosmic Circulation. Repeating the above three times completes a set. After every set, rotate your tongue in your mouth three times and swallow your saliva. Do three sets.

To finish this circulation, lead qi back to your *dantian*. Stand, sit, or lie down calmly and relax your intention. Be as comfortable as possible. Stay in

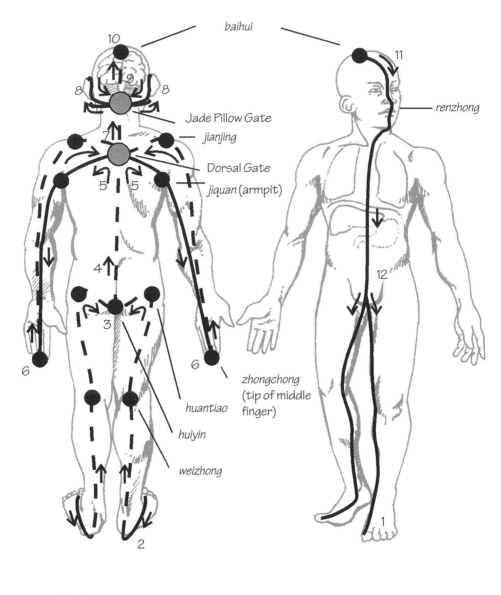

baihui
10
9
8
8
Jade Pillow Gate
7
jianjing
Dorsal Gate
5   5
jiquan (armpit)
4
3
6
6
zhongchong
(tip of middle
finger)
huantiao
huiyin
weizhong
2

11
renzhong
12
1

———— Exhale

— — — Inhale

Drawing 2-15

this state until you feel like stopping. Next, do Part 6 — Concluding Massage from the Fundamentals of Qi Circulation, and massage your rib area before finishing.

4. EIGHT EXTRAORDINARY VESSEL CIRCULATION

The Eight Extraordinary Vessel Circulation is for circulating qi to permeate throughout the body, via the Eight Extraordinary Vessels. It is trained after you have built a solid foundation from the Macrocosmic Circulation which involves only two vessels, the Conception and the Governing Vessels. The Eight Extraordinary Vessel Circulation involves all eight vessels. The path of circulation in this training spreads throughout the body. After a period of training, the meridians and collaterals can be further strengthened to the next level. All diseases can be eliminated, bringing your mind and body to an even higher level of qigong attainment.

The Eight Extraordinary Vessels and their respective paths for this circulation training are listed below; and the path of circulation is shown in Drawing 2-16.

Conception Vessel: Begin at your *huiyin*, up your abdomen, along the center line of your chest, to your lower lip.

Governing Vessel: Begin at your coccyx, up to your sacrum, along the middle of your spine, up along the middle of your neck, up to the top of your head, to the top of your lip.

Thrusting Vessel: Begin at your groin, up through part of the Kidney Channel (sacrum and lumbar), to your chest.

Girdle Vessel: A complete circle around your waist.

Yin-Maintenance Vessel: Begin at your shoulder, along the inside of the arm, to the tip of your middle finger, one on each side.

Yang-Maintenance Vessel: Begin at the tip of your middle finger, along the outside of your arm, to your chest, one on each side.

Yin-Activation Vessel: Begin at the inside of your ankle bone, up along the inside of your leg and thigh, to the side of your abdomen, to side of your chest, until your face, one on each side.

Yang Activation Vessel: Begin at the outside ankle bone, up along the outside of your leg and thigh, to the back side of your rib cage and shoulders, to your face, one on each side.

Notes:

Some of the vessels described in this training are different from the medical explanation of the paths. The descriptions used are based on the traditional Daoist training method.

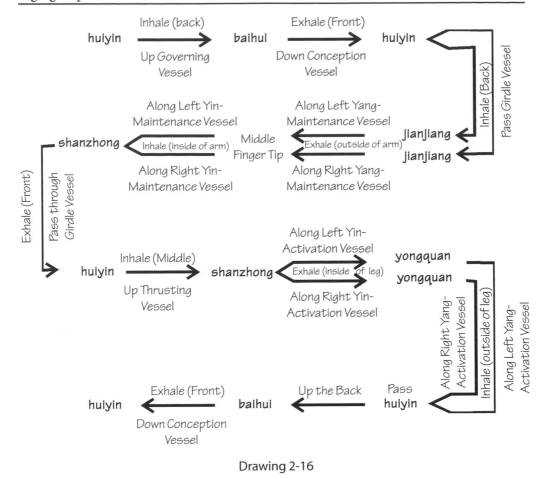

Drawing 2-16

Posture and Intention:

Posture: Start your training standing. After you are smooth with the paths, then you may go on to train while sitting or lying down. Initially, follow the intention and breathing described below. As you become smoother with the circulation, you may then reduce the inhalation and exhalation frequency, without affecting the qi circulation.

Intention: (Use Drawing 2-16 as a reference.) Lead qi from your *huiyin* and finish at your *huiyin*. In this circulation training, you will pass your *huiyin* three times, pass your *baihui* two times, pass your palms once, pass the bottom of your feet once, pass your collarbone once, and pass your *shanzhong* twice.

Change your breathing every time you pass a point, a total of 10 breath changes or 5 complete inhalations and exhalations. A complete circulation is achieved every time you complete the path. You can practice as many circulations as you wish.

5. 14 MERIDIAN CIRCULATION

The 14 Meridian Circulation is the complementary circulation technique to the Eight Extraordinary Vessel Circulation. When you have completed these two circulations, you will have smoothed out the entire body's energy pathways. Before beginning to learn this circulation, you will need to familiarize yourself with the 14 Meridians, their flow patterns, their primary points, and the points where your breathing changes.

A total of 108 different points are involved in this training. It is very important to remember all of them. Appendix A contains a set of acupuncture charts for your reference. When your intention is back to your *huiyin*, stay sitting calmly, forget about everything, and let go of all intentions. Stay in that state for a few minutes.

Drawing 2-17 shows the qi flow pattern from one channel to the next and the time period when the qi is most predominant in that channel. By following the qi circulation pattern in your training, you can greatly improve the flow of qi in your channels.

Posture and Intention:

Posture: Sit or stand.

Intention: Use the points listed below and Drawing 2-17 as a reference. During each inhalation and exhalation, pay attention to one point or the pair of points. Begin at your *huiyin*.

Conception Vessel: *changqiang, mingmen, dazhui, baihui, renzhong*

Governing Vessel: *chengjiang, shanzhong, shenque, qugu, huiyin*

Lung Channel: *zhongfu, yunmen, chize, lieque, taiyuan, yuji, shaoshang*

Large Intestine Channel: *shangyang, hegu, shousanli, quchi, binao, jugu, jingfutu, yingxiang*

Stomach Channel: *chengqi, dicang, xiaguan, touwei, daying, quepen, burong, tianshu, qichong, biguan, liangqiu, zusanli, jiexi, chongyang, lidui*

Spleen Channel: *yinbai, gongsun, sanyinjiao, yinlingquan, chongmen, daheng, zhourong, dabao*

Heart Channel: *jiquan, shaohai, tongli, shenmen, shaofu, shaochong*

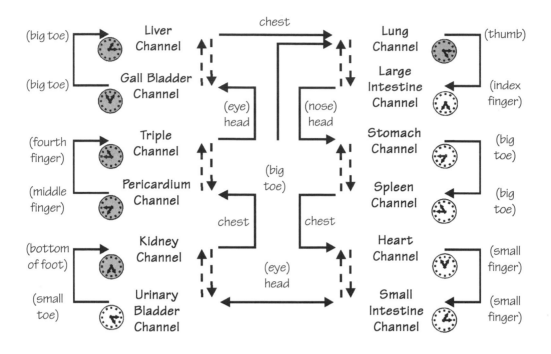

Drawing 2-17

Small Intestine: *shaoze, yanglao, xiaohai, tianzong, tianchuang, quanliao*

Urinary Bladder Channel: *jingming, tongtian, dashu, fengmen, geshu, xiaoliao, weizhong, kunlun, shenmai, zhiyin*

Kidney Channel: *yongquan, rangu, fuliu, henggu, shufu*

Pericardium Channel: *tianchi, quze, neiquan, daling, laogong, zhongchong*

Triple Burner Channel: *quanchong, zhongzhu (hand), waiquan, tianjing, yifeng, jiaosun, ermen, sizhukong*

Gall Bladder Channel: *tongziliao, fengchi, jianjing, riyue, jingmen, daomai, huantiao, fengshi, yanglingquan, qiuxu, qiaoyin (foot)*

Liver Channel: *dadun, taichong, zhongfeng, zhongdu (tibia), jimai, zhangmen, qimen*

Conception Vessel: *guanyuan, huiyin*

6. SUNRISE AND SUNSET CIRCULATION

As the name implies, it is a circulation training for practicing during sunrise (5 - 7 A.M), and sunset (5 - 7 P.M.). This circulation training focuses on the front of the body, energizing the five viscera and the six bowels. It takes advantage of the sun's energy, radiation, magnetic field, and other energy of nature to strengthen the organs and its functioning. The specialized emphasis of the Sunrise and Sunset Circulation training complements the other Daoist qigong presented earlier in this chapter. It can bring your training to an even higher level.

Posture and Intention:

Posture: Stand, sit, or lie down.

Intention: Use the raising and lowering of your *Adam's Apple* to assist in your breathing. Your breathing should be slow, soft, fine, even, deep, long, continuous, and natural.

Inhale: lead qi from your *dantian*, to the left side of your abdomen, to the left side of your chest, past your left collar bone, up the right side of your face to your left *Taiyan* (temple), to your *Yintang* (eye bridge).

Exhale: lead qi from your *Yintang*, to your right *Taiyang*, down the right side of your face, past your right collar bone, to the right side of your chest, to the right side of your abdomen, back to your *dantian*.

This completes a cycle of qi circulation. Repeat 36 times. Then reverse the circle. That is, inhale and lead qi up the right side of your body, and exhale down the left side of your body. Repeat 24 times. A total of 60 circles.

2.4. Level Three

There are many high level training methods. As you approach higher level qigong training, it becomes increasingly important that you have the guidance of qualified teachers. In this section, we will discuss the Gathering the Spirit Method and the Seven Star Big Dipper Method. These training methods must be taught from teacher to students. Our purpose for discussing these methods is to bring your awareness to the available training methods as you progress in your learning and evolution. The qigong in this section will cover the Converting Bone Marrow to Qi.

Gathering the Spirit Method is also referred to as the Absorbing Light and Gathering Qi Method. This method has been taught only through word of mouth and face to face, from teacher to students, without any written words. It is a high level cultivation method. It is a classic method that trains the physical body and cultivates the spirit simultaneously.

Light or aura is an expression of qi in higher vibration. Qi is the foundation of life, and light is the foundation of the spirit. Qi is still within the three dimensional space where the physical body lives, and has not gone beyond the restriction of matter. Light on the other hand has the characteristics of the higher dimensions. There are also many qualitative levels of light.

Daoists believe that humans have three finer spirits and seven baser spirits. The cultivation of the spirit is for fostering the seven baser spirits into Yin Spirit and the three finer spirits into Yang Spirit. Then combine the Yin Spirit and the Yang Spirit and cultivate them into Original Spirit.

The nurturing of the Original Spirit and the expression of the extraordinary abilities are accomplished in the light form. "Without light, your attainment will not reach a high potential. Without light, the cultivation of immortality has no immortal potential". This method is an effective method for cultivating light.

The key to this method is with the path of *light-qi* circulation. In this training, the cultivator absorbs the light of the cosmos to nourish the body; and adjusts, supplements, and repairs the deficiencies or damage of the body. The training follows the path of the nervous system. The benefits are easily seen. The circulation also passes through the forehead, the pituitary gland, the pineal gland, the adrenal gland, prostate gland, thymus gland, thyroid gland, tonsil, and all the other important glands in the body.

Many of the gland functions decrease with age. In high level qigong training, it is necessary to reactivate the proper functioning of these glands. The pineal gland is of high importance. It is strongly related to the *opening* of the Heavenly Eye (Third Eye). The reactivation of the pineal gland is very critical in the maintenance of human energy, and in slowing down the aging process. This method absorbs the *light-qi* into the body to flush, massage, lubricate, nourish, and reactivate these glands. The activation of all these glands will bring them back to a youthful and vital state.

This method uses conscious breathing as a *switch* and uses the mind as a *force* to apply the *light-qi*. The *upper-dantian* is the warehouse for the storage of the light. It is necessary to gather Spiritual Light (light-qi) if one is to nourish the Original Spirit. To be connected to the astral planes, it is also necessary to open the Heavenly Eye in your forehead.

This method was a well guarded secret in the past. It is especially important for people beginning to cultivate the Dao after middle age. If your body is automatically activated to move, it is referred to as a Spiritual Movement. Don't be alerted or nervous. It is a normal reaction to the training. The traditional training time was between 1:00 and 11:00 A.M. Another training time is be-

Figure 2-12

tween 5:00 and 7:00 P.M. The location of your practice should be an area with an abundance of healthy flowers and trees, and with plenty of fresh air.

Seven Star Big Dipper Method is an other high level qigong training. It must also be transmitted from the teacher to the student. It is especially important for a married man in high level training. This training can bring the body back to the health and vitality of a teenager.

1. CONVERTING BONE MARROW TO QI

The complete name for this method is Fostering Shen into Void — Converting Bone Marrow to Qi. There are many different methods of training this qigong from one school to the next. Here we will present the one that has been passed down to us.

Posture:

Stand with your feet shoulder width apart, knees slightly bent, grab the floor with your toes, hold up your anus, keep your back straight, relax your chest, and round your back. Raise your arms up in front of you with your arms bent in and palms facing down (Figure 2-12).

Relax your fingers and coil them in slightly, as if you were pushing on a ball on the surface of water. Tuck your chin in slightly, and press your tongue gently on the palate of your mouth. Keep your upper body relaxed and the lower body firm, while keeping your weight evenly distributed over your legs, but slightly more weight on the ball of your foot than your heel.

Part 1. Circulating Qi

Procedure:

Step 1. Practice the Microcosmic and Macrocosmic Circulation, one then the next, for a total of 20 minutes.

Step 2. Use your mind to lead the qi from your big toe into the ground as if you were throwing a fishing net to catch a fish. Then *pull the net back in* from the ground, lead the qi into your body from your *yongquan*.

Lead the qi up the tibia and fibula, as if water were filling a container. Continue filling your bones with qi, up past your knees to your femur (thigh bone), to your pubic bone, hip bones, and enter the spinal column from your coccyx.

Next, lead the qi up your sacrum, to your lumbar vertebrae, to your thoracic vertebrae, to your cervical vertebrae, into your brain, and to your ears. Then lead the qi to your collarbones, shoulder blades, and ribs. Finally lead the qi to your shoulder bones, to your humerus, past your elbow, to your ulna and radius, to your wrist, and to your finger bones.

At this point, the bones in your body are filled with qi. You will feel as though your bones are as heavy as lead. Your body feels like a thousand pounds; and your feet feel rooted to the ground with the force of a thousand pounds.

Notes:

During your inhalation, draw your abdomen in and lead the qi upward. During your exhalation, your abdomen pushes out slightly and stops leading your qi. When leading your qi, keep your body relaxed, mind calm, and natural. Breathe slowly and evenly. Your mind should be actively leading the qi up your body.

Part 2. Condensing Qi

Procedure:

Step 1. When qi fills throughout your bones, bring your mind to your *dantian*. Breathe naturally and maintain the containment of qi in your bones. Contain the qi in your bones for 3 to 9 breaths. As you get smoother in this training, gradually increase the length of containment to 27 breaths.

Figure 2-13   Figure 2-14   Figure 2-15

Step 2. Then overlap your hands over your *dantian* and bend your upper body forward from your waist; exhale, and lead the qi from your bones, past your *mingmen* to your *inside-dantian* (Figure 2-13). You may need to repeat bending and leading the qi a few times, to lead as much qi to your *inside-dantian* as you can. At this time, you will feel your abdomen area filled with qi — qi pulsating in your *dantian*. You will feel the qi build up from the Converting Bone Marrow to Qi method, is much higher than the Fostering Jing into Qi methods.

Part 3. Distributing Qi

Because the Converting Bone Marrow to Qi method builds up a high level of qi, you will have to circulate the qi after Condensing the Qi in your *dantian* before finishing this training.

Procedure:

Procedure: Inhale deep into your lungs, draw your abdomen in, and use your mind to radiate the qi from your *dantian* to your entire body. Feel your body expanding like a balloon filled with air; and floating off the ground. Let your arms naturally move away from your body (Figure 2-14).

Exhale, push your abdomen out slightly, and use your mind to lead the qi back to your *dantian*. Feel your body condensing as though your entire body shrunk into a tiny point in your *dantian*. Lower your arms back down, with your arms rounded in front of you and your palms facing down (Figure 2-15).

Figure 2-16

Repeat 3 to 9 times, initially. As you get more comfortable with the training, gradually increase to 27 breaths.

Part 4. Finishing

Procedure:

Overlap your hands on your *dantian*. Pay attention to your breathing for 27 cycles. Breathe softly, slowly, deep, and long (Figure 2-16). Use either the Nourishing or Releasing finish described below.

Nourishing Finish — for people who show *insufficiency symptom-complex*. Men, lead the qi to the left side of the abdomen. Women, lead the qi to the right side of the abdomen. When you feel qi has been collected in the designated area, walk around for a few minutes.

Releasing Finish — for people who show *excessive symptom-complex*. The technique for men and women are the same. Disperse qi through your big toes into the ground. Walk for a few minutes.

Book 3:

Buddhist Qigong

3.1. Buddhist Philosophy and Training Concepts

Buddhism is not just a religion, but also a major part of the Chinese culture. Like Daoism, Buddhism can also be generalized into religious and nonreligious parts. The nonreligious part of Buddhism consists of the customs and culture that are inherent in Chinese society. Many Chinese follow the philosophy of Buddhism as a part of their culture and way of life, not necessarily as a religion. Buddhist Qigong is a part of the culture that has been widely practiced by the Chinese people. For many religious Buddhist, Buddhist Qigong assists them in their pursuit of buddhahood (enlightenment or realization). For others, it is a means of attaining better health, higher self-awareness, and developing the higher potentials of the mind and body.

Buddhism originated in ancient India, from the teachings of the first Buddha, Sakyamuni. He was born in 620 B.C. and left this physical plane in 543 B.C. There are many different sects of Buddhism. They can be generalized under two main systems, Mahayana and Hinayana Buddhism. Under Mahayana Buddhism the attainment of buddhahood is presented within the framework of two vehicles, Sutrayana and Tantrayana. Under each of the two vehicles are different sects and under these sects are different traditions. The Qigong in Book Three will focus on the Tantrayana cultivation of Mahayana Buddhism (Tantric Buddhism).

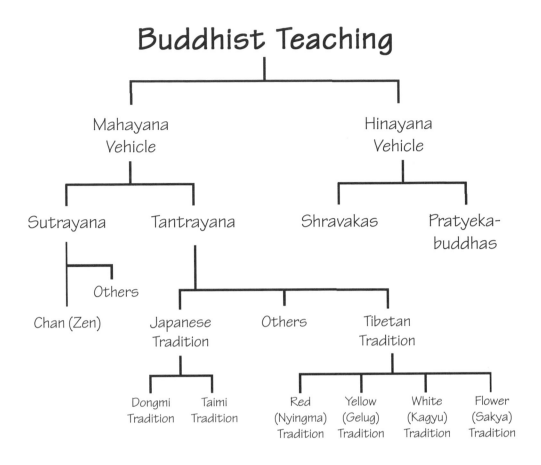

Buddhist Teaching

Chart 3-1

Tantric Buddhism includes: Tibetan, Dongmi, and Taimi. Tibetan Buddhism covers many areas including, Tibet, Nepal, the Plateau of Tibet, Mongolia, Northeastern India, and Northeastern China. Within Tibetan Buddhism are four major traditions: the Red (Nyingma), the Yellow (Gelug), the White (Kagyu), and the Flower (Sakya). Dongmi Buddhism and Taimi Buddhism are subdivisions within Japanese Tantric Buddhism (Chart 3-1).

Tantric Buddhist cultivation involves the cultivation of the Esoteric Abilities of the Body, Speech, and Mind, to reach nirvana. Because their practices are very profound, this sect of Buddhism gradually became known as Mizong in China. Mizong literally means the Secret Doctrine. The implication, however, is not due to the secretive nature of the practice, but due to the extensive and profound nature of the practice.

Tantric Buddhist Philosophy and Training Concepts

One of the significant differences between Buddhism and any other religion, is the fact that there are thousands of Buddhist sutras. Even though there are thousand of sutras, the fundamental principle of Buddhism consists of the doctrine of *karma (cause and effect)* and *shunyata (Emptiness)*. Karma states that all things in the cosmos are the result of cause and effect. Because all things in the cosmos are interrelated by this principle, nothing has an inherent existence on its own. Since nothing exists on its own, it is *Void* of independent existence — *shunyata*. Void or emptiness are not to be confused with nothingness as in the English language; it is the interrelation of cause and effect. Because there is karma (cause and effect), there is shunyata (emptiness, Void, no inherent existence by itself).

Buddhism believes that not only material things are a result of the karma and shunyata; but the human spirit is also a result of karma and shunyata. Our spirit, mind, intention, are all a result of our family, school, society, and environment. This is very apparent in our daily encounters, where we are affected emotionally by what others say or do.

The Buddhist view of the cosmos includes both the View and the Viewer. That is, the View and the Viewer are one. From the Viewer's perspective, the View can't exist without the Viewer. Therefore, the view must begin with the Viewer. Then the focus must be placed on the Viewer to discover the true nature of the View. If this Viewer is *I*, then *I* can't exist independently from the existence of things that *I* observed, the View. It is like a coin, where there is no such thing as a one sided coin. We can't know something exists, if we don't exist. Similarly, nothing exists if there is not an observer, *I*, to *know* that things exist. The relationship of *I* and the other things in the cosmos are dependent on each other to exist. Without one, there is not the other. It does not matter what subject matter we are talking about, it is all the product of our *presence*, that gives it its *existence*.

Tantric Buddhist cultivation involves actively engaging in and experiencing to attain enlightenment. They follow the doctrine of *karma* and *shunyata* to their realization. The cultivation of these doctrines, can generally be divided into two parts: cultivating the *wisdom* to see that all things lack inherent existence and purifying the karmic causing sources — our body, speech, and mind. That is, through what we do, what we say, and what we think, we cause some sort of effect.

Tantric Buddhists believe that everyone can attain buddhahood . They believe that to achieve buddhahood, one cannot solely rely on philosophy and discussion. The physically unexperiential, words inexpressible, and the mind incomprehensible aspects of buddhahood, are categorized into the Three Esoterics: the Esoteric Abilities of the Body, the Esoteric Abilities of Speech, and the Esoteric Abilities of the Mind. The cultivation of the Three Esoterics is to purify the Three Karma. The three karmic causing agents: our body, speech, and mind; involve all the activities of life including human actions and thoughts, good and bad. Tantric Buddhists believe that by cultivating the Three Esoterics they will be able to purify the Three Karma, escape the cycle of reincarnation, and gain enlightenment.

It does not make any difference which Tantric Buddhist Sect we speak of, the cultivation methods will all include cultivating the Three Esoterics. The Three Esoterics are an integral part of each other, and are not to be separated. The Esoteric Abilities of the Body, Speech, and Mind must be done together to produce the highest results. These symbolic expressions involving the Three Esoterics allow the entire being to achieve an esoteric experience that interacts directly with nirvana.

Cultivating the Esoteric Abilities of the Body — Tantric Buddhists believe that the human body contains many profound and esoteric abilities that can link with the cosmos. By using ancient traditional hand and body seal training methods, the practitioner will be able to unlock the hidden abilities within and achieve a union of human and the cosmos, and attain realization. Hand seals are a sign language in Tantric Buddhism. The hand seals are formed with the two hands intertwined, with the right hand symbolizing wisdom and the left hand symbolizing calmness. Each finger, from your pinkie to your thumb, symbolizes earth, water, fire, wind, and the *Void* respectively.

Body seals are accomplished by positioning the body in different postures. In Indian Yoga, forms of body seals have been practiced since ancient times. Pressing the heel against the *huiyin* point and gently pressing the chin against the chest are examples of body seals. Body seals are practiced along with hand seals, mantras, and visualization.

The seals represent a pledge and commitment to transcend karma and achieve enlightenment. They are symbolic methods used to attain a communication between the cultivator and the greater consciousness. In Tantric Buddhist Qigong, the ten fingers connect with the cosmos externally, and connect to the organs internally. Making hand seals are also like fine tuning a radio to receive the broadcast of a radio station.

The Tantric Buddhist Qigong training involves three energy channels and seven energy centers (chakras). The three channels are the Middle, Left and Right Channels. The Middle Channel is the most important. Its color is blue, located inside the spinal cord. It runs from the Sea Bottom (perineum area) up to the top of the head. Along either side of the Middle Channel is the Left and Right Channel. The Left Channel has a red color and connects at the bottom, to the right testicle in men. The Right Channel has a white color and connects at the bottom, to the left testicle. In a women, the Left and Right Channel connect to the right and left ovaries. The three channels are not visible to the eyes.

130

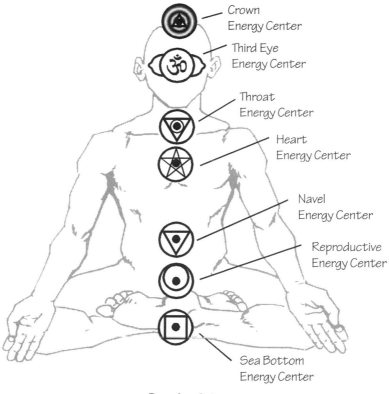

Drawing 3-1

They can only be felt by practitioners after energy channels are open. Different individuals may have different sensations with these energy channels. Some may feel the Left and Right Channels intertwining in a wave like pattern around the Middle Channel.

The seven energy centers are the Sea Bottom, Reproductive, Navel, Heart, Throat, Third Eye, and Crown Energy Centers (Drawing 3-1). The Sea Bottom Energy Center is located around the *huiyin* area. It is also known as the *Root Chakra*. The Sea Bottom Energy Center is the energy and power source of all the other energy centers. It is represented by a four petal lotus. Ancient Indian Yogis believed that a Spiritual Snake, coiled up into three and one-half loops, sleeps in this area with its head pointing down.

The Reproductive Energy Center is located at the root of the reproductive organ. It is represented by a six petal lotus. It manages the sex glands, ovaries in women, testicles and prostate gland in men. The Navel Energy Center, located around the belly button, is represented by a ten petal lotus. It manages the spleen, liver, pancreas, and adrenal gland. The Heart Energy Center, located around the heart, is represented by a twelve petal lotus. It manages the thymus gland, heart, and lungs. The Throat Energy Center, located at the throat, is represented by a sixteen petal lotus. It manages the thyroid gland, tonsils, and salivary gland. The Third Eye Energy Center, located around the eye bridge, is symbolized by a two petal lotus. It manages the pituitary gland. The Crown Energy Center, located at the soft spot on top of the head (most apparent on a babies' heads), is represented by a one thousand petal lotus. This symbolizes the one thousand energy radiation emitting from this energy center.

The method of cultivation in the Esoteric Abilities of the Body is to awaken the *dormant fire* of the Sea Bottom Energy Center; expand that *fire, one* energy center at a time up to the Crown Energy Center; and enter into a tranquil state. This will allow the *nectar* generated to flow down all over the body. This nectar serves to nourish the body, attain a state of peace and joy, heal illness, strengthen the body, extend the life, develop extraordinary abilities, and reach enlightenment.

Cultivating the Esoteric Abilities of Speech — The Esoteric Abilities of Speech involves chanting mantras. It is not necessary to understand the meaning of the words or sounds of the mantras. It is important, however, to have a strong belief and focus while chanting. By sincerely reciting the mantra of realization, the practitioner can attain unlimited merit. Science today has not been able to explain the mysterious connection between sounds and life, and the power of sound. What we do know is that the vibration from sound can cause an avalanche; it can calm the mind; it can put people to sleep; it can make people happy or sad; and it can even kill. Sound can stimulate the growth of plants, and pleasant music can even help cows produce more milk.

Mantra means *Truth*. In Buddhism, *Truth* are words of the Buddha. Also, the internal, unspoken real thoughts in our mind are also considered as *Truth*. Spoken words often contain some arrogance and tinted truth. The unspoken thoughts are the real truth. Human thoughts, considered the unspoken truth, are hard for others to comprehend. In human languages, thoughts are first processed in our brain, translated into words, then expressed by our mouth. A mantra can be expressed with or without words. There are many mantras for bringing health and good fortune, and preventing misfortunes. A mantra contains pledges and wishes without any pretense. It is the true expression of the *heart*.

Over the centuries, great masters of the Tantric Buddhist Sect passed down many mantras. The special tones vibrate the qi channels in the body and bring about the hidden potential within. When chanting mantras, the soundwave of the chant also makes the energy in the body respond to it. A high level of wisdom and extraordinary abilities can be aroused by combining the frequency of sound, the qi in our body and the cosmos, to produce unbelievable power.

The mantra, OM AH HUM, contains the principal syllables of the Sanskrit language. OM is the fundamental sound of the energy behind the origin of the cosmos. It contains unlimited ability. To the human body, it is the sound within the head. When we cover our ears with our hands, it sounds like the sound made from the heart and the circulation of the blood. This sound clears the mind and raises the vitality of spirit. It can also cure the common cold, and illnesses related to the head. It can help bring the energy of the cosmos into the body from the head, and increase wisdom. All things in the world, with or without form, are the expressions of OM. OM is the eternal immortal sound.

AH is the fundamental sound of the growth of life in the beginning of the cosmos. It contains unlimited ability. AH is the first sound — the sound made by all life in the beginning. When one learns how to utilize the sound AH, one can open the knots in the body's channels and clear the chronic diseases of the organs.

HUM is the fundamental sound of the hidden potential of life. It is the sound of material things; it is the sound in the *dantian*. Chanting this sound can vibrate and open the knots in the channels, and inspire new links to life, and bring about health and longevity. The mantra, OM MA NI PAD ME HUM, of Avalokiteshvara, the Bodhisattva of Compassion, starts with OM and ends with HUM. The four sounds in between, MA NI PAD ME, are derivatives and variations of AH.

Different sounds have different frequencies. Some sounds are clear and even, and comfortable to listen to. Some sounds are like a sharp knife, piercingly painful to listen to. Some sounds are inspiring, some sounds are very soft and pleasant, and some sounds are loud and annoying. All of these sounds continuously echo with our consciousness, creating energy interactions that further echo with the energy of the cosmos.

Cultivating the Esoteric Abilities of the Mind — This cultivation utilizes visualization to purify the mind. It is the most important of the Three Esoteric cultivation methods. This is because both the cultivation of the Esoteric Abilities of the Body and Speech, utilize the mind to develop its higher potentials. There are many visualization methods which cover a very broad area. Visualization techniques are not visualizing for the sake of visualizing. Visualization is used to reach a state of *Void* in thought, to enter a meditative state, and attain the union of human and the cosmos. When visualizing, one condenses one's thoughts, by concentrating on one visualization to eliminate all other thoughts. Once all scattering thoughts are stopped, then visualize Void: body void, mind void, all void. When this state is achieved, the spiritual power of the cosmos will be able to flow through your body. You will then be able to *melt* into the Void of the cosmos. That is the union of ourselves with the cosmos — developing peace and luminosity.

Tantric Buddhist Qigong can change the practitioner. With training, one can produce strong intentions and develop extraordinary abilities; by stimulating the conscious, subconscious, and super conscious. Combining our drive for

133

excellence with the different levels of our consciousness, we can unlock our hidden potential and gain an upsurge of spirit and higher wisdom.

Tantric Buddhism believes that humans are inherently enlightened, but live in this confusing and crazy world. When one cultivates properly, one can use the powers within to attain realization. They also believe in fate; but they don't believe that destiny is fixed. Fate is fixed only because of the karma of previous lives that effect this life. Humans can change the outcome of the next life, eventually escaping the cycle of reincarnation and attaining liberation. This is a very optimistic approach towards life. However, life is hard to come by. A Buddhist saying compares the opportunity of being in this life to the amount of dirt stuck in one's finger nails relative to the amount of mud on this planet. Treasure this life, and cultivate unceasingly.

Contents in Book 3

The Tantric Buddhist cultivation methods are very extensive and profound. In this book we can only present a small part of its profound methods. It is said in Chinese, "Buddhism contains immeasurable greatness". We will introduce some of the basic, but important, and well-known Tantric Buddhist Qigong methods which originated from Tibet. In Section 3.2., we will discuss The Seven Keys for Sitting Meditation that will help you attain a calm abiding state for qigong training. Section 3.3. includes six Tantric Buddhist Qigong methods to develop the Three Esoterics.

The qigong methods in Book 3 are a cumulation of Master Liang's Tantric Buddhist Qigong training, beginning over thirty years ago. He learned some of these training methods from his Tibetan friends; and some from his teachers and friends during his travels and quest for knowledge. With over thirty years of compiling, teaching, researching, and his own training, Master Liang has made many *enlightening* realizations to add to the value of the materials presented here. Most of the training is unchanged from the traditional methods. Some methods are changed slightly to better suit the needs of today's people.

3.2. The Seven Keys for Sitting Meditation

Entering a calm abiding state is a very important step in Tantric Buddhist Qigong. A calm abiding state is achieved by gradually reducing the scattering thoughts in your mind and by focusing the mind on one intention. A calm abiding state is achieved when your body feels like floating clouds in the sky, your qi flows without restriction, and your body feels transparent. The tranquil feeling you feel when you enter a calm abiding state can not be fully described with words. This is a state of ultimate wisdom, great luminosity, and absolute consciousness of the cosmos. Often times, after a few hours of meditation, it feels as though it were a few minutes. Many people, through the practice of qigong have this type of experience. However, this type of experience doesn't necessarily mean a state of tranquillity. When one is able to attain a calm abiding state, this experience becomes more and more apparent. Many Chinese meditators often say, "One day in the *heavens* is like one year on earth." Implying that one day in heaven for people who have reached enlightenment is like one year on earth for the unenlightened.

In Tantric Buddhist Qigong, qi in the human body can be divided into different categories according to its flow and its functions. There is qi that supplies the basis of life, qi that flows downward, qi that flows horizontally, qi that flows upward, and qi that flows all over. The Seven Keys for Sitting Meditation are guidelines to assist the different categories of qi to flow in their proper paths and perform their proper functions. They are also initial guidelines for the mind and body to achieve a calm abiding state, and a preparation for Tantric Buddhist Qigong practices in Section 3.3.

1. *Sitting in Full or Half Lotus*: Full Lotus is accomplished by crossing both feet with the bottom of the feet facing up. The Half Lotus posture is accomplished by crossing one leg over the other leg. Sitting in this posture, regulates breathing, providing a smoother path for the qi flowing downward, to enter the middle channel easier; and eliminates annoyances resulting from jealousy.

2. *Making the Tranquil Hand Seal*: This seal is accomplished by overlapping one hand on top of the other hand, and pressing the tip of your thumbs lightly together, with palms facing up. Men left hand on top and women right hand on top. Then place the hand seal in front of your dantian. This posture allows the qi that flows horizontally to enter the Middle Channel easier, and eliminates annoyances resulting from anger.

3. Straighten the back and spreading the shoulders. Keep the spinal column erect, while maintaining its natural curvature. Relax the diaphragm, to allow spiritual energy to reach all over the body. Spread shoulders slightly to allow the qi that flows all over the body, to enter the Middle Channel easier; and to eliminate annoyances resulting from infatuation.

4. Press your chin slightly towards your throat. This will allow the qi that flows upward, to enter the Middle Channel easier, reducing absurd thinking; and eliminating annoyances resulting from greed.

5. Touch your tongue to the palate of your mouth and focus your eyes in front of you, about 170 centimeter away (about 70 inches). Eyes open or half open. This will allow the qi that supplies the basis of life, to enter the Middle Channel easier; and eliminate annoyances resulting from arrogance.

6. Silence your mouth. Exhale carbon dioxide and inhale fresh air. Attain peace and stability of the facial features (ears, eyes, nose, mouth, and heart). To a meditator, the feelings arising from the five facial features should not be thought of as right or wrong; nor good or bad. Only in a neutral state will the meditator attain peace of mind. This state is like a sleeping baby, most peaceful and calm. But, it is not a state of daze. Do not misunderstand daze as a tranquil and calm abiding state.

7. Silence your mind. The mind must be at peace and stable. Don't think about the past, don't think about the future, and don't think about now as you are engaging in meditation.

3.3. Tantric Buddhist Qigong

1. NINE SEGMENT BUDDHIST BREATHING

The training of the Nine Segment Buddhist Breathing *(Jiujie Fofeng)* is to allow the meditator to focus their mind on the breathing. Using the mind to concentrate on breathing, to eliminate all other thoughts. With time and cultivation, the body will become clean and pure, and combine with the Great Luminosity of the Cosmos. This method is used for entering into calmness, by using one thought to eliminate all thoughts.

Part 1. Preparation

Movement , Visualization, and Mantra:

Step 1. Follow the Seven Keys for sitting meditation, and make the Tranquil Hand Seal or the Priceless Vessel Seal (Drawing 3-2).

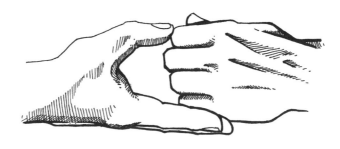

Drawing 3-2

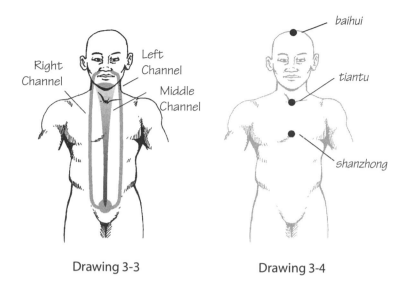

Drawing 3-3   Drawing 3-4

Step 2. Visualize that your body is transparent. Within the body, there are three channels — the Left Channel, the Right Channel, and the Middle Channel (Drawing 3-3).

The Left Channel connects to your left nostril and the Right Channel connects to your right nostril. The Middle Channel is like a trumpet, large on the top and narrow at the bottom. The top reaches the base of the brain and the bottom reaches the *huiyin*.

Step 3. Visualize that there is a statue of Buddha in front of you, emitting white light, or you may simply visualize that there is a huge white light. Inhale, raise both hands over your head, bring the palms together above your *baihui* point (Drawing 3-4 and Figure 3-1) and chant OM. Lower both hands down to your *tiantu* point at your throat area and chant AH (Figure 3-2). Continue lowering your hands until your *shanzhong* point and chant HUM (Figure 3-3).

Step 4. Next form your hands into the Priceless Vessel hand seal, lean your body forward, and place your hand seal in front of your head (Figures 3-4 to 3-6). The white light emitting from the Buddha and the qi of the cosmos enter your body from everywhere. Stay in that position for a few seconds then sit back up and continue with the next exercise.

137

| Figure 3-1 | Figure 3-2 | Figure 3-3 |

| Figure 3-4 | Figure 3-5 | Figure 3-6 |

Part 2. Regulating the Body

Movement and Visualization:

Step 1. *Rotating Your Upper Body*: Place your hand on top of your knees. Rotate your upper body from left to right, three times (Figure 3-7). Then right to left, three times.

Step 2. *Massage Your Back and Waist*: Make fists with your hands and place your fists on the kidney area, with your thumbs on top. Inhale, move your fists up against your back; exhale, move your fists down against your back. Next, bring your fists forward along your waist (Figures 3-8 and 3-9).

Figure 3-7

Figure 3-8

Figure 3-9

Figure 3-10

Figure 3-11

Figure 3-12

Then place your fist on top of your thighs with your palms facing up, middle finger and thumb touching each other (Figure 3-10). Inhale, straighten your arms and waist. Exhale, relax.

Step 3. *Light Hitting*: Relax your left palm on top of your knee. Gently hit the top of your head with your right palm, continue to the left side of your neck, to your left shoulder, to the outside of your left arm, to the back of your palms. Then hit the inside of your arm up until the left side of your chest, then down to your abdomen (Figures 3-11 to 3-15).

Next reverse the direction of the light hitting. Hit from your abdomen to the left side of your chest, down the inside of your left arm, to the left palm, the back of your palm, up the outside

Figure 3-13

Figure 3-14

Figure 3-15

Figure 3-16

Figure 3-17

Figure 3-18

of your left arm, to your left shoulder, to the left side of your neck, and back to the top of your head.

Repeat Step 3, three times . Then do Step 3 with your left palm on the right side of your body.

Step 4. *Finger Tapping*: Continue with your left palm, move down to the right side of your head, to the back of your head, then to the left side of your head. Next, bring your left palm forward to your forehead (Figure 3-16)

Continue moving your palm down to your nose and begin tapping the left side of your nose with your fingers. Tap down your head to your throat, down along the Middle Channel, down the inside of your left leg, to the back of your left foot (Figures 3-17 to 3-21).

Figure 3-19

Figure 3-20

Figure 3-21

Next, repeat Step 4 with your right hand on the other side.

Part 3.

Stages 1, 2, and 3 can be practiced individually or can be practiced in order.

Stage 1. Movement and Visualization:

Preparation: Relax your arms, and bend your body forward, three times. Each time, exhale all the impurities from your mouth while making the *ha* sound.

Step 1. With your mouth closed, press your left fourth finger on your left nostril, and use your right nostril to inhale. When you inhale, turn your head and torso towards your left (Figure 3-22).

Visualize Buddha, all the Bodhisattvas, and your masters/teachers, are illuminating in ten directions (N, E, S, W, NE, SE, SW, NW, up, and down). A white light emitting from them, enters your body through your right nostril. You may simply imagine that white light enters your right nostril.

Step 2. After filling your body with white light, press your right fourth finger on top of your right nostril, hold your breath and turn to face forward (Figure 3-23).

While holding your breath, visualize white light flowing from your Right Channel down to the Sea Bottom Chakra (*huiyin* area), and into your Left Channel. Then flows up your Left Channel to the left nostril. All the blockages, diseases, aches

141

Figure 3-22   Figure 3-23   Figure 3-24

and pains, and poisons in your body are transformed into black qi.

Step 3. Release your left nostril and exhale the black qi (Figure 3-24). Repeat Steps 1 to 3, three times.

Step 4. Next repeat steps 1 to 3, on the opposite side. That is, inhale with your left nostril and exhale with your right nostril, etc. Also, repeat three times.

Step 5. Relax your hands on your knees. Inhale with both nostrils. White light from your Left and Right Channels meets together at the Sea Bottom Chakra. Hold your breath and visualize white light flowing up the Middle Channel to the Crown Chakra (*baihui* area), then back down to the See Bottom Chakra. Then divides into two, up your Left and Right Channels. Exhale all the black qi out of the nostrils. Repeat three times.

There are a total of 9 inhalations and exhalations from Steps 1 to 5 in Stage 1. Practice 3 sets, a total of 27 inhalations and exhalations. The first 9 times, breathe very lightly and finely. The second 9 times, start making sounds with your breathing. The last 9 times, make even louder sounds with your breathing and rotate your body further as you turn, when doing Steps 1 to 4.

Stage 2. Movement and Visualization:

Posture: Sit as described in the Seven Keys for Sitting Meditation. Form the Tranquil Hand Seal and place it below your navel. As an alternative, you may place the back of your palms on top of your thighs, coil your middle and fourth fingers in towards your

Figure 3-25

thumb, while keeping your index and pinkie almost straight (Figure 3-25). Keep your shoulders relaxed.

Step 1. Inhale, visualize white light entering your right nostril. As white light enters your nostril, it changes into a red light down the Right Channel to the Sea Bottom Chakra (*huiyin* area), and up your Left Channel. Exhale, visualize black qi discharging from your left nostril.

Step 2. Inhale, visualize white light entering your left nostril. As white light enters your nostril, it changes into a red light down the Left Channel to the Sea Bottom Chakra, and up your Right Channel. Exhale, visualize black qi discharging from your right nostril.

Step 3. Inhale, visualize white light entering both nostrils. As white light enters your nostrils, it changes into a red light down both the Right and Left Channels to the Sea Bottom Chakra, and soars up your Middle Channel to your Crown Chakra (*baihui* area). Back down the Middle Channel to the Sea Bottom Chakra, up along the Left and Right Channels. Exhale, visualize black qi discharging from both nostrils.

Step 4. Repeat Step 2. That is, inhale from your left nostril and exhale from your right nostril, etc.

Step 5. Repeat Step 1. That is, inhale from your right nostril and exhale from your left nostril, etc.

Step 6. Repeat Step 3. That is, inhale from both nostrils and exhale from both nostrils, etc.

Step 7. Repeat Step 3. That is, inhale from both nostrils and exhale from both nostrils, etc.

Step 8. Repeat Step 1. That is, inhale from your right nostril and exhale from your left nostril, etc.

Step 9. Repeat Step 2. That is, inhale from your left nostril and exhale from your right nostril, etc.

Your breathing should be slow, fine, long, and continuous. Practice 3 sets, a total of 27 inhalations and exhalations.

Stage 3. Movement and Visualization:

Posture: The same as in Stage 2.

Step 1. Inhale, visualize white light entering your right nostril up to the right side of your brain, passing through your right temple and down your Right Channel to the Sea Bottom Chakra. Then up your Left Channel. Exhale, visualize black qi discharging from your left nostril.

Step 2. Repeat Step 1, except visualize gray qi discharging from your left nostril.

Step 3. Repeat Step 1, except visualize white qi discharging from your left nostril.

Step 4. Inhale, visualize white light entering your left nostril up to the left side of your brain, passing through your left temple, down your Left Channel to the Sea Bottom Chakra. Then up your Right Channel. Exhale, visualize black qi discharging from your right nostril.

Step 5. Repeat Step 4, except visualize gray qi discharging from your right nostril.

Step 6. Repeat Step 5, except visualize white qi discharging from your right nostril.

Step 7. Inhale, visualize white light entering both nostrils, up to your temples and down both your Left and Right Channels to the Sea Bottom Chakra, and soaring up your Middle Channel towards your Crown Chakra (*baihui* area). Then back down passing your eye bridge. Exhale, visualize black qi discharging from the tip of your nose.

As an alternative, visualize that the light goes back down the Middle Channel, and back up the Left and Right Channels before you exhale.

Step 8. Repeat Step 7, except visualize gray qi discharging from the tip of your nose.

Step 9. Repeat Step 7, except visualize white qi discharging from the tip of your nose.

Your breathing should be slow, fine, long, and continuous. Practice 3 sets, a total of 27 inhalations and exhalations.

Part 4. Visualizing the Void

Posture and Visualization:

Posture: Same as the Preparation Posture in Stages 2 and 3.

Visualization: After practicing the Stages in Part 3, visualize that Buddha is emitting white light in front of you, and you are also emitting white light. White light is entering your body from everywhere, and white light is emitting from all over your body.

Then visualize that you and Buddha are one. The objects surrounding you are disappearing one at a time. You are dissolving into the clear blue sky. The duration of this practice depends on you. It can be as long or as short as you wish, depending on how you feel. When you are ready to end this training, visualize that the surrounding objects are reappearing in their original positions one at a time, and your body is also returning to its original state.

Part 5. Closing

Movement, Visualization, and Mantra:

Step 1. Inhale, raise both hands over your head, bring them together, and chant the OM sound as you lower your hands. When your hands reach your *tiantu* point on your throat, chant the AH sound. Continue lowering your hands and chant the HUM sound when your hands reach the *shanzhong* point, midway between the two nipples. This is the same as Figures 3-1 to 3-3.

Step 2. With your right hand massage from the back of your head, to the left side of your head, to the left side of your neck, to your

| Figure 3-26 | Figure 3-27 |

left shoulder, down the back of your left arm, to the back of your left palm, to the front of your left palm, up the inside of your left arm, to the left side of your chest, to your abdomen, along your left leg, to your toes and out. As your hand leaves your toes, chant the HUM sound (Figures 3-26 and 3-27). Next, do the mirror image of this massage, with your left hand on the right side of your body.

Step 3. Rub your palms together, massage your face and your head. Next place your palms behind you, over your kidney area. Straighten and bend your legs 7 to 9 times. This concludes the Nine Segment Buddhist Breathing Qigong.

2. PRECIOUS VESSEL QIGONG

Precious Vessel Qigong *(Baopingqi)* is best when practiced after exhaling the impurities from the Nine Segment Buddhist Breathing Qigong, but before Visualizing the Void. It can also be practiced at anytime by itself, except one hour before and after midnight, and at noon time. Also, don't train when you are too full or too hungry. This qigong is divided into four steps: Brimful, Vanishing, Clearing, and Arrow Techniques. It is also divided into four types of breathing patterns: Leading the Breath, Brimming the Breath, Distributing the Breath, and Shooting the Breath.

Movement and Visualization:

Step 1. *Brimful Technique*:

Leading the Breath: Visualize that *spiritual-breath* and *spiritual-qi* are surrounding you. Inhale from both nostrils gently and slowly, deep down into the lower parts of your lungs. At the same time, pull your stomach in and hold up your *huiyin* area. This will allow the qi from above to press down, while making the qi from below lift up. The two qi meet at the area four fingers below the navel. It is like two lids closing from the top and bottom openings of a cylinder, storing qi within.

Brimming the Breath: Push your abdomen out. While still holding your breath, allow the qi to spread all over the body, filling every pore and hair in your body.

Distributing the Breath: After Brimming the Breath for a while, inhale a few more short breaths to completely fill your lungs, making the air in them tight, full, and evenly distributed.

Step 2. *Vanishing Technique*: While still holding your breath, visualize qi entering your Middle Channel until your heart, and all the impurities become *luminous wisdom qi*.

Step 3. *Clearing Technique*: Still holding your breath, visualize qi dispersing all over your body, filling each and every pore and every strand of hair, and out through the pores.

Step 4. *Arrow Technique*: *Shooting the Breath*: Visualize the qi that entered the Middle Channel soars up to the Crown Chakra, but doesn't soar past your Crown Chakra. Exhale from your nose gently, then heavier, and finally exhale as though you are shooting arrows out with your breath. At the same time, visualize that all the pores in your body are also letting out the qi. (Only visualize the qi soaring up to your Crown Chakra once during each practice session. Other times simply visualize qi discharging from your nose without soaring to the Crown Chakra)

Notes:

Steps 1 to 4 are accomplished in one breathing cycle. Practice 18 to 36 breathing cycles each session. When you practice Precious Vessel Qigong, it is best if you exhale the same amount with both nostrils. If you breath more with your left nostril than your right nostril, you may continue to practice. If, however, you breath more with your right nostril than your left nostril, don't practice this qigong.

According to Tantric Buddhism, each breath is associated with one thought. During the change in breaths, there is also a change in thought. The saying, "Mind and breath depend on each other.", came from this reasoning. The cultivation method of Precious Vessel Qigong is for cultivating the mind. Ultimately, allowing the mind to become independent, without being affected by breathing. Even though, there may still be other thoughts, they are not affected by your breathing. The breathing pattern in the Precious Vessel Qigong makes your breathing stop temporarily. This will also stop conscious thoughts and allow you to enter a state of cultivation.

After a period of dedicated Precious Vessel Qigong training, your qi will become abundant and the mind will be calm and peaceful. From the qi entering the Middle Channel, the area four fingers below the navel will radiate with a red ball of light — known as the *Luminous Spot*. With practice, the *Luminous Spot* will become bigger and bigger. Use your mind to lead the ball of red light from the *Luminous Spot* up to the Crown Chakra. This will greatly increase the benefits of your training.

3. ACHIEVING THROUGH SPIRITUAL FLAME

Achieving Through Spiritual Flame *(Lingre Chengjiufa)* is the first of six parts of the Tibetan Achieving Methods. The other five achieving methods are: Achieving Through Visualization, Achieving Through Dreams, Achieving Through Pure Light, Achieving Through Middle Yin, and Achieving Through Reverse View. Achieving Through Spiritual Flame is the foundation of the six achieving methods.

Spiritual scorching must be felt in the cultivation of this qigong, or else, all will be in vain. After a period of training, if a practitioner should lose their color, and their hands and feet feel cold, it means the method of cultivation was not done correctly. We will be presenting the Seventy Breath Method and the One Hundred and Eight Breath Method. You can choose either one for your training. Beginners should practice 6 times a day. After experiencing the *spiritual flame*, you may reduce the frequency.

Achieving Through Spiritual Flame can eliminate cold limb problems. General problems associated with the body will also be healed from the *spiritual flame*. The circulation of the spiritual scorching fire is capable of opening knots in the channels. From the build up of the *spiritual flame*, the body will have a comfortable, light, peaceful, and warm sensation. Your confidence will increase and absurd thoughts will disappear. You will be experiencing may different states of being. Sometimes you will also experience hallucinations and enter the illusory world. Don't insist on searching for these feelings or states. Be natural.

Achieving Through Spiritual Flame was a closely guarded secret. It is one of the foundations of the Tantric Buddhist cultivation method. Without the initiation with the *spiritual flame*, all will be in vain. When you first begin to train the spiritual flame method, you must practice six times a day. Every time, do seventy or one hundred and eight cycles of breathing depending on which method

Drawing 3-5

you choose to do. Once you have attained the feeling of the *spiritual flame*, you can then reduce the frequency of your meditation.

When the *spiritual flame* is developed to an effective stage, the practitioner will be able to eliminate illness and physiological damage. It is also possible to gradually attain the abilities of the Five Openings: the Opening of Clairvoyance, the Opening of Clairaudience, the Opening of Telepathy, the Opening of the Spiritual State, and the Opening of Precognition/Regression.

Some People will experience the luminosity of different lights and circles of lights surrounding the body. After hard cultivation training, the nine orifices in the human body (two eyes, two ears, two nostrils, mouth, anus, and urethra or penis) and the throat, tongue, lips, and chin will not be affected by the bad influences of your surroundings. Your will and memory will be open. The internal body will be extremely healthy and happy. Externally you will able to see, hear, and sense all experiences.

The test for the attainment of *spiritual flame* for cultivators in Gansu, Sichuan Province is to meditate naked in the snow for several hours until the snow surrounding you melts. Otherwise, you can't pass the test.

Seventy Breath Method:

Movement and Visualization:

Preparation: Sit in accordance with the Seven Keys for Sitting Meditation. Visualize the area four fingers below your navel is a character that looks like Drawing 3-5. This character represents Yin. Visualize it as red in color and flickering like a fire in a stove. This fire is warm and cozy. If you are unable to visualize this character, you can simply visualize a small red dot that is flickering. Visualize it as the vitality of your life force.

Use long, slow inhalations. Inhale from both nostrils into your Left and Right Channels. Use your mind to lead the qi down to the red dot. Use this qi as a bellow to expand the red dot, as if you were fanning a fire. At the same, time visualize wind blowing on this red dot or red character. The red dot is getting bigger, redder, and hotter each time you inhale.

Your exhalations should also be slow and long. Visualize that blue smoke is discharging from your nose just like a wood stove discharging blue smoke out the chimney.

Follow this method to inhale (about 5 seconds) and exhale (about 5 seconds). Coordinate your visualizations with your inhalations and exhalations. Every inhalation and exhalation counts as a complete breathing cycle.

Step 1. After ten breathing cycles — the flame reaches your Navel Chakra.

Step 2. After ten more breathing cycles — the area around your Navel Chakra is filled with scorching qi *(spiritual flame)*.

Step 3. After ten more breathing cycles — the warmth of the flame spreads down to the lower body until your toes.

Step 4. After ten more breathing cycles — the flame now reaches the Heart Chakra.

Step 5. After ten more breathing cycles — the flame now reaches the Throat Chakra.

Step 6. After ten more breathing cycles — the flame now reaches the Third Eye Chakra.

Step 7. After ten more breathing cycles — the flame now reaches the Crown Chakra.

When the *spiritual flame* reaches the Crown Chakra, the Bodhisattva's Heart Moon Liquid (Nectar) will begin to flow down your tongue where it touches the palate of your mouth. This Nectar is known as the Water from the Heaven's Yard in Daoist practices. The Nectar is clear and cooling. The *spiritual flame* and the Nectar mutually enrich each other. The spiritual scorching of the Crown Chakra and the downward flow of the Nectar, are the method of combining fire and water to mutually nurture each other.

Drawing 3-6

One Hundred and Eight Breath Method (optional):

Some people practice one hundred and eight cycles of breathing instead of seventy cycles of breathing. To begin, sit in accordance with the Seven Keys for Sitting Meditation. Visualize in the Crown Chakra, at the top of the Middle Channel, that there is a character as in Drawing 3-6. This character represents Yang. It is white in color and is shaped as if it was ready to release Nectar.

Inhale, visualize that *spiritual-breath* is entering your nose, down along your Left and Right Channels until four fingers below your navel, and then begins to rise up the Middle Channel. Visualize that the character at the Crown Chakra turns into a red flame about half a finger in length, with the tip pointed and burning with luminosity. The character turns like a spinning wheel. Exhale, visualize blue smoke discharging out of your nose. With every inhalation, expand the *spiritual flame* from your breathing up half a finger length.

Step 1. After eight breathing cycles — the *spiritual flame* reaches the Navel Chakra.

Step 2. After ten more breathing cycles — the area around the Navel Chakra is all filled with *spiritual flame*.

Step 3. After ten more breathing cycles — the *spiritual flame* extends down from your navel to the lower part of your body, until your toes.

Step 4. After ten more breathing cycles — the *spiritual flame* reaches the Heart Chakra.

Step 5. After ten more breathing cycles — the *spiritual flame* reaches the Throat Chakra.

Step 6. After ten more breathing cycles — the *spiritual flame* reaches the Crown Chakra passing the Third Eye Chakra.

Step 7. After ten more breathing cycles — the character in the Middle Channel and the Crown Chakra is melted by the *spiritual flame*. The melted character changes into Nectar and drips down, filling from the Crown Chakra to the Middle, Left, and Right Channels.

Step 8. After ten more breathing cycles — the Nectar fills the Throat Chakra.

Step 9. After ten more breathing cycles — the nectar fills the Heart Chakra.

Step 10. After ten more breathing cycles — the nectar fills the Navel Chakra.

Step 11. After ten more breathing cycles — the nectar fills the entire body until your fingers and toes.

Some Experiences you may have while training :

First Stage: The chakras in your body open due to *spiritual flame*. The opening of the chakras are filled by the Nectar that contain spiritual power from the *spiritual flame*. You may feel a slight pain in the chakra areas. This is called Experiencing the Pain or Experiencing the Warmth.

Second Stage: The chakras are shrinking. The nectar is increasing and filling into the chakras, developing a state of peace and joy. This is called Experiencing the Development of Extreme Happiness.

Third Stage: From the internal peace that you have achieved, you sense all external appearances as peace and happiness. Many different states begin to appear in front of you. Let it be and continue your *spiritual flame* training.

4. THE GREAT PERFECTION — THE HEART ESSENCE

The Great Perfection — The Heart Essence *(Dayuanman Xinsui)* is a basic cultivation method of the Red tradition in Tibetan Buddhism. It is also the most important initial approach in their cultivation. It is called "the tantra with no other higher than it." It is also one of the most important cultivation methods of the Yellow, Red, White, and Flower Traditions of Tibetan Buddhism. People with high achievement in this training generally will have one or two visible signs. One is health and longevity, the other is the ability to achieve a *rainbow body*, the spontaneous manifestation of light and a rainbow of colors when they leave this physical plane.

This technique came from Lama Achok Trungpa (Azong Zhuba) of the Angzang Temple in Sichuan Province. It is a cultivation that channels the sun's light energy. It is accomplished by calmly visualizing the luminous spots of the cosmos, and sending out *homing* signals from your *heart* (mind) to the luminous spots of the cosmos. Bringing it in and storing it within your body strengthens your body's power source, increases your body's immune system, and slows down aging. From the decades of storing the sun's light energy, when you die, you can use the control of your *heart* (mind) to disintegrate the cells and molecules of your body. This will release a rainbow like radiance. Except for your hair and nails, all other parts of the body will be transformed into the light essence of the elements, that make up the physical body.

Train during sunrise and sunset. When the sun is too bright, it will hurt the eyes. Select an area where you can see the sun easily and without many distractions. You can train while standing or sitting, in Full or Half Lotus.

Stage 1. Precious Vessel Qigong

Movement, Visualization, and Mantra:

Step 1. After training the Precious Vessel Qigong for a period of time, a *Luminous Spot* (a red ball of light) will appear at the location about four fingers below the navel. Use your mind to lead this red ball of light up to the top of your head.

Step 2. When you have accomplished some definite results from the Precious Vessel Qigong, you should begin to chant the mantra, OM AH HUM, one thousand times a day to build up your concentration and perseverance.

Stage 2. Guiding and Absorbing Technique

The Guiding and Absorbing Technique uses the mind to lead the light. It captures the energy of the cosmos and brings it back to your head; distributing it throughout your body, to strengthen the energy in your body.

Movement and Visualization:

First Month: Face the sun but don't look straight into the sun and visualize that the sky is filled with light spots and circles of luminescent lights (white, red, blue, green; more white, less green). These lights are known as *External Luminous Spots*. Visualize a spot of white light emerging from the top of your head. Use your mind to lead the spot of white light out to the *External Luminous Spots* and unite with them. Then use your mind to bring them back together to your head. Repeat many times.

Second Month: Still face the sun and visualize that the sky is filled with light spots and circles of luminescent lights. When you begin to see circles of light, visualize a spot of red light rising from your Third Eye. Use your mind to lead it out to the *External Luminous Spots* and unite with them. Then use your mind to bring the spot of red light back to your Third Eye. Repeat many times.

Third Month: Still face the sun and visualize that the sky is filled with light spots and circles of luminescent lights. When you begin to see light spots and circles of light, visualize a spot of blue light emerging from the tip of your nose and rising up. Use your mind to lead it out to the *External Luminous Spots* and unite with them. Then use your mind to bring the spot of blue light back to the tip of your nose.

Stage 3. Luminous Spot Technique

When you feel you have achieved some definite results from Stage 2, then go on to train Stage 3. You can train this technique either sitting or standing. The training time is unrestricted. The best time to train is during the early morning before the sun gets too bright.

Many Tibetan Tantric Red Tradition cultivators who have trained this method has been recorded to have glorious results. According to the Chinese book, *The Brief Introduction to Rainbow Body Documentary of Tibetan Buddhism*, there were over 40 cases of rainbow bodies during the deaths of cultivators from the Tang Dynasty (618-906 A.D.) to the 20th century. This book was written by Sogyal Tulku (Suolang Dunzhu) of the Religious Research Department within the College of the Tibetan Scientific Society.

Movement and Visualization:

Step 1: Face about 30 degrees off the sun (up, down, left, or right). Don't stare straight into the sun. Visualize the *Luminous Spots* in the sky. Move the large *Luminous Spots* and the small *Luminous Spots*. Next cover the small *Luminous Spots* with the large stable *Luminous Spots*.

The *Luminous Spots* are sparkling like a necklace made of gem stones. You can see the sky composed of circles of light with multiple brilliant rainbow colors releasing great luminosity. This is the source of the cosmos' energy radiation.

When the above scenery appears, don't immerse your thoughts in it. Allow it to disappear naturally. Just let it be. This is the experimental step in visualizing the *Void*.

Step 2: Visualize the *Luminous Spots* on cloudy days

Step 3: Visualize the *Luminous Spots* from candle lights, light bulbs, the moon, and of the night. When you visualize the *Luminous Spots* at night time, you can see beautiful scenery like the luminous reflections of lanterns on the Yangtze River.

Step 3 Requires at least three years of training, twice a day. Gradually increase the time you visualize the *Luminous Spots*. Once you are able to see the source of the cosmos's energy radiation, use your mind to lead the red ball of light from your Precious Vessel Qigong training to the source of the cosmos's energy radiation and unite them.

Then use your mind to retrieve the cosmos's *Luminous Spot* to your Crown Chakra. At this point, your training can be considered to have accomplished Great Perfection. The Great Perfection — The Heart Essence method gives you an opportunity to greatly absorb the sun's energy, allowing you to unite with the cosmos.

5. ARMOR PROTECTION FROM NEGATIVE ENERGIES

There is a saying in Chinese, "*Dao* (your ability and attainment) may be one foot tall, but *Evil* (harmful negative energies) are ten foot tall; when your *Dao* is ten feet tall, *Evil* may still be above your head." Tantric Buddhist cultivators need to always protect themselves from *negativity* around them, pathogenic influences, and all the other bad influences that are detrimental to your *vital-qi*, from entering your body. Armor Protection from Negative Energies (*Pijia Hushenfa*) is a must for all cultivators. It is best if you practice this technique before you go to sleep, to parties, to funerals, to public gatherings, or when visiting the sick.

Part 1. Armor Protection

Movement, Visualization, and Mantra:

Step 1. Make the Vajrasattva Seal by interlocking your fingers and placing them next to your eye bridge (Drawing 3-7 and Figure 3-28). Chant the mantra of Vajrasattva, OM BORULAN ZHELI, seven times.

Step 2. Press the Vajrasattva Seal on your eye bridge, then press on your throat, on your heart, on your left shoulder, on your right shoulder, and back to your eye bridge.

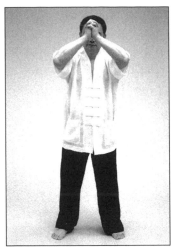

Figure 3-28

Drawing 3-7

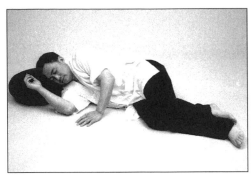

Figure 3-29

Step 3. Separate your palms and place them next to your sides. Visualize that the Vajrasattva is holding a scepter for subduing evil, and transforms its body into four; one in front, one in the back, one to your left and one to your right. Visualization is very important. The more faith and experience one has, the greater the results.

Part 2. Practice Before Going to Sleep

Movement, Visualization, and Mantra:

Step 1. Lie down in bed in the Lucky Posture — lie on your right side with your heart on top (Figure 3-29). It's like a lion's sleeping posture.

Step 2. Chant the mantra of Vajrasattva, OM BORULAN ZHELI, seven times. Or, chant the six-syllable mantra of Avalokiteshvara, OM MA NI PAD ME HUM, seven times.

Step 3. Visualize a powerful red beam of light emitting from your throat into the sky. This powerful red beam of light is like a mosquito net totally enclosing your body. You are sleeping within in it.

Notes:

The achievement of the Armor Protection from Negative Energies depends on your own earnest efforts to cultivate virtue and get rid of evil. It depends on *righteous-qi* (righteous thoughts and actions).

6. THE NINE ESOTERIC SEALS

The Nine Esoteric Seals *(Jiuzi Miling)* can release the latent potential of your mind. It is also known as the Nine Character Hand Seals. Each of the nine seals are accompanied by a command character. The nine command characters are: *Lin Bing Dou Zhe Jie Zhen Lie Zai Qian*. These nine words originated from the work, *Baopuzi*, Chapter 17, written by Ge Hong during the Eastern Jin Dynasty (317-420 A.D.). It stated: "Wish and vocalize, *'Lin Bing Dou Zhe Jie Zhen Lie Qian Xing*. Say them regularly, all evil will be kept away'." What it meant is that by saying these nine words regularly, you will be able to avoid all evil and allow your inner potential to surface.

Dongmi, one of the Tantric Buddhist Sects, influenced by the Chinese Tantric Buddhism, also uses these words. However, when the words were passed down to Dongmi, the last two characters were changed. Instead of copying the last four characters as *Zhen Lie Qian Xing* they were copied as *Zhen Lie Zai Qian*. However, the effectiveness is not altered. Most people that train the Nine Esoteric Seals adopted the characters from Dongmi. This will also be the characters we use in this book.

Every word has a specific hand form and intention. When training the Nine Esoteric Seals, you will need to coordinate your intention with the hand seals. The hand seals and intentions are:

Lin - Immovable Foundation Seal. Making the Lin Seal (Drawings 3-8 and 3-9) maintains an unmoving and unenticed mind, while expressing a strong body and strong spirit.

By not allowing anything to disturb your training, gives you a strong body and strong spirit, which is needed to be a person with extrasensory perception.

Drawing 3-8   Drawing 3-9

Bin - Great Vajrasattva Seal. Making the Bin Seal (Drawings 3-10 and 3-11) expresses the life force for extending life and returning to the age of innocence, by developing the Sea Bottom Chakra. The Sea Bottom Chakra is the extrasensory location for improving health and increasing energy. This area stimulates the sex gland; and strengthens physiological,

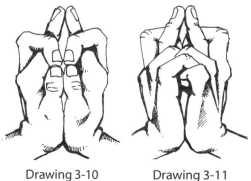

Drawing 3-10   Drawing 3-11

mental, and spiritual aspects, thus preventing illness from attacking your body. Training this seal, gives the practitioner three to five times more energy, than an average person; giving a practitioner a stronger driving force, action force, and creativity.

Dou - External Lion Seal. Making the Dou Seal (Drawings 3-12 and 3-13) makes you brave, determined, and courageous. When encountering difficulties, it gives you a stronger will to tackle the problem. This seal also develops the Reproductive Chakra — the area that eliminates fear and develops determined conviction.

Zhe - Internal Lion Seal. Making the Zhe Seal (Drawings 3-14 and 3-15) expresses the power of your ability to control your own body and other's bodies at will. It develops the Navel Chakra. When you are able to control this area, you will be able to control all other areas of your body. The practitioner who trains this area can emit fire-like energy. The extrasensory ability from your training can heal your own illnesses as well as other's illnesses.

Jie - External Binding Seal. Making the Jie Seal (Drawings 3-16 and 3-17) expresses the ability to know and regulate the human heart, and develops the Heart Chakra. The Heart Chakra is located at your chest area. It is closely linked to the thymus gland, heart, and lungs. This area can open the extrasensory abilities of your heart.

Zhen - Internal Binding Seal. Making the Zhen Seal (Drawings 3-18 and 3-19) expresses the gathering

Drawing 3-12   Drawing 3-13

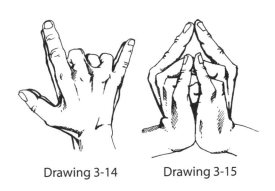

Drawing 3-14   Drawing 3-15

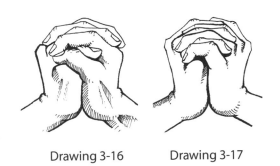

Drawing 3-16   Drawing 3-17

158

of rich, magnanimous love and respect for all, into one's body, showing the merciful heart of Vairocana; and developing the Throat Chakra. The Throat Chakra located at the throat area, is very closely related to the thyroid gland. Sluggishness or vigorousness (metabolic rate) in one's life are governed by the hormone generated from the thyroid gland. Training this area can maintain youth, and give one extrasensory hearing.

Lie - Wisdom Fist Seal. Making the Lie Seal (Drawings 3-20 and 3-21) expresses the kindness of relieving other's pain, and cultivates one's extrasensory abilities.

Zai - Sun Chakra Seal. Making the Zai Seal (Drawing 3-22) expresses the ability to use your extrasensory abilities at will and develops the Third Eye Chakra. This Chakra, located around eye bridge and the pituitary gland, control the functioning of all the other endocrine glands in the body. This area is very important in both Daoist and Buddhist cultivation. Developing this area is very critical to achieving special and extrasensory abilities.

Qian - Priceless Vessel Seal. Making the Qian Seal (Drawing 3-23) expresses a state of Buddha — a supernatural state, and develops the Crown Chakra; and produces a brilliant luminosity in your brain. This area controls all other areas. During training don't think about anything or recite any mantra. You should be in a state of no imagery and no thought.

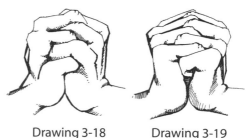

Drawing 3-18   Drawing 3-19

Drawing 3-20   Drawing 3-21

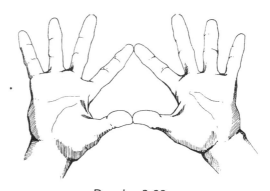

Drawing 3-22

Drawing 3-23

159

Figure 3-30

Figure 3-31

Figure 3-32

Part 1.

Movement, Visualization, and Mantra:

Step 1. Stand with your feet shoulder width apart, facing south. Bring your palms together in front of your chest and chant three times: OM NAMO BENZI Sakyamunifo and all the Enlightened Families (Figure 3-30).

Step 2. Lower both palms down to your sides. Then up over your head above your *baihui* point, clap your palms together, and chant OM. Lower your palms together down to your throat level and chant AH. Continue lowering your palms down to your chest level and chant HUM (Figures 3-31 to 3-33). Prepare to do the hand seals in front of your chest and recite the command characters.

Step 3. Make the Immovable Foundation Seal and recite Lin (Figure 3-34).

Step 4. Make the Great Vajrasattva Seal and recite Bin (Figure 3-35).

Step 5. Make the External Lion Seal and recite Dou (Figure 3-36).

Step 6. Make the Internal Lion Seal and recite Zhe (Figure 3-37).

Step 7. Make the External Binding Seal and recite Jie (Figure 3-38).

Step 8. Make the Internal Binding Seal and recite Zhen (Figure 3-39).

| Figure 3-33 | Figure 3-34 | Figure 3-35 |

| Figure 3-36 | Figure 3-37 | Figure 3-38 |

Step 9. Make the Wisdom Fist Seal and recite Lie (pronounced *lee-a*) (Figure 3-40).

Step 10. Make the Sun Chakra Seal and recite Zai (Figure 3-41).

Step 11. Make the Priceless Vessel Seal and recite Qian (Figure 3-42).

Step 12. Separate and lower both palms down and up to your sides, until shoulder level with your palms facing down. Then circle both palms forward, bend your elbows, and bring your palms next to your chest, while maintaining your palms facing down. Rotate your palms until they are facing your chest and point your fingers toward the center of your chest (Figures 3-43 to 3-45).

Figure 3-39

Figure 3-40

Figure 3-41

Figure 3-42

Figure 3-43

Figure 3-44

Lower your palms down to your *dantian* with your fingers still pointing inward. Straighten your palms and place them over the bottom side of your ribs for 1-2 minutes or until you feel the qi sensation at your liver area. Next move your palms in circular path, three times (Figure 3-46).

Step 13. Continue from above, turn your palms until your palms are facing up. Lift your palms up until shoulder level, then rotate your palms until they are facing out and push forward (Figures 3-47 to 3-49).

Step 14. Bring both palms back together in front of your chest, fingers pointing up, next to your chest (Figure 3-50). Change your palms into the External Binding Seal (Figure 3-51). Hold that posture

Figure 3-45

Figure 3-46

Figure 3-47

Figure 3-48

Figure 3-49

Figure 3-50

for a few seconds, then thrust the seal forward until your arms are straight (Figure 3-52).

Step 15. Separate your palms to your sides with your palms facing down. Rotate both palms up and begin raising them up. When your palms are about shoulder width apart, clap them together (the louder the better) over your head and keep them together (Figures 3-53 to 3-55).

Part 2.

Movement and Visualization:

Step 1. Make the Immovable Foundation Seal above your head. Lower this seal down along the center line of your nose, inhale, and

Figure 3-51

Figure 3-52

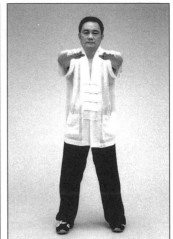
Figure 3-53

Figure 3-54

Figure 3-55

Figure 3-56

silently recite the word Lin. Continue lowering this seal until it is in front of your chest (Figures 3-56 and 3-57).

Visualize that the life force of the cosmos is wrapping around your body. You have been transformed and have become the Vajrasattva. Even the strongest wind from all eight directions can't move you. Nothing can puzzle you; and your wisdom is boundless and limitless (Breathe naturally during the visualization).

Chant the mantra: OM BORULAN ZHELI

Chant the mantra: OM FURILUO SADUOFU AH KANG

Step 2. As you exhale, point the seal forward and extend your arms until they are straight As you straighten your arms, change

Figure 3-57

Figure 3-58

Figure 3-59

Figure 3-60

Figure 3-61

Figure 3-62

the seal into the Great Vajrasattva Seal (Figures 3-58 and 3-59). As you are completing the extension of your arms and changing the seal, lift your right foot up, stomp down, and recite Bin (Figure 3-60).

Then raise your left foot up, stomp down, and recite Bin (Figure 3-61). Bring the seal back next to your chest and point the seal upward (Figure 3-62) (During combat keep the seal pointing towards your strong adversary).

Visualize that you are using the Three Esoterics to become one with the Wrathful Meditational Deity. Your face is expressing the enraged look of this meditation deity, ready to destroy all your strong evil adversaries and obstacles (Breathe naturally during the visualization).

Figure 3-63   Figure 3-64   Figure 3-65

Step 3. As you exhale, raise the seal up along your nose over your head until your arms are straight. Change the seal to the External Lion Seal. Your face expresses the look of a lion engaging an adversary, and is ready to growl (Figure 3-63). Recite Dou.

Visualize that you are using the Three Esoterics to transform yourself into the Vajrasattva. Your body is displaying the color white. You are wearing the precious crown of five wisdoms on top of your head (an infinitely dignified composure). Your body is emitting the brilliance of a multiple of colors. Your *heart* is filled with the valor of the Vajrasattva. Your *heart* is like that of a valiant lion without fear. You have the strength like that of a lion. No one can defeat you. Your power is unlimited and boundless, equal to that of the overflowing life force within the cosmos (Breathe naturally during the visualization).

Chant the mantra: OM FURILUO SADUOFU AH KANG

Inhale and begin lowering the seal along your nose down until your chest level (Figure 3-64). Point the seal forward and thrust your arms forward, as you exhale. Then bring the seal back next to your chest as you inhale.

Step 4. With the seal pointing up, raise it up over your head, and change the seal into the Internal Lion Seal and recite Zhe (Figure 3-65). Lower the seal down along your nose until your chest level (Figure 3-66).

Visualize that you are using the Three Esoterics to become one with Vairocana. The *heart* (mind) of Vairocana is like that of a lion king. Your *heart* is responding and also becomes the

166

Figure 3-66

Figure 3-67

Figure 3-68

Figure 3-69

Figure 3-70

Figure 3-71

lion king. The lion king will devour all the laziness, all the anger, and all the discontent in your heart.

Chant the mantra: OM MA NI PAD ME HUM

Step 5. Point the seal forward (Figure 3-67). Thrust your arms forward. Point the seal up slightly and change the seal to the External Binding Seal and recite Jie (Figures 3-68 and 3-69). Next bend your elbows slightly, then thrust the seal forward again, and let out a loud *heng* sound to vibrate the Heart Chakra (Figure 3-70 and 3-71).

No visualization.

Chant the mantra: OM MA NI PAD ME HUM

| Figure 3-72 | Figure 3-73 | Figure 3-74 |

| Figure 3-75 | Figure 3-76 | Figure 3-77 |

Step 6. Change the seal to the External Binding Seal and recite Zhen. Then bring the seal back next to your chest (Figures 3-72 and 3-73).

Visualize that you are using the Three Esoterics to call the Vajrasattva to assist you in a successful career. You are becoming the Vajrasattva.

Chant the mantra: OM FURILUO SADUOFU AH KANG

Step 7. Point the seal up and raise the seal up over your head (Figures 3-74 and 3-75). Release the interlocking fingers and press your palms together with fingers pointing up (Figure 3-76).

Figure 3-78

Figure 3-79

Figure 3-80

Figure 3-81

Figure 3-82

Figure 3-83

Lower both palms to your sides until they are even with your shoulders, palms face down. Rotate your palms to face forward as you bring your arms horizontally forward, arms straight. When your palms are about a shoulder width apart, quickly clap them together, the louder the better (Figures 3-77 to 3-79). Then make the Wisdom Fist Seal and recite Lie (Figure 3-80).

No visualization and no mantra.

Step 8. Bring the seal back next to your chest. Point the seal down, then back up. Raise the seal up over your head (Figures 3-81 to 3-84). Change the seal to the Sun Chakra Seal and recite Zai (Figure 3-85).

| Figure 3-84 | Figure 3-85 | Figure 3-86 |

| Figure 3-87 | Figure 3-88 | Figure 3-89 |

Lower the seal down to your chest level, then back up until your forehead. Touch your thumbs gently on your eye bridge (Figures 3-86 and 3-87).

Visualize that the moon is full and is taking up half of the sky. Your body is getting bigger and closer to Vairocana. You are entering Vairocana. You are becoming Vairocana, situated within the full moon.

Step 9. Change the seal to the Precious Vessel Seal in front of your eye bridge and recite Qian. Lower the seal down next to your chest and stay there for a while (Figures 3-88 and 3-89).

No visualization and no mantra.

Figure 3-90

Figure 3-91

Figure 3-92

Figure 3-93

Figure 3-94

Figure 3-95

Step 10. Stand in front of a wall and do a handstand (Figure 90). Start with just a short time. Gradually increase the time. (Standing on your hands is another method of making the Zai Seal.)

Step 11. After completing the handstand, stand up on your feet and relax your body. Bring your hands together in front of your chest with your fingers pointing up, and stay there for a while (Figure 3-91). Point your fingers down and lower your palms until your thigh level (Figure 3-92). Let all the impurities drain out of your body through your toes and the bottom of your feet.

Step 12. Move your palms to your sides, up over your head, press them together over your head, and chant OM. Lower your palms to your throat level and chant AH. Continue lowering your palms until your chest level and chant HUM (Figures 3-93 to 3-96).

171

| Figure 3-96 | Figure 3-97 | Figure 3-98 |

Figure 3-99

Step 13. Next point your fingers down and move them down next to your *dantian*. Separate your palms, but keep your fourth fingers touching. Stay there for a while (Figure 3-97). Release the fingers that are touching, face your palms together without touching, and nourish your qi for a while before finishing (Figure 3-98).

Step 14. To finish bring your palms together next to your chest and chant three times: OM NAMO BENZI Sakyamunifo and all the Enlightened Families (Figure 3-99).

Notes:

Vajrasattva is the indestructible, brave, and courageous bodhisattva, with an earnest effort to cultivate virtue and to get rid of evil. Vajrasattva is also known as the Bodhisattva of the Three Indestructibles. The three indestructible qualities are Fearlessness, Decisiveness, and Immovableness, which gives the power to cultivate virtue and to get rid of evil.

Fearlessness is not being afraid, even when one is facing problems and obstacles. The more setbacks one gets, the more courageous and brave one becomes. The bigger the obstacle one overcomes, the happier one gets. If one doesn't have problems, one helps others solve their problems. Because one is made up of an indestructible body, one can't be injured or infected by diseases.

Decisiveness is being free from doubt or wavering even when one is faced with objections, degradation, or obstacles. One becomes even more brave and continues forward. Because one has the wisdom of the Vajrasattva, one can see through the intentions of other's objections, degradation, and obstacles. One further elevates one's courage and puts forth more effort to accomplish one's goals and objectives.

Immovableness is being incapable of being moved by any obstacle. Just as the Tai Mountain will not budge, one will not let any unmeaningful or insignificant events move them. If one is always disturbed by worldly affairs, unable to shake off vanity, other's attacks and criticisms, easily moved by mundane and insignificant events, one will not be able to successfully become one with the *Dao (Tao)* and reach enlightenment.

Book 4:

Emitting, Absorbing, and Healing Qigong

4.1. You Have the Ability to Emit Qi

The ability to emit qi is not something mystical. Many people used to believe that it would take ten to twenty years to be able to emit qi. One of the reasons this might have been true, was that the older generation masters were more conservative in their teaching. Students often had to stay with one master for ten to twenty years before the master was willing to share the keys of the training to the student. This is no longer the case today.

Every person, has the ability to emit qi. An individual's potential, of course, depends on the condition of one's health. Strong and healthy individuals can emit stronger qi. Sick or weak individuals emit weaker qi. With qigong training, everyone can improve their ability to emit qi. Many of the authors' students are senior citizens in their sixties, and seventies. With only a few months of qigong training, they all can emit strong qi, and their bodies have become healthier and stronger. Their emitted qi can pass through several people, pass through walls, and many other materials.

Emitted qi can be used for healing your own illness or others' illness. From the other qigong methods you have practiced in other parts of this volume, you will have built a solid energetic foundation and have a strong storage of qi and you will have the ability to emit qi. With the ability to emit qi and with the understanding of the healing principles, you too can heal yourself and others.

To be able to emit strong qi, one must also be able to generate qi and absorb qi from nature. We live in nature and are part of nature. We depend on nature for survival. Air, food, water, and the sun, are essential life sustaining ingredients. Prolonged deficiency of any of them will result in catastrophic illness and loss of life. Since we are part of a greater cosmic whole, the study of human energy can't be separated from cosmic energy. Since humans and nature are very closely linked, any changes in nature will directly or indirectly affect the human body. The importance of our interaction with nature can't be over emphasized.

The relevant adaptation of the human body to the environment is one of the basic theories in TCM. This theory states that the physical body and the physiological phenomena of the human body, as well as, the pathological changes are constantly adapting to the changes of the environment. The training in Book 4 can significantly enhance the adaptability of the human body to the changes in the environment, as well as, develop your ability to emit qi and absorb qi.

Specifically, in Section 4.2., we will present the methods to unify the cosmos and the human body, both basic and advanced methods. In Section 4.3., we will present methods to emit your qi. To encourage and increase your confidence in emitting qi, we will start Section 4.3. by first introducing the method for building and testing qi. This will allow you to experience your own qi emission.

When you have felt your qi emitting out, you will have more confidence in the rest of the training. After you are able to emit and absorb your qi back to your body, training with a partner and with a group of people will further develop your sensitivity and ability to emit qi. In Section 4.4., we will focus on absorbing qi from natural objects. In Section 4.5. we will introduce methods to develop your healing ability, including methods to feel other's qi, see auras, and methods for healing people, followed by a method to ward off negative energies in Section 4.6.

4.2. Unifying the Cosmos and the Human Body

From the foundation you built in the other qigong training, your circulation of qi in the channels will have become smoother. The focus on this section is to enhance the unification of your body with the cosmos. This section contain two training methods. The Basic and the Advanced Methods of Unification with the Cosmos. The Basic Method of Unification with the Cosmos is the foundation and the preparation for the Advanced Method of Unification with the Cosmos.

1. THE BASIC METHOD OF UNIFICATION WITH THE COSMOS

Part 1.

Preparation

Step 1. Stand with your feet shoulder width apart. Your *baihui, huiyin*, and the midpoint of the two *yongquan* points should be vertically aligned (Figure 4-1).

Step 2. Relax the entire body, especially your *Huizhong*, the center of wisdom. *Huizhong* is located at the slight indentation of your forehead, just above the eye bridge. This area is like the *window* of your body that can emit qi and other extraordinary substances. It is also a window for absorbing qi from the cosmos.

Relaxing your *Huizhong* means opening this window. To open this window, gently stretch the area with a light smile. In other words, you should get in a pleasant mood. The pleasant feeling is from the inside. This will develop your potential and increase your wisdom.

Step 3. Relax the *huiyin* area. This area is an important passage and pivot for qi circulation. Relaxing this area will also assist in relaxing the lower abdomen. After relaxing the *huiyin* area a warm and tingling sensation will develop. Relaxing the *huiyin* area strengthens the body and helps to prevent illness.

Step 4. Bend both knees slightly, and tuck your sacrum in slightly to reduce the curvature of the spine.

Step 5. Keep 70% of your weight on your heels. This way your toes and *yongquan* points can be more relaxed.

Part 2.

Any movement of the spine affects the entire body, including the organs. Moving the spine can enhance the flow of qi in the Conception and Governing Vessels, and the Urinary Bladder Channel in the back of the body. The Urinary Bladder Channel in turn can directly interact with the internal organs. Each and every vertebrae should move in the spinal exercise. The spinal exercise also directly stimulates the brain. By paying attention to the spine, you are also *washing your marrow* — the process of using your mind to lead the qi, and use the qi to cleanse the marrow.

| Figure 4-1 | Figure 4-2 | Figure 4-3 |

Spinal Exercise:

Step 1. Start from the sacrum, do forward wavelike movements, one vertebra at a time, up your spine to your head (Figure 4-2). Pay attention from your *huiyin* to your *baihui* and look internally to the movements of your spine.

Then reverse the direction of the movement by moving your spine, from your head down to your sacrum. Pay attention from your *baihui* to your *huiyin*, and look internally to the movements of your spine. This completes one revolution. Do 3 revolutions. Let your arms move forward and back naturally.

Step 2. Continue from above. Do sideways snakelike movements from your sacrum up to your head, one section at a time, from your *huiyin* to your *baihui* (Figure 4-3). Pay attention from your *huiyin* to your *baihui* and look internally to the movements of your spine.

Then reverse the direction of the movement by moving your spine, from your head down to your sacrum. Pay attention from your *huiyin* to your *baihui* and look internally to the movements of your spine. This completes one revolution. Do 3 revolutions. Let your arms move side to side naturally.

Step 3. Continue from above. Do circular movement from your sacrum up to your head, one section at a time, from your *huiyin* to your *baihui* (Figure 4-4). Pay attention from your *huiyin* to your *baihui* and look internally to the movements of your spine.

| Figure 4-4 | Figure 4-5 | Figure 4-6 |

Then reverse the direction of the movement by moving your spine, from your head down to your sacrum. Pay attention from your *baihui* to your *huiyin* and look internally to the movements of your spine. This completes one revolution. Do 3 revolutions. Let your arms move naturally.

Step 4. Continue from above. Combine Steps 1 through 3. Move your spine in all possible directions, from your sacrum up to your head, one section at a time (Figure 4-5). Pay attention from your *huiyin* to your *baihui* and look internally to the movements of your spine.

Then reverse the direction of the movement by moving your spine, from your head down to your sacrum. Pay attention from your *baihui* to your *huiyin* and look internally to the movements of your spine. This completes one revolution. Do 3 revolutions. Let your arms move naturally.

Part 3.

Posture and Visualization:

Posture: Raise your hands up to your head level with your palms facing your temples or each other (Figure 4-6).

Visualization: The pure essence of the universe is entering your body through your *Huizhong* filling your body. Your body is dispersed throughout the universe and becomes one with the universe. Then forget about your body and breathing. Forget about everything and immerse yourself in a state of *Void*. Move your fingers and toes slightly during your visualization.

Discussion:

After you have stood in this posture for 5 to 10 minutes your shoulders will feel a little sore from holding your hands up. Your body may begin to move automatically. The automatic movements of your arms and spine will reduce the soreness in your arms. Some people may automatically do very graceful dancing and Taijiquan movements. Some may move repeatedly in one direction, laugh, or cry. Some people will not move at all. Most people will move slightly.

The movements are the result of the qi balancing action in the body. The paths that are restricted may be uncomfortable or painful. When the restrictions are removed, the discomfort or pain will have been eliminated. If there was any emotional trauma hidden within, one may cry or laugh. This is an expression of releasing emotional stress. Once released, the body will feel much better and illness may be cured.

People without any illness, will generally have very graceful movements. Their face will show a smile, expressing a cheerful expression. Some people will be able to see many different colors at the *Huizhong*. Some people will smell incense. Some people will automatically do acupuncture massage on themselves. Some people will be able to do movements that they normally would not be able to do. During training, one will be able to bring about the hidden potentials within. After training one will feel light and agile, filled with vitality, and energy circulating smoothly. Illness will have been prevented, and health and longevity attained.

This training is attempting to attain a proper flow of qi through stillness. From stillness comes movement. With training one attains a balance of *yin-yang*, smooth flowing qi pathways, and a regulation of the five emotions — joy, anger, worry, pensiveness, and fear. This will improve physiological functions and the spirit of vitality. Which in turn, will prevent and heal illness, extend the years, and increase your wisdom.

Some people may feel hot, sweaty, and tingling all over. Some people will feel cold in the arms and legs. These are all possible sensations from the training. Don't be afraid. The reason for these different sensations is the significant differences in the condition of an individual's physiological and psychological health. Even in the same individual, the condition of one's mind and body fluctuates from day to day. Don't be surprised if your movements are not the same each time you train.

People that are unable to calm down for the training, and people that are distracted by other people's movements may also not have any movement. The more one thinks of movements, the less chance you will move. Keep in mind that even though you may not have any movement during the training, you will still gain benefits. During any qigong training, it is imperative that one does not pursue sensation or movements, just be natural. Even when the physical body doesn't move, so long as the qi is moving internally, you will benefit from the training, just the same.

Finishing:

> When qi has moved through the restrictions in the body, the movements will naturally stop. As your body stops moving, men place their left hand on the *dantian*, with their right hand on top of their left hand. Women place their right hand on their *dantian*, with their left hand on top of their right hand. Keep your intention at your *dantian*. This will retain the qi in your body instead of it dispersing out of your body.

> The length of time required for the *Finishing* will last until the body stops moving or until you no longer feel the sensation of qi all over your body. Be patient. If you are too eager to finish; you may feel your body wanting to twitch, and after doing other movements you may feel unable to stop easily. Even though this will not constitute any big problem, it may not be a good feeling and you may feel tired. To remedy this condition, you should do Part 3 again. This time be patient and complete the *Finishing* properly. Then with your eyes open, do deep breathing 10 times or more. During your exhalation, gently make the *ha* sound.

Notes:

A. Wear loose clothing with flat and soft sole shoes. Remove your watch, glasses, and other jewelry that may affect your training. Find an open area without tables or chairs close by. The best place is one that is clean, quiet, and with plenty of fresh air.

B. The best time to practice is during the early morning hours. It is also good to practice in the evening between 11 P.M. and 1 A.M. However, it is recommended that you have a partner training with you, during the evening hours.

C. Make sure to keep warm during your practice. While training, your pores are open. You may catch a chill, if you allow cold air to enter your pores.

D. Stay away from distractions such as children, television, radio, and the telephone. These interruptions can cause uneasiness after practice.

E. Refrain from drinking and eating cold drinks and food, shortly before and shortly after practice. Warm water or tea is recommended after practice.

F. Women should not train this qigong during their period, or while pregnant. Individuals with heart disease and individuals with mental conditions should refrain from practicing Part 3 of this qigong.

G. After you have practiced this qigong for a while, you will have the automatic movement, shortly after your hands are raised. To stop, these individuals can gently use their intention to stop, and will be able to stop the movement easily. When you are in a bad mood, unhappy, feel uneasy, or are catching a cold, do this qigong for 10 minutes or more, you will feel lighter and discomfort will disappear.

Some people during the early stages of their training are unable to control their movement, and are unable to stop once the body starts moving (During other still meditations, some people may also have this problem). Therefore, it is recommended that you have an instructor or a partner with you when you train. After a few times, you can then practice on your own.

H. When doing the *Finishing*, you must be patient, don't hurry the process. Wait until the qi sensations disappear before concluding the training. If you are unable to stop the movement, do one or all of the following: 1. Open your eyes wide and do deep breathing 10 or more times. 2. Have your partner grab a hold of your wrist and squeeze the *neiguang* and *waiguan* points simultaneously, until your movement stops. Then walk for a few minutes. 3. Have your partner, grab a hold of your *quchi*, *hegu*, and *dazhui*, and *jianjing* points; or use cold water to wash your face. 4. Have your partner gently brush down the back of your body, from your head down to your toes, then from your shoulder down to your hands. Repeat until the movement stops.

2. THE ADVANCED METHOD OF UNIFICATION WITH THE COSMOS

The Advanced Method of Unification with the Cosmos is based on the Tantric Buddhist discipline. It has been well documented and presented by Master Liu Han-Wen in his work on Chan and Tantric Buddhist Qigong in China, under the chapter called *Wisdom Qigong*. This method takes your mind up to the limits of the sky and down to the roots of the earth, and sideways to the limitless reaches of the cosmos. We have also included another Tantric Buddhist Qigong method that uses your qi spiraling out and uniting with the cosmos. The Advanced Method of Unification with the Cosmos takes the Small Cosmos (human) into the Great Cosmos to unify the two.

The Basic Method of Unification with the Cosmos trains the body to activate the qi. The advanced method allows the practitioner to further feel the correspondence between the body and the cosmos, and its benefit to health. During this training, you will be nourishing your qi and combining with the cosmos' qi. Your qi will regulate itself with the cosmos' qi to eliminate illness and attain health; developing your body's potential, and cultivating a higher intellect. Some individuals may also develop amazing abilities.

Part 1. Beginning

Preparation and Movement:

Preparation: Stand with your feet shoulder width apart and turn your feet out slightly. Tuck your sacrum in slightly, to reduce the curvature of your spine at your waist. Raise your arms up with your palms facing each other, in front of your face, as in Figure 4-6.

As an alternative, you may place your hands in front of your chest or abdomen. Lift your head up slightly and keep your neck straight. Shift most of your weight on your heels. Relax your *huiyin*. Your posture should be comfortably expanded and expressing a feeling that your qi is *embracing the great lakes and mountains*.

Movement: Continue from above, with your eyes half closed, for about 3 minutes. While standing, move your fingers and toes gently. Gradually extend the movements to your wrists, elbows, and shoulders; heels, knees, and hips; sacrum, lumbar spine, thoracic spine, and cervical spine. With practice, you will be able to move the entire body with ease. When your spine moves, all other parts (organs, other joints, and muscles) move. The emphasis is on the movements of the organs. The joints and muscle movements are secondary. Let them move naturally; don't force them.

As you move your body, pay attention to your joints from top to bottom; then from bottom to top continuously. Keep your muscles as relaxed as possible and listen to the sounds your body makes in a state of relaxation. Breathe naturally, be aware of your breath, but don't focus on it.

Part 2. Relax, Expand, Let Go, and Retrieve

Movement and Visualization:

Step 1. *Relax your huiyin for about 1 minute.* Stand in the same Posture as in Part 1. To be able to relax the entire body, you need to first relax your *huiyin.* When your *huiyin* is relaxed, you will be able to relax the rest of your body, to attain better blood and qi circulation. The *huiyin* is the pivotal point of qi circulation. It is the point where yin and yang energy passes. In the entire process of this training, your *huiyin* should always be relaxed. From this, you will reach a comfortable and cheerful state. Maintain this state throughout your practice - keep your *inner smile* radiating.

Step 2. *Expand your Huizhong for about 2 minutes. Huizhong* in Chinese means *center of wisdom.* It is also called *Huimu,* meaning *eye of wisdom.* It is located at the indentation of your forehead, slightly above the area between your eyebrows. When your *Huizhong* is expanded, you will be able to express your inner smile physically. This way you will be relaxing your five emotions: worry, anger, fear, joy, pensiveness.

Expanding your *Huizhong* is also known as cultivating the *body* and *heart* by improving physiological and mental functions. *Huizhong* is a *window* to the universe. Individuals with a high level of qigong training can accomplish amazing tasks from the *spiritual light* emitted from their *center of wisdom.* Coordinating the expanding of your *Huizhong* at the top, and relaxing your *huiyin* at the bottom, to connect yin and yang, allows the yin and yang energies to transport smoothly, from one to the other.

Step 3. *Let go of your whole body for about 2 minutes.* Visualize and look far into the grand sensory of the sun, moon, mountains, lakes, rivers, oceans, and the rest of the cosmos through the *eye of wisdom.* From the relaxing of your *huiyin* and expanding of your *Huizhong,* relax and spread your muscles, bones, skin, and hair, to the farthest reaches of the cosmos. Breathe together with the cosmos, be one with the cosmos.

Step 4. *Retrieve back to guanyuan (outside-dantian).* Bring your attention back from *the distance.* Pass through your *center of wisdom,* along your spine and into the space within your abdomen. Retrieving is a prerequisite for storing. You will need to use both your ears and eyes to *listen* to and *focus* on your *guanyuan*. Overlap your palms on your *guanyuan*, men with their left hands in and women with their right hands in. Close your eyes and look at your *guanyuan* internally. This is called *"Return the Shen to your body; qi will automatically come back"*.

Discussion and Notes:

When you are practicing Steps 1, 2, and 3, maintain a comfortable and cheerful feeling. The cheerful feeling should come from your inner smile. Internally, your physical body should be as relaxed as possible; and externally, let go as far as you can. Also, maintain the gentle swaying of your body.

This training first requires you to relax, expand, and let go, then retrieve. It starts from building up qi internally, then absorbing qi from the cosmos. Utilizing the energy of the cosmos to attain the ability to retain your own energy without leakage. During your practice, you will first feel your arms and legs fill with qi, then your entire body fill with qi.

You may have qi sensations like warmth, heat, tingling, itching, swelling, slight aches, lightness, heaviness, largeness, smallness, emptiness, void, or limbs swinging and jumping. Sometime you may see shooting stars, thunder, bright sunshine, the moon, or rainbow colors. These are all natural and common sensations. Don't be nervous or worry about them. Just let them be. However, don't search for any specific sensations during practice, be natural. It is very important to be natural. When you are natural everything will be fine.

Once you have familiarized yourself with this training, you no longer need to set your body in any specific posture. You can practice indoors or outdoors, as you wish.

Part 3. Absorbing Energy from Above and Below

Movement and Visualization:

Step 1. *Absorbing energy from below.* Stand in the same posture as in Part 1. Place your attention at your *guanyuan* and begin bringing your attention downward. Continue to bring your attention out of your body in three paths, from your *huiyin* and the two *yongquan* points at the bottom of your feet. Bring your attention slowly down and gauge how deep the earth is.

Penetrate all the way through the earth and *see* what it *looks* like on the other side of the earth and pick up qi from the earth. Then bring your attention back in three paths to your *yongquan* and *huiyin*.

Step 2. *Absorbing energy from above.* Continue from above, combine the three paths into one at your sacrum, and up along your spine. When your mind reaches shoulder level, again divide into three paths up through your two *jianjing* points (located on top of your shoulder, the midpoint between the first thoracic vertebrae and the edge of your shoulder, one on each side), and your *baihui* points up to the sky. Continue up and gauge how high the sky is. All the way up to the stars, to pick up qi from the sky.

Then bring your attention back down to your *baihui* and *jianjing* points. Down along your spine and out of your huiyin and the two *yongquan* points. Continue down slowly as before to the other side of the earth, to pick up qi from the earth.

Step 3. Repeat Steps 1 and 2 a total of three times. On the third time, after you pick up qi from the sky, bring your attention back to your *baihui* and *jianjing*. Then down along your spine to your *mingmen* and back to your *guanyuan (outside-dantian)*. Place your palms over your *guanyuan*, men left hand in and women right hand in.

Close your eyes and internally *look* at your spine down to your *guanyuan*, and *listen* to your *guanyuan* to increase your qi sensations.

Discussion and Notes:

Raise your attention up to the sky to pick up *yang-qi* to supplement your own qi. Penetrate down to the earth to pick up *yin-qi* to nourish your blood. This training will assist you in feeling the unification of humans, earth, and the sky. Your spine is filled with bone marrow, connects to your brain, and energetically connects with your kidneys. In this training, you are using your spine as the center, and use your mind to lead the qi up and down to interact with the cosmos. When qi permeates all over your body, you will feel your *baihui* and *jianjing* connecting to the cosmos. The qi connecting to the *huiyin* and *yongquan* points can also be felt. You may also feel an energy beam from the earth up to the sky with your body within the beam.

During practice, occasionally you may *hear* thunder sounds and bird sounds, and smell the fragrance of flowers. These are sensations you may have in addition to the sensations you felt in Part 2. This is due to the further activation of qi in your channels, and the result of qi flowing stronger through your channels to balance the *yin-yang*.

186

Part 4. Absorbing Energy from Six Directions

Movement and Visualization:

Step 1. Stand in the same posture as in Part 1. Bring your attention to your *guanyuan* point on your abdomen. Lead your attention out to your left, right, front, back, up, and down, all at the same time. Visualizing that you are being attracted by the cosmos to the farthest reaches of the cosmos. Then bring your attention back from the distance to your abdomen. Repeat three or more times.

Step 2. Then overlap your palms on your *guanyuan (outside-dantian)*. Bring your mind back to the inside of your abdomen *(inside-dantian)*. Close your eyes, look internally at your *inside-dantian*, and *listen* to it.

Part 5. Absorbing Energy by Spiraling

Movement and Visualization:

Step 1. Continuing from Part 4, sit down on a chair (you may stand or lie down if you like). Keep your palms on your *guanyuan*. Condense your qi in your *inside-dantian* into a small ball and begin spiraling up from behind, and down in front of you; then again, up, and down. Moving into a bigger and bigger spiral, to the size of your body, the size of the earth, and to the size of the cosmos. Keep rotating until the entire cosmos is spiraling with you.

After a while, begin spiraling smaller and smaller until your attention is back to your *inside-dantian*. Keep the qi spiraling inside of your *dantian*. Even after you finish this training, you should still maintain the spiral in your *inside-dantian*. This will give you the benefits as if you were training continuously.

Discussion and Notes:

A. Parts 4 and 5 are supplements to Part 3. After training for a long period of time, your qi will become very strong and many different sensations will begin to occur. The points on your body will have a thrusting, jumping, shrinking, expanding, warmth, hotness, coolness, and/or tingling sensation. You may also *see* some *external scenery* and other special sensations.

187

B. You will feel the qi inside you invigorated, and the qi from outside filling into your body from all directions. This training can increase your sensitivity. When your sensitivity increases, you will become aware of other people's energy patterns, especially when you come into close proximity of an individual who is ill.

C. Try to avoid anybody or anything that may affect your training or cause you to feel unable to protect yourself. When practicing in a group, stay at a distance between each other to reduce interference from one another.

D. If you should feel uncomfortable from the continuous spiraling of the qi in your *inside-dantian*, then stop the spiraling completely. Patiently wait until the qi has completely stopped spiraling in your *dantian*. This is the general way to finish a session of training. Individuals with high qigong accomplishments, are in a constant state of qi cultivation. This of course depends on the depth and length of time one has invested in qigong practice.

4.3. Emitting Qi Methods

The primary focus of this section is to introduce methods for increasing qi for emission, ways to train and emit qi, and ways to use the emitted qi to heal some common illness. We have included parts of *Emei Dragon Qigong*, *Emei Dapeng Qigong*, *Shaolin Internal Power Qigong*, *Cross Space Power Qigong*, and a combination of Tantric and Chan Buddhist Qigong.

1. BUILDING AND TESTING QI

Part 1. Building Qi

Procedure:

Step 1. Stand comfortably with your feet about a shoulder width apart. Relax your shoulders. Raise your palms over your head and bring them together, at the same time vocalize the sound OM. Lower both palms together, down to your throat and vocalize the sound AH. Continue lowering your palms together until your chest and vocalize the sound HUM (Figures 4-7 to 4-9).

Step 2. Then point your fingers down, separate your palms with your palms facing each other. Lift both palms up, until your fingers are pointing forward and elbows are bent (Figures 4-10 to 4-12).

Figure 4-7

Figure 4-8

Figure 4-9

Figure 4-10

Figure 4-11

Figure 4-12

Next, lift both elbows back and up, while naturally lowering your forearms until your palms are facing back. Bend your knees slightly (as low as you feel comfortable with your feet pointing in slightly, or pointing forward). Move your elbows and wrist towards your back until your fingers are pointing towards your waist, palms facing up, but without touching your waist. Hold that position for about 5 seconds (Figures 4-13 and 4-14).

Step 3. Squeeze your elbows back towards each other as you point your fingers forward (Figure 4-15). Hold for a few seconds. Next, relax your shoulders and allow the relaxation of your back muscles to push your arms forward, until your elbows clear your torso. Then, rotate your palms until they are facing down (Figures 4-16 and 4-17).

Figure 4-13   Figure 4-14   Figure 4-15

Figure 4-18

Figure 4-16   Figure 4-17

Relax your fingers and form them into a stair pattern (base of your thumb presses in slightly and your index finger is higher than the other three fingers). Stay in this posture for at least 10 minutes (Figure 4-18). The longer you stay in this posture, the stronger your qi sensation will be.

Step 5. *Closing.* Lift both palms up next to your collar bones and change your palms into fists, as you inhale and straighten your legs. Then breathe out slowly as you open your fists and push your palms down to your *dantian* level in a natural standing position (Figures 4-19 and 4-20).

If you are going to practice other training after the Building Qi posture, don't do the Closing yet. Do the Closing only after you have finished a session of practicing.

Figure 4-19   Figure 4-20

Discussion and Notes:

Breathe naturally. Don't pay attention to any specific area. When you raise your palms over your head and vocalize the sound OM, visualize that the *pure essence* of the universe is entering your body through your *baihui*. Then, as you continue with the palm movements and vocalizing the AH and HUM sounds, bring the pure essence down to your throat, your chest and into the rest of your body.

When you squeeze your elbows back towards each other, it stimulates the 12 Channels in your body and smooths out the qi flow. As you point your fingers forward, you also stimulate your Girdle Vessel which in turn stimulates your Conception and Governing Vessels. This increases the flow of qi in your 12 Channels. The Girdle Vessel is like a belt that wraps around your waist. It interacts closely with the three yin channels and three yang channels in your legs, as well as, the Conception and the Governing Vessels. This can greatly increase the flow of qi between the upper and lower parts of your body.

The pigeon toe stance can increase the emitting force of your qi more than with your toes pointing forward. Together with the squeezing of your arms which condenses the qi and blood; when released, a strong force of qi will flow out through your arms. This will increase the flow of qi in the three yin channels and the three yang channels in your arms. When the qi flow increases in your palms and fingers, you will feel a warm, swelling, and tingling sensation. Maintain this standing posture to enhance your blood and qi flow as long as you wish.

According to Traditional Chinese Medicine, when qi and blood are flowing smoothly, then there will be no aches and pains; when qi and blood are not flowing smoothly, then aches and pains result. Standing posture practice can help you achieve smooth flowing qi to attain health and heal illness.

Figure 4-21 Figure 4-22 Figure 4-23

Part 2. Testing Qi

Procedure:

Step 1. Continue from the standing Building Qi posture, cross your arms in front of each other with your right forearm on top of your left forearm, palms facing down. Your arms don't touch. Point the *neiguan* point of your right forearm at the *waiguan* point of your left forearm (Figure 4-21).

Neiguan point is located on the center line of your forearm, two thumb widths from your wrist. *Waiguan* is on the opposite side of your *neiguan* point on the back of your forearm. Pay attention to the sensations between the two points for about 30 seconds.

Next rotate your arms until your palms are facing up. This time, point the *waiguan* point of your right forearm at the *neiguan* point of your left forearm (Figure 4-22). Again, pay attention to the sensations between the points for about 30 seconds.

Step 2. Move your forearms closer to your body and bring your right palm over your left palm. Point the *laogong* point of your left arm at the back of your right palm (Figure 4-23). Pay attention to the sensations between your palms for about 30 seconds. Feel the different sensations between the front of your left palm and the back of your right palm.

Step 3. Rotate your right palm over until it is facing your left palm, as if you were holding a ball between your palms (Figure 4-24).

Figure 4-24

Figure 4-25

Figure 4-26

Pay attention to the sensations between your palms for about 30 seconds.

Step 4. Pull your palms away from each other until your right palm is at your *renzhong* (between the tip of your nose and your upper lip) height and your left palm is at your *dantian* height. Your palms should still be facing each other (Figure 4-25). Pay attention to the sensations between the palms for about a minute.

Step 5. Bring your palms closer together, but not touching. Then, pull them away from each other again. Repeat three times and pay attention to the varying sensations which result from the different distances.

After three times of pulling your palms away from each other, keep your right palm back at *renzhong* height and left palm at *dantian* height for about 30 seconds. Then point the middle finger of your right hand at the center of your left palm. Gradually, lower your right palm towards your left palm with your right middle finger still pointing at your left palm (Figures 4-26 and 4-27). Pay attention to the sensations on your left palm.

Step 6. Bring your right palm back up and make circular movements with your right middle finger over your left palm (Figure 4-28). Again, pay attention to the sensations on your left palm.

Step 7. Straighten your right middle finger, bring your palms closer together, and rotate both palms until your fingers are pointing forward, as you extend your arms forward (Figures 4-29 and 4-

Figure 4-27

Figure 4-28

Figure 4-29

Figure 4-30

Figure 4-31

Figure 4-32

30). Circle your palms over each other and pay attention to the sensations between your palms (Figure 4-31).

Step 8. Pull your palms away from each other until shoulder width apart. Then rotate your left palm until it is facing down. This will bring you back to the Building Qi posture (Figure 4-32). Repeat the entire Testing Qi practice on the other side. That is, do the mirror image of the procedure described above from Steps 1 to 8.

After you have done both sides and are ready to conclude your practice session, do the *Closing* described in Part 1, Step 5. If you are continuing with your practice, wait until you finish practicing, then do the *Closing*.

194

Discussions and Notes:

From the Building and Testing Qi training everyone can feel very strong qi sensations in their hands. The sensation of a ball of qi between your palms can be felt easily when the *laogong* points on your palms are brought to face each other. The strength of attraction or repulsion between the palms will differ from one person to the next. The sensation becomes even more apparent when the middle finger of one hand is pointing at the *laogong* point of the other hand. Some people will feel pressure on the *laogong*; itching, aching, or tingling sensations. When the middle finger of one hand is drawing circles, the other palm will feel like circles are been drawn on it. These sensations are a test for you to feel the strength of your own qi.

The Building and Testing Qi training is not only for testing your own qi, it also has the potential to heal many illnesses of the organs. This is because the primary movements involved in the training are at the Conception Vessel; the *renzhong, tiantu, shanzhong, zhongwan, xiawan, qihai*, and *dantian* points; and passes through the Girdle Vessel. This exercise can help heal illness associated with the intestines, stomach, menstruation, nocturnal emission, impotence, and palpitation. For others, it is capable of strengthening their health.

2. ROTATING THE QI BALL

After you have built a good foundation through the Building and Testing Qi training, you can further strengthen your internal qi by practicing the Rotating Qi Ball method. Part 1 of Rotating the Qi Ball is done by circling qi around your stomach and abdomen area. This technique strengthens the Girdle Vessel and in turn activates qi circulation in the Conception Vessel. It has the potential to prevent digestive problems, urinary problems, and reproductive system problems. Part 2 is adapted from the *Emei Fire Dragon Rotating the Qi Ball* technique. It increases your qi emitting ability to an even higher level, by strengthening your qi and increasing the qi flow in your vessels.

Part 1. Activating the Girdle Vessel

Procedure:

Step 1. Stand as in the Building Qi posture. Lower your palms slowly to the right side of your body over your liver, but not touching (Figure 4-33). The *tiger's mouth* (the area between your index finger and your thumb), face each other; and your *laogong* points face your liver for 30 seconds to a minute.

Step 2. Shift most of your weight onto your right foot and turn your body towards your left, at the same time, turn your left foot to

Figure 4-33   Figure 4-34   Figure 4-35

your left. While moving your feet, rotate your palms until they are facing down, the tiger's mouths should still be facing each other (Figure 4-34). Your right knee should be bent until it slightly passes your right toes, with your knee and toes pointing in the same direction.

Next, circle your palms counterclockwise in front of your abdomen. Circle at least 12 times counterclockwise, at the rate of about 4 times a minute.

Step 3. After your palms have circled 12 times, rotate your palms until your *laogong* points are at the left side of your body over your spleen, but not touching (Figure 4-35). Stay in that posture for 30 seconds to a minute.

Step 4. Then turn your left foot in and shift most of your weight onto your left foot, as you turn your body to your right and your right foot to your right; at the same time, extend and rotate your palms until they are facing down (Figure 4-36). Your left knee should be bent until it slightly passes your left toes, with your knee and toes pointing in the same direction.

Next, circle your palms clockwise in front of your abdomen. Circle at least 12 times, at the rate of about 4 times a minute, similar to the other side.

Step 5. After 12 circles, return your palms back to the right of your body over your liver. Again, point your *laogong* points over your liver for 30 seconds to a minute (Figure 4-37).

196

Figure 4-36

Figure 4-37

Figure 4-38

Figure 4-39

Figure 4-40

Figure 4-41

Step 6. Turn your body and your right foot in until they are facing forward, rotate your palms until they are facing down, and circle your palms counterclockwise (Figure 4-38). Circle at least 12 times. Then place your palms over your abdomen for 30 seconds to a minute (Figure 4-39).

Step 7. Again, rotate your palms until they are facing down and circle clockwise 12 times (Figure 4-40). After 12 times, place your palms at your abdomen with your *laogong* points pointing at your *dantian* and the tiger's mouths facing each other (Figure 4-41). Stay in this posture for 30 seconds to a minute.

Part 2. Rotating the Qi Ball

Procedure:

Step 1. Continue from above. Extend both palms forward with your right palm over your left, palms facing each other, and your fingers pointing forward. Bend both knees into a Horse Stance. Hold your palms as if you were holding a ball. The fingers of your right hand face the fingers of your left hand, but not touching. Rotate your palms 100 times, as if you had a ball between your palms (Figure 4-42).

The rotation is done by simultaneously pulling the base of your right palm down, in, and rotating your palm until it faces up; while rotating your left palm up, your right palm is facing down (Figure 4-43). This way you change your left palm up and right palm down. Next, repeat the procedure by simultaneously pulling the base of your left palm down, in, and rotating your palm until it faces up; while rotating your right palm up, your left palm is facing down.

When you rotate your palms, the fingers of your right hand and your left hand are always facing each other. Keep your elbows, shoulders, and torso moving naturally as your palms rotate. This will increase your qi and blood circulation.

Step 2. After rotating for 100 times, return your palms to the standing Building Qi posture. If you are finishing this session of your practice, do the *Closing* described in Part 1, Step 5 — Building and Testing Qi. If wish to continue, then proceed to the next training in this section before doing the *Closing*.

3. EMIT AND RETURN QI BACK TO YOUR BODY

Part 1. Embracing the Moon

Procedure:

Step 1. Start from the standing Building Qi posture. Cross your right forearm over your left forearm without touching. Next, point your right middle finger at your *quchi* point on your left arm. Move your index finger up and down 10 times without touching (Figure 4-44).

| Figure 4-42 | Figure 4-43 | Figure 4-44 |

Next, draw circles with your middle finger over your *quchi* point for about 10 times. (*The quchi* point is located at the tip of the elbow line when you bend your elbow.)

Step 2. Straighten the middle finger of your right hand and point your *laogong* point on the *quchi* point of your left arm. Move your right palm up and down slowly, 10 times (Figure 4-45). As your right palm moves up, relax your palm; and as your right palm moves down, flex your palm slightly to open your *laogong* point.

Step 3. Repeat Steps 1 and 2, three times. Pay attention to the sensations of your middle finger, your *laogong*, and your *quchi*.

Part 2. Return Qi Back to Your Body

Procedure:

Step 1. Continue from Part 1. Lower your elbows and raise your palms until your palms are overlapping, but not touching — left palm on the inside, the *laogong* point of your right palm facing the back of your left palm, and the *laogong* point on your left hand faces your *tiantu* point (Figure 4-46). Next, push and pull your right palm, back and forth. Combine the qi emitted from your right and your left *laogong* points into your *tiantu* point. Practice for one minute.

Step 2. Move both palms up until your *laogong* points are facing your mouth (Figure 4-47). Repeat the same push and pull movement with your right palm and emit qi from your *laogong* points into your mouth for one minute.

199

Figure 4-45   Figure 4-46   Figure 4-47

Step 3. Move both palms up to your *Huizhong* and repeat the same push and pull movement with your right palm and emit qi from your *laogong* points into your forehead for one minute (Figure 4-48).

Step 4. Move both palms up to your *baihui* (Figure 4-49). (For a stronger qi sensation, squat down slightly and cross your right leg over your left thigh, with your foot facing up. This will require some balance.) Next, repeat the same push and pull movements with your right palm and feel the emission of qi from your *laogong* into your *baihui* and the sensations on your *yongquan* points for one minute.

Step 5. Separate your palms and lower them down until your palms are facing your ears (Figure 4-50). Next, repeat the push and pull movement with your right palm and emit qi from your right *laogong* point. Pay attention to the sensations on your left palm for one minute.

Step 6. Move your palms to the back of your head facing your *fengchi* points (Figure 4-51). Do the push and pull movement with both palms and emit qi into your *fengchi* points for one minute. (*Fengchi* is located on the side of your first cervical vertebrae.)

Step 7. Move your palms down to your chest (Figure 4-52). Do the push and pull movement with both palms and emit qi into your chest for one minute.

Step 8. Move your palms down to your stomach level (Figure 4-53). Do the push and pull movement with both palms and emit qi into your stomach area for one minute.

Figure 4-48

Figure 4-49

Figure 4-50

Figure 4-51

Figure 4-52

Figure 4-53

Step 9. Move your palms down to your *dantian* level (Figure 4-54). Do the push and pull movement with both palms and emit qi into your *dantian* for one minute.

Step 10. Move your right palm down until your *huiyin* level and move your left palm back facing your coccyx (Figure 4-55). Do the push and pull movement with your right palm and emit qi through your right *laogong* point. Pay attention to the sensations on your left palm for one minute.

Step 11. Finally bring both palms back to the standing Building Qi posture (Figure 4-56) and repeat by doing the mirror image of this training, from Part 1 to Part 2. After you have completed both sides and want to conclude this session of your training,

Figure 4-54

Figure 4-55

Figure 4-56

do the *Closing*. If you are continuing your training, wait until you have finished the next exercise before doing the *Closing*.

Discussion and Notes:

The focus of *Emit and Return Qi Back to Your Body*, as the title implies, is to emit your own qi back to nourish your body. The qi from your body after going through your *quchi* point can pass through your *shaohai* point. Your *shaohai* point can in turn affect the *neiguan* and *laogong* points. This can further the foundation you have built from the standing Building Qi posture, by activating the qi circulation in the three yin and three yang channels on the arms: the Lung, Heart, Pericardium, Large Intestine, Small Intestine, and Triple Burner Channels.

When you emit qi to your *tiantu* point, you are influencing your respiratory system. It is especially advantageous for correcting problems associated with your bronchial tubes and lungs. Emitting qi to your mouth, influences the nerves around your mouth that connect to your brain. This area also connects to your Conception Vessel and directly influences the qi flow in this vessel. When you emit qi to your *wisdom center (Huizhong)*, you can open your *wisdom eye*, and increase your wisdom. Some people can develop special abilities when they emit qi into their *Huizhong*. Emitting qi to this area can also help heal problems associated with your eyes and strengthen them. Emitting qi to your *baihui* allows qi to flow throughout your body, all the way down to your *huiyin* and *yongquan*, and balancing the *yin-yang* to eliminate illness. TCM believes that illness is the result of a qi imbalance within the human body. By balancing your yin-yang qi, you will be able to prevent illness from occurring.

Emitting qi to your ears influences your entire body, especially your organs. It can also help stabilize your nervous system. When you emit qi to the *fengchi* points, you can influence and regulate hormonal production. It can also help prevent a cold. When you emit qi to your chest, your stomach, your *dantian*, and your *huiyin* areas; you can help strengthen and maintain the health of the respiratory, digestive, urinary, and reproductive systems. Therefore, the Emit and Return Qi Back to Your Body technique is also a training for self-healing.

4. QI ENTERS THREE GATES

This training is for increasing your ability to absorb qi and increasing your ability to emit your qi.

Procedure:

Step 1. Continue from the standing Building Qi posture. Rotate your right palm until it faces your left *hegu* point (Drawing 4-1). Push your right hand slowly towards your left hand while keeping your left hand in one place (Figure 4-57).

Then move your right hand below your left hand as you rotate your right palm facing up, and point your middle finger towards the middle finger of your left hand (Figure 4-58).

Step 2. Move your right hand along the center line of your inside left arm. Starting from your *zhongchong* point to your *laogong*, *daling*, *neiguan*, *jianshi*, and *shaohai* points (Figure 4-59).

The *zhongchong* point is located on the medial corner of your middle finger. *Jianshi* is located on the center line of the inside forearm, four finger widths above *neiguan*. *Shaohai* is located on the corner of the elbow line closest to your torso.

Step 3. Next relax your right hand middle finger and pull your hand up towards your right. Then rotate both hands until your *laogong* points are facing each other (Figures 4-60 and 4-61). Hold this posture for 1 minute.

Step 4. Slowly pull your hands away from each other at an angle until your right hand is at the upper right corner of your head and your left hand is at your hip level (Figure 4-62). Keep your *laogong* points facing each other and hold for three minutes.

Step 5. Point the fourth finger of your right hand towards the *laogong* point on your left hand (Figure 4-63). Hold for 30 seconds to 1 minute. Next, straighten the fourth finger of your right hand and point the fourth finger of your left hand towards the *laogong* point on your right hand. Hold for 30 seconds to 1 minute. Then straighten the fourth finger of your left hand.

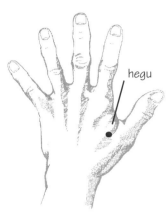

Drawing 4-1

Figure 4-57

Figure 4-58

Figure 4-59

Figure 4-60

Figure 4-61

Step 6. Point the fourth finger on both hands towards each other (Figure 4-64). Hold for 30 seconds to 1 minutes. Then straighten your fingers.

Step 7. Gradually bring your hands toward each other. Then rotate your left palm face down and bring your right hand on top of your left hand (Figures 4-65 and 4-66). Keep your hand about 4 inches away from each other.

Step 8. Move your right hand up along the back of your left forearm to your left shoulder (Figure 4-67). Turn your right palm until it faces your chest and begin lowering it down towards your right.

Figure 4-62

Figure 4-63

Figure 4-64

Figure 4-65

Figure 4-66

Figure 4-67

Continue lowering your right hand until it is next to your liver, while rotating your left hand until it faces in towards your Girdle Vessel, and at the same level as your right hand (Figure 4-68). Hold this posture for 30 seconds to 1 minutes.

Step 9. Extend your palms forward until your hands are back in the starting position, the Building Qi posture (Figure 4-69). Hold this posture for 1 minute.

Step 10. Do the mirror image on the other side.

Step 11. After completing both sides, do the *Closing*.

Figure 4-68   Figure 4-69

Discussion and Notes:

This technique begins by sending qi from the right hand *laogong* point to the left hand *hegu* point. Then continues sending qi in through the *zhongchong* point on the middle finger, along the Pericardium Channel, to *shaohai* point on the Heart Channel, and passes the Girdle Vessel to increase the qi flow.

The moving of the fourth fingers activate the Triple Burner Channel. Also, when you move your one hand along the back of the other hand, you are sending qi up through your Large Intestine and Triple Burner Channels. While you are sending qi through these channels, your other hand begins to turn and face your Girdle Vessel to increase the circulation of qi in the Girdle Vessel, which in turn activates the Conception, Governing Vessels, and other energy pathways. This can significantly increase the flow of qi and blood throughout your body, and increase the potential to absorb outside qi and emit your qi.

This technique increases the interaction between your qi and the qi of the universe, creating a stronger linkage between the two. This ability, in turn builds a solid foundation for emitting qi to heal others, while not being adversely affected during the healing process. This training is also a self-healing method for problems associated with the spleen, liver, and the digestive system.

5. ACTIVATING QI WITH YOUR FINGERS FOR HEALING AND EMITTING

This method is a unique derivative of the *Shaolin Internal Power Qigong* and *One Finger Chan Qigong*. It is also known as *Cross Space Power Qigong*. It utilizes the various combination of finger movements to activate the qi circulation in the energy pathways to attain healing and strengthening effects, and to increase one's ability to emit qi.

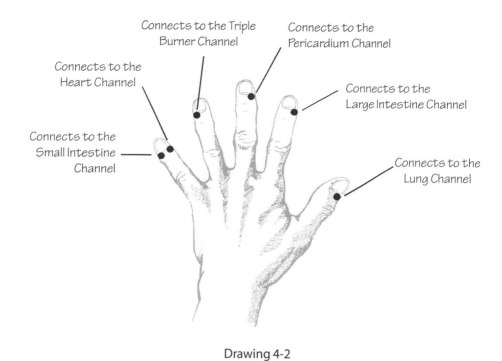

Connects to the Triple Burner Channel

Connects to the Pericardium Channel

Connects to the Heart Channel

Connects to the Large Intestine Channel

Connects to the Small Intestine Channel

Connects to the Lung Channel

Drawing 4-2

According to acupuncture theory, the Lung Channel connects to the thumb, the Large Intestine Channel connects to the index finger, the Pericardium Channel connects to the middle finger, and the Triple Burner Channel connects to the fourth finger, and the Heart Channel and the Small Intestine Channel connects to the small finger (Drawing 4-2). With specific movements of the fingers, one will be able to regulate the qi flow in the connected channels.

Indirectly, the three yin channels on the legs can be activated by the three yin channels on the hand. Similarly, the three yang channels on the leg can be activated by the three yang channels on the hand. The yin channel relationships are: the Lung Channel relates to the Spleen Channel, the Pericardium Channel relates to the Liver Channel, and the Heart Channel relates to the Kidney Channel. The yang channel relationships are: the Large Intestine Channel relates to the Stomach Channel, the Triple Burner Channel relates to the Gall Bladder Channel, and the Small Intestine Channel relates to the Urinary Bladder Channel. Therefore, the movements of the fingers can activate both the channels connected to the specific fingers, as well as, the related channel.

In addition to the yin or yang channel relationship, each finger also has a special relationship to different parts of the body. The thumb is related to the head. The index finger is related to the area between the collarbones and the diaphragm. The middle finger is related to the area between the diaphragm and the navel. The fourth finger is related to the area between the navel and the pelvic bone. The small finger is related to the thighs on down. The 10 fingers are closely connected to the rest of the body. Therefore, the proper movements of the fingers can significantly regulate the functioning of the different part of the body and organ systems.

In Part 1 we will present the finger moving patterns. In Part 2, we will present general finger activating methods for health and preventing illness. In Part 3, we will present healing and prevention methods for specific chronic illness. In Part 4, we will present the emitting and regulating qi method.

Part 1. Finger Moving Methods

Preparation:

Stand in a Horse Stance and hold your hands in front of your body, as in the Building Qi posture .

Basic Finger Movements:

Moving the thumb: From the starting hand position, move your thumb away from your palm, circle down until your thumb is pointing down. Pause slightly, then reverse the circle back to the Preparation posture (Figures 4-70 to 4-72).

Moving the Index Finger: Raise your finger up slightly, then slowly point your finger down until you can't move it anymore (Figures 4-73 and 4-74). Pause slightly, then return to the Preparation posture.

Moving the Middle Finger: Point your finger down until you can't move it anymore (Figure 4-75). Pause slightly, then return to the Preparation posture.

Moving the Fourth and Small Finger: Use the same procedure as in Moving the Middle Finger.

Discussion and Notes:

After moving the fingers return them to the Preparation posture before proceeding to the next finger movements. When repeating the entire process, all ten fingers should be straight and loose before repeating. Follow the specific requirements, one step at a time. If you should feel dizzy during your practice, don't be afraid. Rest for a while and drink some warm water or tea. This will get rid of the dizziness. Don't practice when you are too full or too hungry. Breathe naturally. Don't keep your mind in any specific part of your body. If you are unable to stand up and do the exercise, you can sit on a chair with your feet relaxed on the floor. However, the training time should be increased.

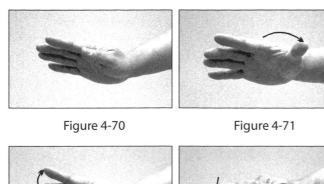
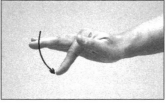

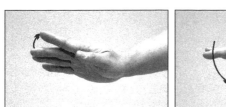
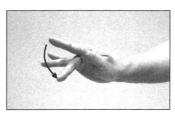

| Figure 4-70 | Figure 4-71 | Figure 4-72 |

| Figure 4-73 | Figure 4-74 | Figure 4-75 |

Part 2. General Finger Activating Qi Methods

Anti-aging and Longevity Method: From the Preparation posture, move your index fingers, your fourth fingers, your thumbs, small fingers, then your middle fingers. This completes one time. Repeat the procedure 5 times. Then stand in the Preparation Posture for five minutes and do the *Closing*.

Getting Rid of Pathogenic Influences and Cancer Prevention Method: From the Preparation posture, move your small fingers, middle fingers, then your thumbs. As you are moving your fingers, gradually move your right forearm under your left forearm while keeping your left forearm in place. When the arms are crossed, simultaneously move your index and fourth fingers on both hands. Then return your right forearm to the Preparation posture. Next, repeat the above movement, but this time cross your left arm under your right arm. This completes one time.

Repeat the procedure 4 times. Then stand in the Preparation posture for 5 minutes and do the *Closing*.

Part 3. Healing and Prevention Methods for Chronic Problems

Specific Condition:

High Blood Pressure Healing and Prevention: Bend your fourth and small fingers at the middle joints, then return to the Preparation posture. Next, move your thumbs. Then move your fourth and small fingers together. This completes one time.

Repeat the procedure 6 times. Then stand in the Preparation posture for 5 minutes and do the *Closing*.

Heart Diseases: Move your small fingers. Then flex and straighten all ten fingers, and relax. Next, move your middle fingers. Then flex and straighten all ten fingers, and relax. This complete one time.

Repeat the procedure 11 times. Then stand in the Preparation posture for 5 minutes.

Stomach and Intestine Diseases: Move your middle fingers, then move your fourth fingers and return to the Preparation posture. This completes one time.

Repeat the procedure 11 times. Then stand in the Preparation posture for 5 minutes and do the *Closing*.

Liver Diseases: Move your middle and fourth fingers at the same time, then return to the Preparation posture. This completes one time.

Repeat the procedure 9 times. Then stand in the Preparation posture for 5 minutes and do the *Closing*.

Mental Diseases: Move your thumbs, your small fingers, then index fingers and return to the Preparation posture. This completes one time.

Repeat the procedure 6 times. Then stand in the Preparation posture for 5 minutes and do the *Closing*.

Headache: Move your thumbs twice, move your small fingers once, then move your thumbs one more time. This completes one time.

Repeat the procedure 11 times. Then stand in the Preparation posture for 5 minutes and do the *Closing*.

Insomnia: Move your fourth and small fingers together 11 times. Then move your index fingers 2 times and return to the Preparation posture. Then stand in the Preparation posture for 5 minutes and do the *Closing*.

Heat Induced Asthma: Move your thumbs and middle finger simultaneously 9 times, and return to the Preparation posture. Next, move your small finger 2 times, and return to the Preparation posture. Then stand in the Preparation posture for 5 minutes and do the *Closing*.

Cold Induced Asthma: Move your thumb and fourth fingers simultaneously 9 times, and return to the Preparation posture. Next, move your middle fingers 3 times, and return to the Preparation posture. Then stand in the Preparation posture for 5 minutes and do the *Closing*.

Low Temperature and Low Thrombocyte: Move your thumbs and small fingers simultaneously 7 times, and return to the Preparation Posture. Move your middle and small fingers simultaneously 6 times and return to the Preparation posture. Then stand in the Preparation posture for 5 minutes and do the *Closing*.

Difficulty Conceiving (for Men or Women): Bring your fourth and small fingers down and hold that position for 15 minutes. Next, bring your middle fingers down and hold while keeping the fourth and small fingers down for another 10 minutes. Hold for a total of 25 minutes, the longer the better. To finish, without returning to the Preparation posture, just do the *Closing*.

Part 4. Regulating Qi by Emitting Qi through Your Fingers

Procedure:

Step 1. Stand in the Preparation posture.

Step 2. Move your fourth fingers and return to the Preparation posture. Move your index fingers and return to the Preparation posture. Move your small fingers and return to the Preparation posture. Move your middle fingers and return to the Preparation posture.

Step 3. Move your thumbs down, circle your hands in, then out, 2 times (right hand counterclockwise and left hand clockwise), and return your thumb to the Preparation posture.

Step 4. Repeat Steps 1 through 3, nine times. Then stand in the Preparation posture for 5 minutes and do the *Closing*.

Notes:

A. Each finger should have moved for a total of 45 seconds to 1 minute. That is, it should take about 5 minutes to finish the 9 repetitions, and 10 minutes to complete the entire exercise.

B. The Triple Burner Channel connects to the fourth finger. Therefore, moving the fourth finger can enhance the qi flow in the Triple Burner which indirectly activates the Girdle Vessel. From the activation of the Girdle Vessel, the Conception and the Governing Vessels will then be activated. When the Conception and the Governing Vessels are activated the 12 Channels will also become more active.

C. The movement of the thumbs can focus qi for emitting. With regular training of this technique, you will feel the qi in your hands get stronger and stronger.

6. EMITTING A QI BALL

Increasing your ability to focus and emit qi is also a way to regulate the viscera and bowels, and limbs. This method came from *Emei Dragon Taiji Qigong*. It was a development with the *Shaolin Internal Power Qigong* as a its foundation, for increasing an individual's ability to emit qi. We will introduce three methods for this training. Each method can be done by itself or with the other two methods.

Method 1. Pushing a Ball of Light into the Earth

Procedure:

Step 1. Stand in the Preparation posture. Inhale, rotate your palms until they face up and begin to raise your hands up towards your chest (Figure 4-76). Visualize that your hands are holding up a ball of light. Next, move your hands to the sides (Figure 4-77). Visualize that your chest is invigorated with qi, and the light ball you are holding is connected to the blue sky.

Step 2. Exhale, rotate and bring your hands down in front of your body (Figure 4-78). Continue to lower your hands as you squat down and move your hands to the sides (Figure 4-79). Visualize that you are pushing a beam of light down into the earth. Feel the equal and opposite reaction of the qi sensation pressing on your palms, as you push the light beam down. The warmth of this reactive qi enters your arms and goes throughout your body.

Step 3. Again, inhale, rotate your hands up, stand up gradually, and raise your hands up in front of your body to repeat the procedure.

If you are only training this method, repeat 50 to 100 times. If you will be practicing this along with the other two methods, repeat 9 times.

Figure 4-76

Figure 4-77

Figure 4-78

Figure 4-79

Figure 4-80

Figure 4-81

Method 2. Emitting Beams of Light

Procedure:

Step 1. Continue from Method 1 (or start from the Preparation Posture). Inhale and raise your hands up in front of your chest (Figure 4-80). Visualize the ball of light on your palm is being magnetized by your *laogong* points and is resting over your head.

Step 2. Exhale, rotate your palms until they are facing down with your fingers pointing at each other, but not touching (Figure 4-81). Then, turn your body to your right as you shift your weight to your left foot, and take a small step to your right with your right foot (Figure 4-82). Next, turn your left foot in, as you shift

Figure 4-82   Figure 4-83

your weight to your right leg and extend your hands forward (Figure 4-83). Your right arm should be straight, left arm bent, and index fingers should be aligned.

As you rotate your palms to face down, visualize the light ball is magnetized to your laogong points below your palms. Then the light ball turns into two light balls. Following the extension of your hands and as you exhale, the light balls become beams of light shooting to a distance and appear as a light dot in the distance. With your eyes half open, focus on this light dot in the distance.

Step 3. Pull your arms back towards your chest with your palms facing down and fingers pointing at each other. At the same time, shift your weight back to your back foot. Pivot your right foot in and left foot out and begin to bow your left foot to your left, and extend your hands to your left. This is the mirror image of the extension on the right side. The visualization is the same.

If you are only training this method, repeat 50 to 100 times. If you will be practicing this along with the other two methods, repeat 9 times on each side.

Method 3. Emitting a Ball of Fire

Procedure:

Step 1. Continue from Method 2 (or start from the Preparation Posture). When your palms are in front of your chest and your weight is evenly distributed on both feet, inhale, extend your arms to the sides with your palms facing forward, and lean back slightly (Figure 4-84).

Visualize the pure essence of the universe is entering your body through your *baihui*, *laogong*, and *yongquan* points into your body. The pure essence transforms into a light ball held by your hands.

Step 2. Exhale, squat down slightly as you bow your body forward, squeeze your arms towards the center, and point your palms forward (Figure 4-85).

Visualize the ball of light becomes two beams of light shooting towards a target in front of you from your *laogong* points. The two beams of light hit the target and ignites it, making the target into a fire ball.

If you are only training this method, repeat 50 to 100 times. If you will be practicing this along with the other two methods, repeat 9 times.

7. EMITTING AND CIRCULATING QI WITHIN YOUR BODY

Emitting and Circulating Qi within Your Body method is another way to train your ability to emit qi back to your body for circulation. The focus will be on sensing your own qi, by emitting and sending your own qi back to your body. The objective will be to increase your qi emitting ability and to increase your sensitivity to feel the circulation of qi inside your body.

With proper training, all living individuals have the ability to emit qi. Healthy individuals, especially those that have practiced martial arts, Taijiquan, and/or other qigong methods will, generally speaking, have a higher ability to emit qi than other individuals. Each person's sensitivity to qi is different. Some people are very sensitive to external qi, some people are not sensitive and have difficulties feeling qi. As a general reference, women have a stronger sensitivity to qi than men; active people have a stronger sensitivity to qi than people that are not active; open and vivacious people have a stronger sensitivity to qi than people that are stubborn. However, with training, everyone can improve their sensitivity to qi.

Procedure:

Step 1. *Sending Qi into Your Laogong Point.* Stand or sit on a chair or crossed leg. Place your palms in front of your body facing each other, a few inches apart. When you begin to feel the qi between your palms, use your right hand to send qi into your left *laogong*

Figure 4-84   Figure 4-85   Figure 4-86

point by pushing your right hand toward your left hand. Then pull away (Figure 4-86).

Repeat the push and pull movement with your right hand. Pay attention to the sensation of qi entering your *laogong* point. Practice for 2 to 5 minutes then change hands, by sending qi from your left hand into your right *laogong* point for 2 to 5 minutes. Compare the sensations between the two sides.

Throughout this exercise, your breathing should be natural; and body should be relaxed, especially your shoulders, elbows, and wrists. Also, when you send qi from one hand to the next, flex the sending palm as it gets closer to the receiving palm. This will open the *laogong* point of the sending palm and increase the qi emission. Relax the palm when pulling away.

Step 2. *Sending Qi into Your Elbow.* Use the same procedure as in Step 1, except your mind is paying attention to leading qi to your receiving elbow instead of paying attention to the *laogong* point. As you send the qi from one hand to the next, use your mind and eyes to lead the qi from the receiving *laogong* through your forearm to your elbow. Do each side until the qi sensation is strong, before proceeding to the next step.

Step 3. *Small Circle.* Use the same procedure as in Step 1, except your mind is leading qi all the way up the receiving arm, and continues through your chest or your back, returns to the sending arm, and back to between the palms. As you send the qi from one hand to the next, use your mind to lead the qi. Do each side until the qi sensation is strong, before proceeding to the next steps.

Step 4. *Small Circulation.* Use the same procedure as in Step 1, except your mind is leading qi from the receiving *laogong* point to the elbow, and to the chest. Keep the qi at your chest for a few seconds, then lead the qi down to your *dantian, huiyin,* and tailbone. Next, lead the qi up your spine, to your head, and down the center line of your head, back to your chest. Then, lead the qi down to the sending arm and back between the palms.

Step 5. *Grand Circulation.* Use the same procedure as in Step 1. Lead the qi from the receiving *laogong* point to your elbow, to your chest, to your *dantian,* to your *huiyin,* up along your spine, to your head, back down to your chest, to your *dantian,* to your *huiyin,* divide into two paths down your legs, and to your *yongquan.* Keep the qi at your *yongquan* for a few seconds, then lead the qi back up your legs, to your *huiyin,* to your spine, to your head, back to your chest, and down the sending arm, back to between the palms.

Discussion and Notes:

A. While leading the qi, your sending palm continues to emit qi into the receiving *laogong* point. Breathe naturally.

B. With the Microcosmic and Macrocosmic Circulation from Daoist Qigong training as a foundation, the qi in your body can be circulated very naturally and easily. If you practice diligently, you will be able to circulate qi any way you wish.

8. EMITTING QI TO AND FROM A PARTNER AND A GROUP

Practice with healthy partners, people that you train with, family members that have done qigong, and/or people that you enjoy being with. People that have practiced qigong for a while are very sensitive to energy. Practicing with ill individuals or people that you dislike can hurt your body.

Part 1. Sensitivity Training

Procedure:

Step 1. Stand facing a partner, with one of your palms facing sideways at one of your partner's palms. One partner uses slow movements, pulling their palm away and bringing it closer, to send qi to the other person. The sensing person can close his or

217

her eyes and pay attention to the sensation. Repeat as many time as you wish. Then change sides.

Step 2. The sender moves the hand slowly around the sensor's palm, while the sensor closes his or her eyes and pays attention to the sensations. Repeat as many time as you wish. Then change sides.

Step 3. The sender draw circles in the direction of the sensor's palm with his or her fingers. The sender gradually increases the distance between his or her hand and the sensor's palm. The sensor closes his or her eyes and pays attention to the sensations. Repeat as many time as you wish. Then change sides.

Step 4. Repeat Steps 1, 2, and 3 by increasing the distance between you and your partner. With practice, you will be able to sense each other's qi from further and further away.

Step 5. When Steps 1 to 4 have been practiced for a period of time, and your sensitivity has increased, practice the training without any specific pattern. That is, the sensor stands comfortably with their eyes closed, and the sender sends qi with their fingers and/or palms with any possible movement. The sensor tries to decipher where and how the sender's qi is being emitted.

Part 2. Two Person Absorbing and Emitting Qi Training

Procedure:

Step 1. Stand facing your partner. One person stands with their palms in front of his or her body, with palms facing up. The other person with palms facing down a few inches above their partner. It doesn't make any difference who's hands are up or down.

Step 2. *Absorbing Qi Training.* Use your mind to absorb qi from your partner's *laogong* points. Your partner relaxes and pays attention to the sensation. When you are absorbing qi from your partner, use your mind and eyes to help lead the qi into your body.

Step 3. *Emitting Qi Training.* Send qi from your *laogong* points into the *laogong* points of your partner. When sending qi, use your mind and eyes to help lead the qi into your partner's body.

Step 4. Change sides and repeat Steps 2 and 3.

Discussion and Notes:

During training both people should feel the sensation of qi. When your qi is being absorbed, you will feel qi draining out of your *laogong* points, or your palms may feel cold. When your partner is emitting qi into your body, you will feel qi entering your body, your hands may feel warm, and/or have a very comfortable sensation. If you do not have these sensations, you must practice more of the *Emitting and Circulating Qi within Your Body* method.

Part 3. Two Person Qi Circulating Training

Your partner must be someone that has practiced qigong, has the ability to emit and absorb qi, and has developed a strong sensitivity to qi through qigong training.

Procedure:

Step 1. Stand facing your partner with your palms facing each others' palms without touching. Your right palm faces your partner's left palm, and your left palm faces on your partner's right palm. Keep your palms at a comfortable level with your fingers pointing up.

Step 2. Use your mind and eyes to lead your partner's qi from both *laogong* points into your arms and to your solar plexus. Practice until you feel comfortable, light, and substantiated. Ask your partner how he or she feels. Then have your partner lead your qi.

Step 3. Use your right hand to emit your qi into your partner's left hand. Keep emitting qi into your partner's body, to his back or chest, then to his right arm, out of his right hand and back to your left hand.

When doing this training both you and your partner will have significant sensations in the hands. When the qi returns to your left hand, you should also have significant sensations in your left palm. Practice for a few minutes, then change to emit qi from your left hand and return it to your right hand. Then have your partner emit qi to you.

Step 4. Lower both arms down to your sides. Use your mind to emit qi from your *baihui* point out to your partner's *baihui* point. When your partner feels the qi entering his or her body, he or she leads the qi down to his or her *yongquan* points, into the ground, then to your *yongquan* points. When you feel the qi return to your *yongquan* points, lead the qi back up your body and again emit qi out to your partner's *baihui* point. Repeat several times before having your partner emit qi to you.

Part 4. Training with a Group of People

After you have familiarized yourself with training with one partner, you should practice with a group of people. Stronger qi sensations can be felt with more people. The benefit can be greater than training by yourself or just with one partner.

Procedure:

Step 1. Practitioners all stand in a circle facing in. Everyone has the same hand facing down and the other hand facing up. If your right palm is facing down, then your left palm should be facing up. In this case, keep your right palm facing down on top of the person to your right's left palm, without touching. Also, place your left palm facing up under the person to your left's right palm without touching.

Step 2. One of you emits qi from one of your *laogong* points into the person next to you and leads the qi through everyone in the circle and back to your other hand. Repeat a few times, then change people, until everyone has a chance to emit and lead qi through everyone else.

Step 3. Next, one of you points one of your fingers towards the palm of the person next to you and draw circles in the air. Everyone pays attention to the sensations, then change people.

Step 4. Everyone relaxes their hands and stands in a comfortable position. One person steps away from the group and emits qi with one palm towards the group. Everyone in the group pays attention to the emitted qi. Gradually increase the distance between the person emitting and the group. Then change people.

Step 5. Everyone lines up facing the same direction. One person stands behind the person at the end or faces the person in the front and emits qi through the people standing in line. Practice to see whether or not the furthest person in line can still feel the emitted qi. Then change people.

Step 6. One person lies down on the floor or on a long bench. One person (sender) emits qi with one hand into the *baihui* point on the person lying down, another person (sensor) places his or her *laogong* points towards the *yongquan* points of the person lying down. The sensor pays attention to the sensations of qi emitted by the sender.

Next, the person at the *yongquan* points becomes the sender and the person at the *baihui* point becomes the sensor and pays attention to the qi sensations. Alternate people lying down, and emitting and sensing qi.

Step 7. Two people lie down with their feet facing each other. A third and fourth person each place one hand next to the *baihui* point on one of the people lying down. The third and the fourth person alternate emitting and sensing qi, and pay attention to the sensations.

Step 8. One person emits qi to a group of people and pays attention to the different sensations on their palms as they emit qi to different individuals. The sensations will differ from man to woman, from a stronger person to a weaker person, from a younger person to an older person.

When you sense qi from different people, pay attention to how the sensations differ from person to person. Do not absorb qi from ill or weak individuals.

4.4. Absorbing Qi Methods

Nature contains a tremendous amount of strong qi sources. The mountains, rivers, oceans, the sun, the moon, the stars, trees, flowers, and bushes, all contain qi that are advantageous to the human body. In this section, we will present the many methods of absorbing qi from nature, from heat sources, and through objects.

1. ABSORBING QI FROM THE SUN

Procedure:

Step 1. When the sun starts to rise over the horizon, extend one of your arms towards the sun, and point your index finger at the sun. Look at the sun from your index finger to the sun. While the sun is still red in color, focus on the sun as it rises completely above the horizon. It is said that with this training, one will be open the *Heavenly Eye*.

| Figure 4-87 | Figure 4-88 | Figure 4-89 |

Step 2. After the sun has risen over the horizon and while the sun is still red, use one of your palms to face the red sun (Figure 4-87). Allow the sun's qi to enter your *laogong* point. The other palm faces down. Allow the red sun's qi to continuously pass through your body and out of your palm that is facing down, for a few minutes.

Step 3. Then use both palms to face the red sun (Figure 4-88). Allow the sun's qi to enter both of your *laogong* points, passing through your body, out of your *yongquan* points, and into the ground.

Step 4. When the sun has changed to a milky white color, turn your back to the sun and stand in a comfortable stance with your arms to your sides. Round your back and arch your chest lightly to open your *mingmen* point (Figure 4-89). When your *mingmen* point is *open*, the entire body will be *open*. With the sun shining at your *mingmen* point, the internal organs and bowels can be nourished and invigorated.

2. ABSORBING QI FROM THE MOON

Procedure:

Stand relaxed, facing the moon. Raise your arms up and face your *laogong* points towards the moon and look at the moon. Use your mind to absorb the qi from the moon through your *laogong* points into your body.

You will gradually feel a pushing pressure on your chest and you may take a few steps backward involuntarily. Your palms will sometimes feel magnetized and you may take a few steps forward involuntarily. Practice for 20 to 30 minutes. If you should feel that the qi is too strong, lead it out of your body through your *yongquan* into the ground.

Absorb the moon's qi only during the 3 days before to 3 days after the full moon.

3. ABSORBING QI FROM TREES

Procedure:

Step 1. Select a healthy tree with a thick trunk. Pine trees and cedar trees are the best. Other evergreens or trees that are filled with leaves, and shrubs are also good. Don't use trees that have lost most of its leaves, and trees that you can't feel any qi from.

The best time to absorb qi from trees is during the day between sunrise to 12 noon. Don't try to absorb qi from trees at night, in the rain, during thunderstorms, or on a cloudy day.

Step 2. Stand facing the side of the tree that is facing the sun, with your back to the sun, and your feet on the root of the tree. Relax your body, place one hand on the trunk of the tree, and the other hand down to your sides, palm facing down (Figure 4-90).

This is a natural absorption method. Within a few minutes you will feel your hands begin to expand, tingle, be slightly sore, or have an electric flowing sensation. Your body may also feel tingling.

Step 3. Stand with both of your palms facing the tree without touching (Figure 4-91). Use your mind to lead the qi from the tree into the *laogong* point on one of your hands, to that arm, and into your body. Then lead it back out of the other arm and out of the *laogong* point.

Before you begin to absorb qi from the tree, locate an area of the tree that you can feel the strongest sensation of qi and face the absorbing palm towards that area.

Step 4. Stand in the same posture as in Step 3. Use your mind to lead the qi into the *laogong* point of one hand, to your chest, to your *dantian*, to your *huiyin*, up along your spine, to the top of your head, again to your chest, then to the other arm and out the other *laogong* point.

Absorb qi from different trees. They will give you different sensations.

Step 5. Stand facing the tree with your hands down to your sides. Relax your entire body (Figure 4-92). Use your mind to lead the qi through your *baihui*, into your body, and out of your *yongquan* points. When leading the qi into your body, your chest should feel comfortable and filled with energy. The whole body should feel tingly, along with many other good sensations.

4. ABSORBING QI FROM FLOWERS AND BUSHES

Procedure:

Stand in a comfortable stance facing flowers or bushes with your palms facing down at the flowers or bushes (Figure 4-93). Use your mind to lead the qi into your *laogong* points, up to your arms, and to your chest. You will have a carefree and cozy feeling.

Try different flowers and bushes. They will give you different sensations. Some can also have different effects on your emotional state.

5. ABSORBING QI FROM MOUNTAINS, RIVERS, ANDOCEANS

Procedure:

Stand in a comfortable stance with your palms facing the source, in front of your body or to your sides. Use your mind to absorb qi through your *laogong*, *baihui*, *Yintang (eye bridge)*, and all the points and pores into your body.

6. ABSORBING QI FROM HEAT SOURCES

Procedure:

Individuals who are weak, always feel cold, and have difficulty feeling qi from any other source except from heat sources, can absorb qi from stove, fires, heaters, etc.

Stand in front of the heat source with your palms facing the heat source. Use your mind to lead the qi from the heat source into your *laogong*, up your arms to your chest, then to your

Figure 4-90   Figure 4-91   Figure 4-92

Figure 4-93

dantian, to your *huiyin*, up along your spine, to your head and back to your chest. Repeat until you feel comfortable.

7. ABSORBING QI THROUGH OBJECTS

Procedure:

Practice with a partner and an object between you and your partner. For example, you or your partner could stand on either side of a wall and one of you could do the sending and the other could do the sensing or one of you could lie down on a bench, and the other emit qi from underneath the bench.

4.5. Develop Your Healing Ability

Qigong practice is not only beneficial for health, personal healing, and longevity. The Daoist and Buddhist Qigong methods are also capable of bringing about an individual's extraordinary potential. To develop this potential, it is imperative to have dedication, faith, perseverance, patience, and time. Extraordinary abilities must be developed naturally. Some people are gifted, and develop extraordinary abilities immediately. Some people may never develop extraordinary abilities in this life time. If it is meant to be, you will have extraordinary abilities with practice. You will have already succeeded when you've attained good health and improved the quality of your life.

In Sections 4.3. and 4.4., we have focused on emitting and absorbing qi methods. The ability to emit and absorb qi can enhance one's own practice. It can also help to heal others and their training. In this section, we will introduce more fundamental training methods to develop and to realize your healing potential. More specifically, in this section, we will focus on developing your palms' sensitivity for healing, developing your ability to see auras, and developing your ability to scan the body. We will also present methods to heal patients.

1. DEVELOPING THE SENSITIVITY OF YOUR PALMS

The human body is an extremely intricate and complex physiological organism complete with extraordinary potential. The human body contains an emitting station much like a radio broadcast station, constantly sending out its biological waves — a manifestation of qi that is not restricted by time and space. The biological waves of an organism contain the complete information of that organism. The human body also contains a receiver much like a radio. With the proper tuning of the human body receiver, one can receive external biological waves.

In this training, you use your mind to tune into the subject's biological waves without touching the subject. After receiving the subject's biological wave signals into the palms, the palms then magnify the signals. Depending on the reaction of the palms, the condition of the subject can be deciphered. Most people have the hidden potential to receive and decipher biological wave signals. With proper practice, they will be able to bring about their hidden potential.

Traditional Training Method:

Practice 1. Practice to develop your sensitivity to plant energy. At dawn, before the sun rises, use your hands to feel, without touching, different trees. Pay attention to the different sensations between different trees.

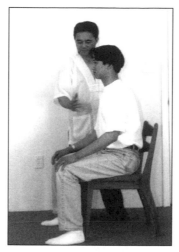

Figure 4-94

Practice 2. Practice to develop your sensitivity to the human body. Move your palms over or around a person's body and find any irregularities (Figure 4-94). Practice on people that you are not familiar with.

Practice 3. Practice to develop your sensitivity to your teacher's energy when he or she is discussing the training. Sit comfortably and relax your body. Place your hands on top of your knees with your palms facing up (Individuals with high blood pressure should have their palms facing the knees without touching).

While listening to your teacher, pay attention to your palms. An activation of the potential in your palms has occurred when your palms have a slight soreness, tingling, warmth, swelling, pain, muscle twitching, or a vibration that harmonizes with the teacher's projecting voice. While reading this book, you can also read it out loud to practice your palms' sensitivity.

Notes:

An energetically sensitive person's palms can easily be activated. Others may have to practice for a period of time to develop their sensitivity. A small portion of people may not be able to feel the qi at all. If you are unable to feel a qi sensation, you should practice other qigong methods in this volume.

Practice 4. Practice using your palms to diagnose a patient's illness. Keep your palm or palms about 1 foot away from the patient. Move your palm horizontal or vertically across the patient. Pay attention to the different sensations, when your palms are over different areas of the patient's body.

The qi sensations on your palms could be a slight soreness, tingling, heat, swelling, pain, muscle twitching, heaviness, itching, coolness, coldness. Sometimes you may also feel a suction pulling your palm or your palm may vibrate.

Beginners must practice as much as possible with different people, and feel the same patterns in similar cases or locations. For example, under normal conditions, the heart area will feel warm, the kidney area will feel cool, the lung area will feel slightly tingly. The other areas of the body will feel an evenness of energy or a slight warmth and tingling. The more you practice, the more experience you will have. By drawing upon these experiences, you will be able to correctly distinguish the differences between normal and abnormal conditions.

Notes:

A. When you are ill, your energy is unbalanced, your hands and feet are cold, it will be very difficult to diagnose another person's illness. You must regain you own health before attempting to diagnose other's illness.

B. Humans have the potential to diagnose illness with their palms. However, the ability of the person to diagnose illness accurately depends on the person's experience. It is recommended that other methods of diagnosis be used in conjunction with palm diagnosis.

2. DEVELOPING YOUR ABILITY TO SEE AURAS

Every person's body has an aura (light). All living things have auras. Even nonliving things have auras. Physicists refer to the aura as a *field*, a space which contains active magnetic or electrical lines. The aura of the human body is the *qi field* of the body. Some individuals are born with the ability to see auras. Others are able to see auras with qigong training, as well as, after a session of meditation. With the ability to see human auras, it is possible to understand the workings in the human body. Depending on the colors and the intensity of the aura around the individual, the condition of the individual can be deciphered.

With the ability to see auras, one can also decipher the depth of another person's energy cultivation. The aura of Laozi was described as purple. The aura of Sakyamuni Buddha and Avalokiteshvara were described as a ring with multiple radiating colors. Drawings of Jesus Christ and the Virgin Mary also showed auras. Indian yogis, Chinese Daoist and Buddhist cultivators all have large beautiful auras.

Training Methods:

Practice 1. Find an area that is light in the front and dark in the back. Point your fingers toward each other without touching. Move your fingers horizontally apart or up and down while concentrating on your finger tips. With practice you will be able to see beams of light extending from your finger tips. The beams of light from one hand will interact with the beam from the other hand, connecting and shearing apart as you move them.

Practice 2. Place your hands in a lighted area with your fingers pointing at the dark area. Relax your entire body and get into a meditative state. Half close your eyes and look at the light (aura) emitting from the tip of your fingers. You may be able to see different colors of light extending from your fingers. Practice as often as you can. When you are able to see the aura with your eyes half closed, then look at the aura without closing your eyes halfway.

Practice 3. Practice looking at people's heads. It will be easier to see people's auras when they are standing in a lighted area with a dark background. First look with your eyes half closed, then open your eyes completely. You may be able to see different colors of light around people's heads. Some people's auras can extend all the way up to the roof. With practice you will notice the auras all around people's bodies.

Notes:

A. Practice everyday to develop your ability to see auras.

B. Generally speaking, white and silver auras on an individual indicate good health. A gray aura is an indication of illness. The darker the tint of gray, the more serious the illness. When the color has become black, it indicates a severe condition.

C. Qigong practitioners and people who meditate regularly have very strong auras. Their aura may be silver-white, yellow, blue, green, gold, purple, or a combination of these colors. Sometimes the aura may be etheric (fog) like. People with qigong training can develop their ability to see auras much easier.

3. DEVELOPING YOUR SCANNING ABILITY

There are many different types of scanning abilities. They include the ability to scan within one's own body, scan inside another person's body, scan objects that are hidden or behind walls, and scan things and events that are far away. The qigong training that can open the Heavenly Eye (Third Eye) can develop one's ability to scan.

The Heavenly Eye is slightly above the midpoint between the eye brows. The pineal gland is located at the intersection of a line from the Heavenly Eye inward and a line down from the *baihui* point. The hormone generated in the pineal gland can slow down aging, regain sexual function, and prevent illness.

In China there have been experiments that have shown that 40% of the children who underwent a specific training, develop the scanning ability. However, their scanning ability was unstable and short lived. Children with scanning ability need to continue to develop and solidify their ability. Before puberty, children can often see things that adults can't see. Adults often think that children are making up stories. In reality, it could be because children's Heavenly Eyes have not degenerated and are still *open*, and they can still see occurrences on the astral planes.

With dedicated practice, some adults will be able to reopen their Heavenly Eye. People that are close minded, restrictive, tense, and too analytical will have a hard time opening their Heavenly Eye. This is because their Personality is overshadowing their deep consciousness. People that can relax easily and enter into a calm abiding state, with little or no worry have a higher potential to open their Heavenly Eye. Some people are gifted, and are born with the Heavenly Eye open, and are able to keep it open into adulthood. In China, these individuals are referred to as individuals with extraordinary abilities. There are many individuals with extraordinary abilities all over the world today.

Traditional Training Methods:

Practice 1. Practice gathering qi methods and methods that focus your attention on your *upper-dantian*. These methods include Golden Light Method, Gathering Spirit Method, Absorbing Qi to Make Up for the Leakage; and emitting qi to your Heavenly Eye, to your *baihui*, and to your temples.

Any training that focuses your attention on your *upper-dantian* is also training that focuses your attention on the pineal gland. After a significant period of practice, qi will have gathered in the pineal gland, activating the Heavenly Eye and eventually reopening it.

Practice 2. Practice Qi Permeating Technique, any of the Daoist qi circulating methods, Golden Light Method, Gathering the Spirit Method, Nine Segment Buddhist Breathing, and/or Achieving Through Spiritual Flame. They are all methods that bring in the pure essence of the cosmos into the body via the pineal gland.

Practice 3. Practice visualization methods. Visualize the teachers that you admire, visualize Buddha, visualize Laozi, visualize Jesus Christ, ... When you visualize them, you are receiving their signals. This type of visualization is also a method to absorb qi, light, and a higher potential. As you gather more and more potential, you will eventually reactivate and open your Heavenly Eye. When your Heavenly Eye is open, you will not only have the scanning ability, you will also be able to receive signals from the astral planes much easier.

Some people also practice looking at themselves in a mirror and are able to reactive their Heavenly Eye this way. Some people are also able to open their Heavenly Eyes by looking at flowers, trees, water, and glass objects.

The Golden Light Method and the Gathering the Spirit Method are also visualization methods that can open your Heavenly Eye.

You may also practice the internal view method by visualizing a red lantern or ball of fire at your *lower-dantian* radiating inside your body. When you have illuminated your body from the inside, then visualize your organs, your bones, your skin. Visualize from up to down, left to right, or anyway you wish. Repeat several times.

Practice 4. Practice vibration methods: such as The Basic Method of Unification with the Cosmos and The Advanced Method of Unification with the Cosmos, and the Head Conditioning exercise in Wushu Qigong. These methods can all vibrate the pineal gland.

Practice 5. Practice with other people. Ask individuals with very strong qi to emit qi into your *baihui*. The emitter uses *sword finger* (index and middle fingers straight, fourth and small fingers coiled in with the thumb on top of them) or their *laogong* point to emit qi into the receiver's pineal gland. The emitter can also gently press their *sword finger* on the receiver's *Yintang*.

4. HEALING METHODS

Methods:

Technique 1. *Removing the illness causing energy.* Enter into a qigong meditative state. Visualize/see the beams of light from the fingers of one hand. Insert the beams into the area of injury,

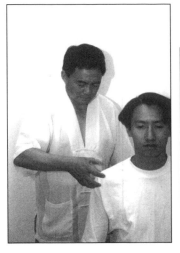

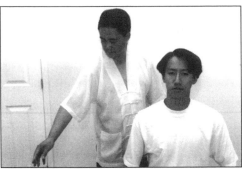

Figure 4-96

Figure 4-95

discomfort, or illness. Rotate your wrist and make a complete circle with the hand to break up the infestation of bad energy (Figure 4-95). Then pull your fingers away from the patient and draw the bad energy out of the patient's body (Figure 4-96). When you feel the bad energy is out, shake your hand down towards the ground and visualize that the bad energy is immersing three feet into the ground.

As you grab the bad energy you may feel sticky, coldness, pinching, and jumping sensations in your hand. You may also feel something is being taken out of the patient's body. Repeat the process until the area you are healing, no longer has coldness, pinching, heat, or any other abnormal sensations.

This healing technique is used to eliminate illness causing energy. It is especially effective for tumors, furuncles, headaches, eye problems, some female illnesses, stomach illnesses, and illnesses that attack sections of the body. The effectiveness of the healing will, of course, be dependent on the healer's ability.

Technique 2. *Emitting qi into the patient.* Place your hand on the ill area of the patient and think with strong intention, "infection is disappearing, pain is removed, and complete recovery is being attained" (Figure 4-97). After 10 to 30 minutes, remove your hand. The patient may feel the illness reduced or has disappeared.

A healthy individual's biological wave frequency is higher than that of an ill individual. The energy in the palm is one of the highest in the human body. When a healer's hand is placed

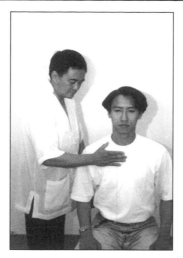

Figure 4-97

on a patient's ill spot, the healer's energetic signals and energy will flow toward the patient and create balance.

When doing a healing, don't place your hands directly on the ill area. Keep a piece of cloth between your palms and the patient.

Technique 3. *Smooth out the qi meridians*. This method helps the patient smooth out their qi meridians by releasing the illness causing energy out of the patient's *laogong* points and/or *yongquan* points. It is especially helpful for healing paralysis, problems associated with women's periods, rheumatism, and other illness resulting from rheumatic fever.

1. Removing Illness Causing Energy. Have the patient lie on his or her back. The healer stands to the right of the patient next to the abdomen area. As you inhale, move the back of your palms up from the patient's feet to the patient's head (Figure 4-98).

Next rotate your palms face down, exhale, and emit qi from your *laogong* points. As you exhale move your palms down towards the patient's feet (Figure 4-99). At the same time, use your mind to lead the patient's illness causing qi out of the patient's body. Next, shake your hands toward the ground to release the bad energy.

Repeat several times, then check the condition of your patient with your palms, and repeat a few more times.

2. Nourishing your patient. Inhale, move the back of your palms up from the patient's feet to the patient's abdomen and

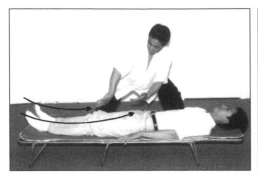

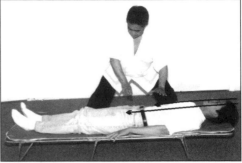

Figure 4-98   Figure 4-99

stop. Then rotate your palms to face the patient's abdomen. If your patient is a man, circle your palms in a clockwise direction above his abdomen. If your patient is a women, circle your palms in a counterclockwise direction above her abdomen.

Notes:

1. The combination of Techniques 1 and 3 can produce even better healing results.

2. When applying Technique 3, don't use the inside of your palms to face your patient, when moving your hands up from the patient's feet to their head. You must use the back of your palms. Otherwise, you will increase the patient's blood pressure.

3. The healer should use their entire body to inhale, and exhale to their *laogong*. The energy you absorb into your body needs to be more than what you are emitting, to be able to sustain your healing endurance and strength.

4. Your ability will gradually increase with more healing sessions.

4.6. Warding Off Negative Energy Method

Any energy that has a bad effect on the human body is negative energy. This includes pathogenic influences and evil intentions projected towards you from other individuals. Sometimes when you enter a place, or when you come in contact with certain objects, or meet certain people you immediately feel uncomfortable. This is because negative energy is bombarding your mind and body.

Methods:

1. Make an attempt to stay away from any place that contains any type of negative energy. When you do feel negative energy coming on,

find out where it is coming from, or from who is projecting it. Try to stay away. This is especially important during your qigong training.

2. When you feel negative energy coming on, the simplest way is to extend your palm in the direction of the negative energy. This way you are making a stopping movement to the negative energy. Then use your mind to deflect the negative energy to the sides. Repeat several times, or until you no longer feel the negative energy bombarding you.

   Practice as often as possible to make it a natural reaction. Sometimes, even your friends may project negative energy when they are in a bad mood. Although it may not be projected at you, you may still feel the affect of the negative energy, when you are in close proximity. You can use these situations as an opportunity to practice.

3. Practice using your mind and eyes without your palms to avoid negative energy. Use your eyes to intercept negative energy projected towards you, then use your mind to redirect it away from you.

4. When you feel negative energy, but don't know where it is coming from, use your strong determination and intention to redirect the negative energy away from you.

5. Using a mantra or prayer along with strong determination and intention can prevent negative energy from entering your body. This is especially effective when encountering mysterious and evil energies. It is very difficult for evil energy to attack individuals with a strong mind and filled with righteous energy.

   15 years ago, when Master Liang was attending the Chinese National Wushu Exhibition, he met the brother of the last Chinese emperor. The former Manchurian prince, Fu Huan, told Master Liang, he had seen many amazing qigong masters in his life when living in the palace. He said that the best technique against any negative energy is to open your eyes wide and continuously recite any *words* that will bring up your vitality of spirit. Nothing will then be able to affect you. His experience shows that everyone with a strong intention can elevate their vitality of spirit and emit very strong qi to protect themselves from negative energy. However, individuals that are weak or lack qi are easily attacked and affected by negative energy.

6. Absorb tree's qi to build a defensive layer against negative energy. Stand facing a big strong tree. Use your palms to locate the strongest area of the tree and absorb the tree's qi into your arms, to your chest,

to your *dantian*, to your *yongquan*, and out to the ground, to the roots of the tree, back to the trunk of the tree and again into your palms. Repeat this qi circulation many times. Then relax your body. Use your mind to lead the tree's qi into your *baihui*, into your body, and out of your *yongquan*, to the roots of the tree, back to the tree trunk, and again into your *baihui*. Repeat many times.

When you are comfortable with the above methods, while still standing in front of the tree, relax your entire body, use your mind to absorb the tree's qi through your *yongquan* points and into your body. Then use your mind to emit the qi out all around your body, building a sustained energy field to protect against negative energy. With determination and regular practice you will be able to build a strong guardian layer of qi to protect you from negative energy.

Book 5:

Wushu Qigong

5.1. Internal Energy Training in Chinese Martial Arts

Wushu (martial arts) practitioners are one of the major contributors to the development of qigong since ancient China. Through their strive for excellence and greater skills for combat readiness, they have made many important discoveries for fighting, as well as, for health and healing. Over the long history of Wushu Qigong development, combined with the already available qigong knowledge, martial artist masters developed their own unique training methods and emphasis.

One of the training methods in *Wushu* is the striking of vital areas, by using focused qi, power, and speed, to subdue a stronger and more powerful opponent. These vital points, when struck with enough force, can reduce the enemy's fighting ability, cause serious injury, or death. Many of these vital points were discovered through generations of combat experiences by martial arts masters. Most of these vital points correspond with the acupuncture points on the qi meridians. The understanding of acupuncture points and meridians give a martial artist a better knowledge of themselves and their opponents.

Today, martial artists, utilize the already available references from acupuncture charts to enhance their martial arts training. They also utilize an understanding of qi flow and qi patterns in the body, as a reference for timing and striking of vital points for the most devastating effect on their opponent. On the other hand, high level martial arts qigong masters have also contributed to medical qigong understanding. Their experience and ability in martial arts qigong and vital point training, gave important insights to the workings and healing of energetic traumas.

Chinese martial art training is very extensive and profound. Each division of martial arts has its stylistic qigong training methods. A Chinese proverb states, "Training the techniques without training internal energy, it is all in vain when one gets old." Martial arts without *gongfu* (training that increases the internal energy accomplishment) is considered "showy boxing with no real strength." Martial arts without internal strength is sufficient as a sport and health exercise. To be effective as a practical fighting art with an energetic foundation, martial artists need to have *gongfu*.

Gongfu is also romanized as *Kung Fu*, which is also a term used for Chinese martial arts. *Kung Fu* literally means time and energy, not martial arts. That is, any accomplishment that requires a lot of time and energy to become proficient is called *Kung Fu*. Therefore, the attainment that you gain through your martial arts training, especially in your qigong training, is the level of Kung Fu you have in Chinese martial arts. Because the dedication and discipline in perfecting the mental, physical, energetic, and spiritual requirements of being a true martial artist are very demanding, the term *Kung Fu* has become synonymous to Chinese martial arts.

Wushu is the proper term for Chinese martial arts. It is usually classified into two divisions, mainly the *Internal Style* division and the *External Style* division. Martial styles such as Shaolinquan, Chaquan, Bajiquan are considered to be External Styles; and Taijiquan (Tai Chi Chuan), Xingyiquan, Baguazhang, Liuhebafa are considered to be Internal Styles. Regardless of the classification, each style has qigong in their training.

Qigong training builds a lasting and solid foundation for the physical body. The conditioning of the physical body manifests the internal energy attainment. Without the proper conditioning of the physical, it will be difficult for the internal achievement to be expressed as a martial art. Conversely, without the internal energy training, the physical body lacks the lasting foundation to back up the physical demands.

Traditional martial arts training has always included qigong as part of their internal energy training. It's not just for fighting. It is also for strengthening the mind and body. A healthy mind and body are the foundation for a proficient martial artist. Their training philosophy can be summarized in one commonly used phrase: "Training the muscles/tendons, bones, and skin externally; training energy *(qi)* internally."

Even though Wushu Qigong is primarily for strengthening the body and for fighting. It has a very important aspect in common with medical qigong.

238

They are both trying to understand the rhythm of human life and its many activities, understand the surrounding environment, use the application of herbs, and use the mind and movements, to lead energy flow.

In *Wushu*, one "Trains the physical to aid the shapeless; cultivates the shapeless to care for the physical." That is, Wushu Qigong is not just for martial arts applications, it is also an excellent way to strengthen the body. Therefore, Wushu qigong is also beneficial for people that are not involved in martial arts training.

In the rest of this book, we will be presenting the Intensive Iron Shirt Qigong training methods to strengthen and develop your body's ability to withstand powerful attacks; followed by offensive hard qigong training, for improving your fighting applications.

5.2. Intensive Iron Shirt Qigong

Iron Shirt and Golden Bell Cover are qigong training that build up the human body's ability to withstand an attack. A Chinese proverb states, "First learn how to take hits, then learn how to fight." That is to say, before one gets involved in free sparring, one should first attain the ability to withstand physical strikes. Iron Shirt training makes your body so strong that it is like you are wearing a shirt made of iron — iron shirt. It is also like your body is covered by a golden bell — Golden Bell Cover.

There are many different ways to develop the Iron Shirt ability. Much of this training will take at least three years to complete. The Iron Shirt training in this section is an *Intensive Iron Shirt Qigong*. If you practice twice a day, once in the morning and once at night, you will attain significant results from this training in thirty days. Of course, if you only train once a day or once every few days, the length of time necessary will increase.

In today's society, we are all very busy. Not everyone can concentrate or has the time to train everyday. From our once a week classroom instruction and training experience, it took three to five months for students to attain significant results. In our Iron Shirt training program, we also include conditioning exercises for the palms, fingers, arms, etc. We will introduce this conditioning training in Section 5.3.

Even though it takes a short amount of time to complete the Intensive Iron Shirt Qigong training, it still needs a long period of continuous training to solidify and maintain your attainment. A Chinese proverb states, "Impatiently rushing produces no result." This proverb implies that when one rushes to complete something, one tends to become bewildered and not be able to achieve one's objective. In other words, what one should be concerned with, is the effectiveness of the training, not the length of time needed in the training. If you simply complete the training in a short period of time and stop training, the *Kung Fu* you attained will not stay with you for very long. People in training often say, "Live until old age, learn until old age."

1. OVERALL BODY CONDITIONING

Part 1. Iron Shirt Preparation Qigong

Procedure:

Step 1. Stand straight with your feet naturally apart and with your arms hanging down to your sides. Relax the entire body. Calm your heart and quiet down your qi. Get rid of all scattered thoughts. Begin to inhale and bring your arms forward, crossing in front of your abdomen with palms facing in — left hand on the inside, right hand on the outside. Continue inhaling and bring your arms up in circular paths in front of your body (Figure 5-1).

Complete your inhalation by lowering your arms until your palms are at shoulder level. At this time, your elbows should be pointing down and your hands change into fists, facing up. Hold your breath for a couple of seconds. Exhale and let out the *che* sound, while thrusting your elbows toward your rib cage area, making contact with the back of your forearm and your rib cage (Figure 5-2).

Step 2. Stand in a high Horse Stance with your palms at your waist. Begin to inhale, bend down, extend your right palm from your right foot towards your left foot. At the same time, change your stance into a high left Bow Stance (Figure 5-3). Continue to inhale, and raise your right arm up over your head as you turn 180 degrees around to your right (Figure 5-4).

Then, hold your breath slightly. Then exhale, let out the *che* sound and thrust your right elbow towards the right side of your rib cage area, making contact with the back of your forearm and your rib cage. At the same time, change your stance into a high right Empty Stance (Figure 5-5).

Step 3. Do the mirror image of Step 2.

Step 4. Repeat Step 1.

Step 5. Do Steps 1 through 4, one more time.

| Figure 5-1 | Figure 5-2 | Figure 5-3 |

| Figure 5-4 | Figure 5-5 |

Part 2. General Upper Body Training

During the conditioning parts of this training, it is best if you have a partner or assistant to help with your training. Hold your breath or exhale when your body is being hit. Stop hitting during inhalation. Start striking lightly, then gradually increase the power during each session. In the first few days, there may be some bruising. Don't be afraid. After a few days, it will disappear. When bruises have disappeared, your skin will not change colors any more. Practice hitting 5 to 7 times each area from the bottom to the top. Make sure that the entire torso is covered when you complete Part 2. You must focus your attention and be serious or else injuries may occur. It is especially important when hitting your kidney area. If you don't have a partner, do it yourself.

This training can also help in curing old injuries, arthritis, some illness; and fill the body with qi to nourish the organs.

Stage 1.

Procedure:

Step 1. *Head Exercise*: Lean your head on a wall (Figure 5-6). Rub your head on the wall about 50 times in each direction. Then turn your body to your right and rub the right side of your head and rub about 50 times in each direction (Figure 5-7). Next, turn your body slightly to your left and rub the left side of your head about 50 times in each direction. Adjust your stance as necessary for better balance.

Start lightly and gradually increase the pressure on your head from light to heavy. This will allow the qi to circulate to the top of your head and return back to the rest of your body. The complete process should take about 5 to 10 minutes.

Step 2. *Upper Body Conditioning with your Palm*:

Front of the Body: Turn until your body is facing up, with your head still pressing on the wall (Figure 5-8). Ask your partner to use either one of his or her palms to hit the front of your body from your pubic bone up to your throat. Continue until the entire surface on the front of your torso has been covered.

Left Side of the Body: Turn to your right until the left side of your body is facing up. Place your right hand on your waist and place your left hand over your head on the wall. Ask your partner to hit you with their palm from your waist up to your armpit and continue striking up your arms until your fingers. Repeat 5-7 times.

Back of the Body: Keep your head on the wall and place both hands on your waist. Then turn until your back is facing up. Ask your partner to hit your back with their palm from your sacrum up until the top of your head. Continue until the entire surface on the back has been covered.

Right Side of the Body: Keep your head on the wall and turn you body until the right side of your body is facing up. Keep your left hand on your waist and place your right hand on the wall above your head. Ask your partner to hit you with their palm from your waist up to your armpit, then up to your fingers. Repeat 5-7 times.

 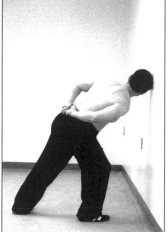 

Figure 5-6   Figure 5-7   Figure 5-8

Step 3. *Upper Body Conditioning with Bamboo Sticks*: Find 15 to 30 pieces of small bamboo sticks and tie them into a bundle. Cut the ends so that they are even, for use as your training tool. The training process with the bamboo sticks is the same as with the palm.

The focus when using the palm hit, are on the surface of the body. Whereas, the focus of the bamboo sticks is on compacting the qi underneath the skin, to build up the resistance to a strike. Condition your body with only the palm and bamboo stick striking for a period of time before proceeding to Steps 4 and 5.

Step 4. *Upper Body Conditioning with a Sandbag*: Make a bag with thick cotton material to hold sand. Fill the bags with 3-7 pounds of sand or more.

After a period of conditioning the body with palm strikes and with the bamboo sticks, add to the training by using the sandbags. The training method with the sandbags is the same as with the palms and bamboo sticks.

After completing the striking training, stand up. Take the sandbag in one hand and hit from your abdomen to your chest for a few minutes. When your body can withstand the pounding of a sandbag that weighs 7 pounds, your body will be able to withstand an average person's punch.

Step 5. *Upper Body Conditioning with a Metal Rod, Metal Strip, and Blade*: From the foundation you achieved with the striking of the palm, bamboo sticks, and sandbags; you can now go on and train with iron rods about 18 inches long, iron strips, and other harder materials to build up your body's qi level to withstand a strike. The method of training is the same with harder tools as it is with the palm, the bamboo sticks, and the sandbags.

When using the metal strip as a training tool, you can start by using the flat surface, then the side and the ends to hit. After training for a period of time hitting with the flat side, then use the narrow edges and the ends. When training with the blade, start by using the back edge of the blade for a period of time. When your body is ready to withstand the sharper edge of the blade, chop down with the blade vertically only.

Chop in small increments and don't slide the blade when chopping down. When you first start training with the blade, you will feel a burning sensation and needle piercing pain during your sleep. This feeling will disappear after a few days.

2. SOLAR PLEXUS CONDITIONING

The solar plexus is one of the weakest areas in the human body. People that have never done any type of physical conditioning, will feel pain in this area, from the press of a finger. With a little more pressure, they will feel like vomiting, muscles cramping, and may even pass out. After training this area, you will not only be able to withstand strikes to this area, you will also strengthen your liver, gall bladder, stomach, and diaphragm. Illness associated with these parts of your body can also be corrected. Once you complete the solar plexus training, you will be able to easily withstand pointy metal objects, such as a spear pressing on your solar plexus.

To develop a high level of tolerance with your solar plexus will take long, hard, and dedicated training. You will be able to build a good foundation to withstand an average person's punch with the methods described, but to attain a high level will require a long period of conditioning. People with high accomplishment in this area are able to place over one hundred pounds of weight on their back while easily suspending their bodies on a stick.

Train your solar plexus only after finishing a session of Iron Shirt Qigong.

Part 1. Lead Qi to Your Solar Plexus

Procedure:

Step 1. Stand in a high Horse Stance. Form your hands into a sword hand — index and middle fingers straight, other fingers coil in and form a circle. Extend your arms straight to your back right

244

Figure 5-9

Figure 5-10

Figure 5-11

corner by pointing your right sword hand in that direction and your left sword hand pointing at your elbow (Figure 5-9).

Inhale, turn your body to your left, while circling your left hand behind you, into a fist pointing down, and circling your right arm to the front, into a fist pointing up. Exhale, change your stance into an Empty Stance and thrust your right elbow towards your solar plexus while letting out the "che" sound and rotate your left arm (Figure 5-10).

Repeat Step 1, three times.

Step 2. Do the mirror image of Step 1, three times.

Part 2. Solar Plexus Training

Procedure:

Step 1. Use a section of stick about 1 inch in diameter. Round one end of the stick into an egg shape. Place the flat end on the wall and press the round end on your solar plexus. Inhale and hold your breath, lean on the stick (Figure 5-11). Start with about 5 seconds and gradually increase the time. Then relax, exhale. Repeat 30 times.

Step 2. Secure one end of the stick on the floor. Press your solar plexus on the end of the stick and suspend your body in space (Figure 5-12). Inhale, and hold your breath as you take your hands off the floor (Figure 5-13).

As your solar plexus gets stronger, you will also be able raise your feet, one at a time off the floor (Figure 5-14). Keep

Figure 5-12

Figure 5-13

Figure 5-14

practicing until you are able to suspend your body completely off the floor, with only your solar plexus supporting your body. When you are able to suspend your body easily, begin pivoting your body around, by pushing off with your feet.

After completing the session, massage your solar plexus for a few minutes.

Notes:

When you let out the *che* sound, feel your qi gathering at your solar plexus. The sound should be emitted at the same time as the elbow thrusts toward your solar plexus. When you exhale, the arm that has the elbow thrusting towards the solar plexus should rotate to increase the solar plexus qi sensation.

3. THROAT CONDITIONING

The throat is also one of the weakest parts of the human body. With a slight poke of the fingers to the throat area, one will find difficulty in breathing; cough, and even pass out. With proper training, our throats can be conditioned to do amazing tasks, such as bend steel rods and withstand sharp objects pressing against it. This training can also help cure some ailments associated with bronchitis, laryngitis, asthma, and other breathing system related illness.

Train your throat only after completing a session of Iron Shirt Qigong.

Figure 5-15   Figure 5-16   Figure 5-17

Part 1. Lead Qi to Your Throat

Procedure:

Step 1. Stand straight and hold your hands in fists. Inhale, step forward with your right leg into a right Bow Stance and bring your arms up over your head (Figure 5-15). Exhale, step forward with your left leg in an Empty stance, while changing your fists into palms and diagonally pushing down to your left (Figure 5-16). At the same time, tuck your chin in, lead the qi up to your head at the *tiantu* point (lower part of the throat), and let out the *che* sound.

Step 2. Repeat the exercise by stepping with your left foot back into a right Bow Stance and bringing your arm back over your head while inhaling. Do a total of three times, then reverse directions and do the other side, three times.

Part 2. Throat Training

Procedure:

Tie a bundle of bamboo chopsticks together (or wood rods). Use the smooth end of the chopsticks and press on the esophagus, the area above the sternum. Place the other end of the stick or rod on the wall (Figure 5-17). Lean your weight on the rod and begin turning the rod with your hand in a circular pattern. Do this for a couple of minutes.

Figure 5-18

Figure 5-19

Notes:

When you first start this training, hold your breath when pressing your throat on the rod. As you get stronger, you will no longer need to hold your breath. After a couple of weeks, try using only one chopstick to press on your throat and see if you can break it in half. As your attainment increases, change the chopsticks into small metal rods. In a traditional performance of throat qigong, a spear is used to demonstrate the attainment of this ability. This technique is called, "Silver Spear Piercing at the Throat" (Figures 5-18 and 5-19).

4. ARMPIT CONDITIONING

The armpit is also another weak area in the human body. Slight pressure on this area, will cause you to feel pain. With proper training, you can increase the resistance of this area. Individuals with a high level of attainment in this training, can break bricks under the armpits.

Train your armpit only after completing a session of Iron Shirt Qigong.

Part 1. Lead Qi to Your Armpit

Procedure:

Step 1. Stand with your feet a little wider than shoulder width apart. Inhale, bend your body to your left, and punch down with your right fist towards your left. At the same time, pull your left hand between your right ear and right shoulder (Figure 5-20).

Straighten your body, lower your left arm and change your left hand into a fist. Bend your body to your right, inhale some more, as you punch down with your left fist towards your right. At the same time, pull your right hand between your left ears and right shoulder.

Again, straighten your body, bring your left fist back to your left, inhale some more, as you again punch down to your left

Figure 5-20   Figure 5-21   Figure 5-22

with your left fist. Once more, bring your right fist back to your left, inhale some more as you punch down to your right with your left fist. This will increase the accumulation of qi on the left side of your armpit.

Step 2. Stand up, change your left fist into an open palm and circle both palms in front of your body, up and out to the sides, twice, while continuing to inhale (Figure 5-21). After two circles, lower your arms, change your palms into fists, and thrust your elbows towards the sides of your ribs, while letting out the *che* sound (Figure 5-22).

Step 3. Repeat Step 1 and 2 on the other side by first punching to your right with your left fist, once; then punch to your left, twice, with your right fist, etc.

Notes:

Steps 1 and 2 are completed in one inhalation and one exhalation. You should have punched once with your right fist to your left, punched three times with your left fist to your right, and circled twice with your arms, without exhaling.

Part 2. Armpit Training

Procedure:

Use a baseball bat or a piece of wood with a rounded end. Place it under your armpit, squeeze and release your armpit, while twisting the bat or wood for a couple of minutes on each side (Figure 5-23).

Figure 5-23

Notes:

Train the armpit conditioning exercises until you no longer feel pain from your squeeze, then begin to train with thin pieces of bricks. When you are able to break thin bricks under your armpit, gradually increase the thickness of the bricks.

5. HEAD CONDITIONING

Part 1. Preparation

Procedure

Step 1. Stand naturally with your hands over your head. As you lower you hands down, visualize that you are in the sky, standing on top of the clouds and holding on to white qi. The white qi is permeating throughout your body, all the way down to your *yongquan*, but not out. Repeat 3 times.

Step 2. Place both hands on top of your *dantian*, men left hand on the inside, women right hand on the inside. Visualize that the inside of your abdomen is filled with white qi, for 3 to 5 minutes. Next, circle your palms on your abdomen, 100 times in each direction.

Visualize with high concentration that qi is circling inside your abdomen. It is best if you can practice three times a day, during the morning, afternoon, and evening. Massaging the abdomen can help accumulate *jing*, *qi*, and *shen* in your abdomen; and strengthen your tendon and fascia layers.

Figure 5-24   Figure 5-25   Figure 5-26

Part 2.

Procedure:

Step 1. Inhale, draw your *huiyin* up and abdomen in. Use your mind to lead the white qi in your *dantian*, up to the top of your head. Hold your breath, hit the top of your head with a sand bag. Then exhale, and relax your *huiyin* and your abdomen.

Repeat 9 times. Then place your palms on top of your *dantian* for 1 minute. Don't hit the top of the head in the morning. Condition the top of your head with objects only during the afternoon and evening.

Begin using sandbags to hit your head. Make sure that the sandbag is loosened up before using it. Lead qi to your head on impact. Start using a 3 pound sandbag. Increase the weight of the bag every 10 days by one pound. When you are able to withstand the impact of a 5-8 pound sandbag, replace the sand bag and gradually start training with a rod, baseball bat (Figure 5-24), and bricks.

Step 2. The *Head Exercise* from the Iron Shirt Qigong Head has already built a foundation for your head conditioning. After training the Iron Shirt Qigong for a couple of weeks, you can begin to condition your head by hitting it on the walls.

Start by hitting very lightly and gradually increase the force of impact, by standing further and further away from the wall, as you lean into the wall (Figures 5-25 and 5-26). The force of impact should not make you feel dizzy or be painful. On the

251

point of impact, either hold your breath or exhale. Train 5-15 minutes each session.

Notes:

It is very important that you start with a very gentle force and gradually increase the force, without causing injury to your head. Haste will cause injury, and lose all that you have attained.

The bricks used in China are made of clay. The bricks made in North America are mostly made of concrete. Be careful when using them.

6. LEG CONDITIONING

It is very painful for the shin to be hit. With proper training, this area can increase its resistance to a strike, and its effectiveness in offense. A front sweep kick with a conditioned leg, in free sparring is very deadly, making your opponent unable to defend.

Part 1. Lead Qi to Your Shins

Procedure:

Step 1. Stand up straight with your hands at your waist. Next, lift your right foot up, turn your foot to your right, and kick down at an angle. As you kick, let out the *che* sound as you exhale (Figure 5-27). Use your mind to lead qi to your leg when kicking. Bring your right foot down, then kick with your left foot. Repeat nine times, on each leg.

Step 2. Stand up straight, bend from your waist, and lower your fingers to the floor (Figure 5-28). Inhale, cross your arms in front of your legs. Exhale, squat down, and fling your fists up and out to your sides, with your elbows pointing down (Figure 5-29). Next stand up, then repeat. Do a total of 3 times.

Part 2. Shin Training

Procedure:

Place one leg on a chair. First use your palm to strike the front of your leg, then use a bamboo stick bundle, sandbag, wooden rods, and metal rod. Start striking lightly and increase the force gradually as your leg gets stronger, without injuring your leg. If you practice daily, it will only take you one month to be able to put a brick on your shin and have someone break the brick with a hammer, without injuring your shin.

Figure 5-27   Figure 5-28   Figure 5-29

Notes:

This training can increase the front of your legs' resistance to strikes. It will be much stronger than someone else without the training. Keep in mind, however, human bodies are not made of steel. Don't hit too hard with metal objects.

7. MUSCLE CONDITIONING

Muscle conditioning is a special training to increase the energy of the body. It is also referred to as a *Thousand Pounds of Great Power Qigong*. This qigong builds on the foundation built from the previous training methods, and assists the practitioners in developing an even higher level of accomplishment.

Part 1. Lead Qi to Your Muscles

Procedure:

Step 1. Stand with your feet parallel. Place your left hand on your waist. Right arm bends with fingers pointing forward next to your chest. Next thrust your right arm forward as you let out the *che* sound with your exhalation.

Hold your breath, then bend your fingers and imagine pulling a heavy object, while bringing your fist next to your chest slowly. Completely exhale, then inhale and lower your right arm down to your side naturally.

Do the mirror image of Step 1 with your left arm.

Figure 5-30   Figure 5-31   Figure 5-32

Step 2. Stand straight with your feet parallel and hands facing each other next to your chest. Next thrust your palms forward as you let out the *che* sound with your exhalation (Figure 5-30). Hold your breath, then bend your fingers and imagine pulling a heavy object while bringing your fist next to your chest slowly (Figure 5-31). Completely exhale, then inhale and lower your arms down to your sides naturally.

Step 3. Place your left hand on your waist. Bend your right arm with your fingers pointing to your right next to your chest. Next thrust your right arm to your right as you let out the *che* sound with your exhalation (Figure 5-32).

Hold your breath, then bend your fingers and imagine pulling a heavy object, while bringing your fist next to your chest slowly (Figure 5-33). Completely exhale, then inhale and lower your right arm down to your side naturally.

Do the mirror image of Step 3 with your left arm.

Step 4. Bend both arms with your fingers pointing to your sides next to your chest. Next thrust both arms out to your sides as you let out the *che* sound with your exhalation (Figure 5-34).

Hold your breath, then bend your fingers and imagine pulling a heavy object, while bringing your fists next to your chest slowly (Figure 5-35). Exhale and lower your arms down to your side naturally.

Step 5. Bend both arms with your fingers pointing up next to your chest. Next thrust both arms up over your head as you let out

Figure 5-33   Figure 5-34   Figure 5-35

Figure 5-36   Figure 5-37

the *che* sound with your exhalation (Figure 5-36). Hold your breath, then bend your fingers and imagine pulling a heavy object, while bringing your fists next to your chest slowly (Figure 5-37). Completely exhale, then inhale and lower your arms down to your sides naturally.

Part 2. Muscle Training

Procedure:

Step 1. First practice all the other Lead Qi techniques described in this section.

Step 2. Tie a cotton rope tightly around the bulky muscle areas of your body. Exhale, let out the *che* sound, and tense your muscles to break the rope. Gradually increase the amount of tied rope around your muscles. As your attainment gets higher, replace the cotton rope with thin gauge wire.

Notes:

When wrapping the wire around your body, don't keep the wire on for too long. If you are unable to break the wire within 5 breaths, you should remove some of the wire and try again. Keeping the wire on too long will damage your *original-qi*. Be careful and increase the amount of wire gradually.

8. GROIN CONDITIONING

The groin area of men cannot withstand a forceful strike without training. With proper training, one can increase the resistance to a strike. For middle age and older individuals, this training can also improve and cure problems associated with the degeneration of sexual functions.

Procedure:

Step 1. Massage the testis: Rub your palms together until they are hot. Then place them around your penis and testis, massage 100-300 times.

Step 2. Massage the Girdle Vessel: Place your right palm over your *dantian* and left palm on your *yaoyangguan* point on your Governing Vessel, located on your lower back between your 4th and 5th lumbar vertebrae.

Massage the *dantian* and *yaoyangguan* about 100 times or until they are hot. Then place your hands on each side of your waist and massage 100 times or until they are hot. This technique can strengthen the kidneys and improve the kidney function.

Step 3. Place your palms on your lower back, maintain contact and circle your palms to the front. Next use one of your palms, gradually over time, slap lightly to heavily, the area from your pubic bone down to your groin, for 5-15 minutes.

Step 4. *Pulling*: Use both hands and grab a hold of the base of the penis, pull up and circle from right to left, 30-50 times; then left to right, 30-50 times. Then pull forward and release 30-50 times. Next massage the *dantian* area until it is hot.

Step 5. *Hitting with the Edge of your Palms and Bamboo Stick Bundles*: After training Steps 1-4 for a period of time, then train step 5. Use the edges of both palms, alternately striking your crotch to your groin. Practice 5-15 minutes.

This will increase the contraction power in the area around the testis, making the area stronger and able to withstand external attack. After a period of time, use the bamboo stick bundle to condition the groin area.

Notes:

The best time to train is when you wake up in the morning and before going to bed at night. You can train while lying down, sitting, or standing. When you first start training, you will feel slight pain in the testis. The weaker your kidneys, the more obvious the pain. With steady practice, your *kidney-qi* will increase and the pain will decrease.

If your goal is only to gain better health from this training, you should practice more of Steps 1 to 4. As a martial arts conditioning exercise, you will need to practice more of Step 5. Self-control is necessary in this training, to avoid turning it into masturbation.

5.3. Hard Qigong for Powerful and Effective Applications

Qigong for offense primarily involves the training of the arms, elbows, legs, knees, palms, and fingers for martial arts applications. It includes both internal qigong training and physical training. Internal qigong builds the foundation and increases the internal power emission. Physical training strengthens the hardness of specific areas and increases the power delivery potential. Both internal qigong and physical training must be practiced. Without either one, the training can't be completed.

Most of the hard qigong training, are divided into stages. Set aside a regular time each day or week for your training. Train each stage until your body has achieved the *goal* of that stage before proceeding to the next. The *goal* of each stage is to be able to do the exercise easily. Use common sense during your training. After each session of your training, wash the area involved in the training with hot water, and/or use iron palm or bruise liniment to massage the joints and the contacting surfaces. You can't hurry your progress. The only thing that can give you more achievement in your training is a steady input of *time and energy* — the meaning of Kung Fu.

1. QIGONG FOR DEVELOPING INCREDIBLE STRENGTH

This Qigong should to be practiced before any hard qigong training in this section, to increase the effectiveness of your training.

Procedure:

Step 1. *Nourishing Your Qi*: Stand comfortably straight with your arms naturally at your sides. Breathe through your nose. Inhale, use your mind to lead the *pure essence* of the cosmos and the earth into your body, through your *baihui* and *yongquan* points to your *dantian*. Exhale, keep your mind at your *dantian*.

Repeat Step 1, 36 times.

Step 2. *Opening and Closing your Pores*: Continue from above. Inhale, use your mind to lead the pure essence of the cosmos and the earth into your body through the pores of your body. Then use your mind to contract all your pores, as if you were binding your body tightly and condensing the *pure essence* into your *dantian*.

Hold your breath for a few seconds. Exhale, disperse qi from your *dantain* all over your body. Relax all your pores and discharge all the impurities from your body, through your pores, out to the cosmos. Relax the entire body and feel as though you have melted into the cosmos and become one with the cosmos.

Repeat Step 2, 36 times.

Step 3. Stand comfortably with your arms naturally at your sides. Tuck your chin in slightly. Mentally push your *baihui* up and condense your qi at your *dantian*. Maintain this position for about 1 minute.

Step 4. *Holding the Heaven*: Inhale through your mouth and begin lifting your palms up (Figure 5-38). Continue lifting your palms up until your eye level. At this time, turn your palms to face you with your thumbs pointing up. Contract your entire body, grip the floor with your toes, hold your abdomen in, and expand your chest.

Use your mind to lead the *pure essence* of the cosmos into your body through your *baihui*, two *laogong* points on your palms, and two *yongquan* points on the bottom of your feet. This technique is also called "*Admitting Qi from the Five Centers*."

Figure 5-38　　　　　　　Figure 5-39　　　　　　　Figure 5-40

Then hold your breath, close your mouth, use your throat to swallow the qi into your *dantian*, as if you were swallowing food. Next, rotate your palms until your palms are facing forward, with your thumbs pointing down. Relax the entire body and begin extending your abdomen out. At the same time, use your mind to lead the qi from your *dantian* up the Conception Vessel to your *baihui*.

Exhale through your mouth, rotate your palms until your palms are facing up, and extend until your arms are over your head (Figure 5-39). Tighten your body while extending your abdomen out. Use your mind to lead qi from your *baihui* down to your ears, then to your armpits, and to your *laogong* points.

Lower your arms naturally and repeat Step 4, 18 times.

Step 5. *Extending the Wings*: Inhale, use the same movements and intention as in Step 4. Then hold your breath, close your mouth, use your throat to swallow the qi into your *dantian*, as if you were swallowing food. Next, rotate your palms until your palms are facing forward, with your thumbs pointing down. Relax the entire body and begin extending your abdomen out. At the same time, use your mind to lead the qi from your *dantian* down to your *huiyin*, then up along the Governing Vessel to your *baihui*.

Next, exhale, and extend both palms slowly to your sides (Figure 5-40). Tighten your entire body, while extending your abdomen out. Use your mind to lead the qi from your *baihui* down to your ears, then to your armpits, and to your *laogong* points.

Lower your arms naturally and repeat Step 5, 18 times.

Step 6. *Push the Mountain*: Inhale, use the same movements and intention as in Step 4. Then hold your breath, close your mouth, use your throat to swallow the qi into your *dantian*, as if you were swallowing food. Next, rotate your palms until your palms are facing forward, with your thumbs pointing down. Relax the entire body and begin extending your abdomen out. At the same time, use your mind to lead the qi from your *dantian* up the Conception Vessel to your *baihui*. Then back down along the Conception Vessel to your *dantian*, down to your *huiyin* and continue up along the Governing Vessel to your *baihui*.

Next, exhale, and drop your elbows and extend both palms slowly forward (Figure 5-41). Tighten your entire body, while extending your abdomen out. Use your mind to lead the qi through your *baihui* down to your ears, then to your armpits, and to your *laogong* points.

Lower your arms naturally and repeat Step 6, 18 times.

Step 7. *Push the Ground*: Inhale, use the same movements and intention as in Step 4. Then hold your breath, close your mouth, use your throat to swallow the qi into your *dantian*, as if you were swallowing food. Next, rotate your palms until your palms are facing forward, with your thumbs pointing down. Relax the entire body and begin extending your abdomen out.

Relax the entire body and press your tongue gently on the roof of your mouth. The intention while holding your breath is to use the mind to lead the qi from your *dantian* up the Conception Vessel to your *baihui*. Then back down along the Conception Vessel, back to your *dantian* and down to your *huiyin*. Separate into two paths down the front and inside of your legs to your *yongquan* points on the bottom of your feet. Next back up along the back of your legs to your *huiyin* and along the Governing Vessel to your *baihui*.

Next, exhale, and rotate your palms face down and bend from your waist, as you lower your palms to the floor. Touching the floor with the base of your palms and fingers pointing at each other (Figure 5-42). Use your mind to lead the qi from your *baihui* down to your ears, then to your armpits, and to your *laogong* points.

Stand up slowly and repeat Step 7, 18 times.

Figure 5-41   Figure 5-42

2. IRON FIST TRAINING

Stage 1.

Procedure:

Step 1. *Golden Ox Plows the Field*: Lie on the floor with your fists about a shoulder width apart and use them to support your upper body (Figure 5-43). Inhale, straighten your arms and move your hips up and back until your body forms an inverted V shape (Figure 5-44). At the same time, use your mind to lead the qi from your arms to your *dantian*.

Then, hold your breath, bend your arms, and swing your body down and forward. Straighten your arms again, as you arch your back and lift your upper body (Figure 5-45). At the same time, use your mind to lead the qi from your *dantian*, to *your huiyin*, to *your baihui*, and to *your shanzhong*.

Next, exhale, bring your body back down to the starting position (Figure 5-46). At the same time, use your mind to lead the qi from your *shanzhong* along the inside of your arms to your *laogong* points. Repeat as many times as you are able. Build up the repetition gradually.

Step 2. *Punch Layers of Paper*: Hang a stack of paper (a telephone book with the cover removed is an excellent recyclable choice) on a wall or on the floor. Use your fists to punch the stack of paper (Figure 5-47). Remove the pages as you punch through

Figure 5-43

Figure 5-44

Figure 5-45

Figure 5-46

the layers. Build up the times you punch, gradually, without injuring your fists.

Stage 2.

Procedure:

Step 1. *One Arm Push Ups with your Fist*: Use your right fist to support your body, both your body and your right arm should be straight (Figure 5-48). Inhale, use your mind to lead the *pure essence* of the universe from the outside of your right arm to your *baihui*.

Then, hold your breath as you bend your right arm and lower your body down (Figure 5-49). At the same time, use your mind to lead the qi from your *baihui* along your Conception Vessel down to your *dantian*.

Next, exhale, hold up your anus, testis (in male), and push back up until your right arm is straight. At the same time, use your mind to lead the qi from your *dantian* up to your *shanzhong*, and along the inside of your right arm to your right fist. Practice as many times as you can, then repeat with your left arm.

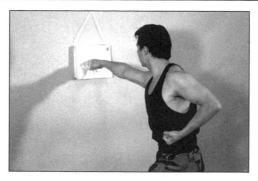

Figure 5-47

 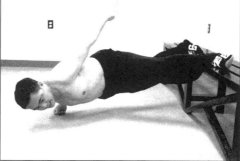

Figure 5-48   Figure 5-49

Step 2. *Punch an Iron Sand Bag*: Hang an iron sandbag at chest level. Inhale bring your mind to your *dantian*. Exhale, punch the bag with your fist; while using your mind to lead the qi from your *dantian* to your *shanzhong*, past your armpit, and through your punching arm to your fist. Punch until your fists are warm and you can not punch any more, but before your skin ruptures.

Stage 3.

Procedure:

Step 1. *A Single Arm Handstand with Your Fist*: Lean on the wall and do a single arm handstand with one fist (Figure 5-50). Use your mind to lead the qi from all over your body to your fist during your exhalation. Hold this posture for as long as you can on one side, then change to the other side.

Step 2. *Punching a Brick Wall or Trees*: Use the same procedure as in *Punching an Iron Sand Bag*. Make sure that the wall or the tree is smooth, and doesn't rupture your skin, during your training.

Figure 5-50   Figure 5-51   Figure 5-52

3. IRON PALM TRAINING

Preparation:

Lead Qi to Your Palms: In a standing position, inhale, settle your palms with your fingers pointing forward and palms face down. At the same time, use your mind to lead the qi from your *dantian* to your palms. Exhale, relax your palms, keep your mind at your palms, and don't allow the qi to escape out of your palms. Imagine that your palms are immersed in warm water. The water gets hotter and hotter, as your palms also get redder and hotter. Do 36 breathing cycles.

Stage 1.

Procedure:

Step 1. *Golden Ox Plows the Field*: Use the same procedure as in Iron Fist training, except with palms instead of fists supporting the body.

Step 2. *Push the Mountain*: Stand at an arm length away from the wall, with your finger tips touching the wall. Exhale through your nose, hold up your *huiyin*, and grab the floor with your toes. At the same time, use the movements of your shoulder to push your arms forward and strike the wall with your palms (Figures 5-51 and 5-52).

As you strike the wall, use your mind to lead the qi from your *dantian* to your *shanzhong*, separate into two paths to each armpit, along the inside of your arms and to your *laogong* points. Then, inhale, and relax your entire body and bring your palms back to the starting position. At the same time, lead the qi from your palms back to your *dantian*. Repeat until your arms and palms are sore and red.

Stage 2.

Procedure:

Step 1. *One Arm Push Ups with your Palm*: Use the same procedure as in Iron Fist training, except with your palm supporting the body.

Step 2. *Palm Strike an Iron Sandbag*: Place an iron sandbag in front of you at abdomen level. In the beginning, wrap thick layers of cotton cloth on the iron sand bag to protect your palms. As your palms get stronger, gradually remove the layers of cloth on the bag.

Face the iron sandbag, inhale, raise your arm up over your head and lead the qi to your palm. Exhale, squeeze the base of your thumb towards your pinkie and hit the bag, contacting with the meaty part of your palm. When hitting the iron sand bag do not hold back. Hit as hard as you can to increase your power.

When you hit the bag, use your mind to lead the qi through the bag. Practice until one palm is red, hot, and sore; then do the other palm. Follow the same procedure as above, using the inside edge of your palm and the back of your palm.

Stage 3.

Procedure:

Step 1. *Single Arm Handstand with Your Palm*: Use the same procedure as in Iron Fist Training, except use your palm instead of your fist.

Step 2. *Hit a Brick or a Rock*: Use the same procedure as the training with the iron sandbag. Be careful not to injure your palms.

Then, hold a brick or a rock with one hand and hit it with the other palm. Alternate hands.

Figure 5-53   Figure 5-54

Figure 5-55   Figure 5-56

4. EAGLE CLAW TRAINING

Preparation:

Step 1. Stand in a Horse Stance with your arms extended to your sides, palms face down (Figure 5-53). Inhale, lead qi from the outside of your arms to your *baihui*, and down along the Conception Vessel to your *dantian*. Exhale, lead the qi from your *dantian* along the inside of your arms to your finger tips. Repeat 36 times.

Step 2. Stand in a Horse Stance with your arms extended in front of you, palms face down. Flex your wrists from side to side, 10 times (Figure 5-54). Repeat until you complete 10 breaths.

Then inhale, change your palms into fists and pull back towards your chest as though you were pulling something very heavy towards you (Figure 5-55). Exhale, push your palms forward, and lead qi to your *laogong* points (Figure 5-56). Repeat Step 2, three times.

Figure 5-57

Figure 5-58

Figure 5-59

Step 3. Change your stance into a left Bow Stance. Extend your right arm forward with your fingers spread apart, and left arm extended behind you with your fingers spread apart, both palms face down. Flex your wrists from side to side 10 times (Figure 5-57). Repeat until you complete 10 breaths.

Then inhale, change your palms into fists and pull back towards your chest as though you were pulling something very heavy towards you (Figure 5-58). Exhale, push your palms down, and lead qi to your *laogong* points (Figure 5-59).

Repeat Step 3, three times.

Step 4. Change your stance into a right Bow Stance and repeat the mirror image of Step 3.

Stage 1.

Procedure:

Step 1. *Golden Ox Plows the Field*: Use the same procedure as in Iron Fist and Iron Palm training, except with fingers, instead of fists or palms supporting the body.

Figure 5-60   Figure 5-61

Step 2. *Rotate Chopsticks*: Bundle a handful of chopsticks together. Grab a hold of the chopsticks with both hands and twist the bundle in opposite directions with your hands (Figure 5-60). Alternate the direction of your twist. As you twist the chopsticks, lead the qi from your *dantian* to your *laogong* points.

Step 3. *Grabbing the Vessel*. Use a vessel with an opening, the size of your palm. Stand in a Horse Stance and place the vessel in front of you. Grab a hold of the vessel with one hand and lift it up and down slowly (Figure 5-61).

When you grab the vessel, inhale, hold your breath, and hold up your *huiyin*. When you put the vessel down, relax your body and exhale. Repeat Step 3, 36 times or more on each side.

An empty vessel is easy to do. You should increase the weight of the vessel everyday by placing a handful of sand in the vessel, until the vessel is filled with sand.

Stage 2.

Procedure:

Step 1. *One Arm Push Ups with your Fingers*: Use the same procedure as in Iron Fist and Iron Palm training except with fingers supporting the body.

Step 2. *Winding Weights:* Tie a piece of rope on a short piece of stick and the other end on a heavy object. The length of the rope should equal the distance between your arms and the floor when your arms are extended in front of your body, while standing in a Horse Stance. The weight of the object depends on the strength of the individual.

Figure 5-62   Figure 5-63

Stand in a Horse Stance, grab a hold of the stick with both hands and extend your arms forward. Wind the rope until the weight is completely up (Figure 5-62). Then release the weight down and repeat several times. Next reverse the winding direction, repeat several times.

Step 3. *Tossing an Iron Ball*: Use an iron ball that weights about 10 pounds or more. Stand in a Horse Stance. Toss the ball up and grab it with the other hand. Alternate sides until you are tired (Figure 5-63).

Stage 3.

Procedure:

Step 1. *Single Arm Handstand with Your Fingers*: Use the same procedure as in Iron Fist and Iron Palm training, except use your fingers instead of your fist or palm. Start with 10 fingers supporting the body. Very gradually reduce the supporting fingers from 9 to 1 finger, as you get stronger with training and time (Figure 5-64).

Step 2. *Tossing an Iron Sandbag*: Prepare an iron sand bag that weighs 10 pounds or more. Stand in a Horse Stance. Toss the iron sand bag up and grab it with the other hand. Alternate sides until you are tired.

You can train with the bag in many ways. You can toss it between people or individually. You can use a light bag to train your accuracy, or you can train with a heavy bag for power.

Figure 5-64　　　　　　　Figure 5-65

Step 3. *Pushing Bricks*: Stand in a Horse Stance. Hold a brick in each hand (two bricks if the brick size is small). Alternate extending one brick in front of your body and the other back to your chest (Figure 5-65). Do 100 times each training session.

5. STEEL FINGER TRAINING

Preparation:

Step 1. *Lead Qi to the Fingers*: Sit or stand comfortably. Extend your arms to your sides even with your shoulders, with your palms facing to the sides. Relax your hands, inhale, bring your palms in towards your chest with your palms facing each other. At the same time, lead the pure essence of the universe into your *laogong* points and down to your *dantian*.

Exhale, rotate your palms out and extend your arms again to the sides. At the same time, lead qi from your *dantian* to your fingers.

Repeat Step 1, 36 times.

Step 2. *Lead Qi to the Index and Middle Fingers*: From a standing position, place your arms naturally down to your sides. Inhale, hold your hands into fists, and raise them up to the side of your eyes with the eye of your fist facing back (palm faces in). (The eye of the fist is the area between your index finger and thumb). At the same time, lead the *pure essence* of the universe into your *baihui* and raise your heels up.

270

Hold your breath, lower your heels down, and *swallow* the qi down to your *dantian*.

Exhale, extend your arms to your sides while straightening your index and middle fingers. At the same time, lead the qi from your *dantian* to *shanzhong* (midpoint between your nipples), past your armpits, and to the index and middle fingers.

Then lower your arms down to your sides and repeat Step 2, 36 times.

Step 3. *Lead Qi to the Index Fingers*: From a standing position, place your palms facing up at your hip level with your index fingers pointing at each other. All other fingers are coiled in. Inhale, raise your palms up to your chest level and rotate your hands to face up while maintaining your index fingers pointing at each other. At the same time, lead the *pure essence* of the universe into your *baihui* as you raise your heels up.

Hold your breath, lower your heels down, and *swallow* the qi down to your *dantian*.

Exhale, raise your hands up over your head while maintaining the palms facing up and index fingers pointing at each other. At the same time, lead the qi from your *dantian* to your *shanzhong*, past your armpits, and to the index fingers.

Then lower your arms down to your sides and repeat Step 3, 36 times.

Stage 1.

Procedure:

Step 1. *Untying Rope*: Find a piece of rope about 1 yard long and make 9 dead knots on the rope. Stand in a Horse stance, hold on to the knots, and extend your arms forward. Inhale and lead the qi from all over your body to your *dantian*. Exhale and lead the qi from your *dantian* to your fingers. Repeat until you feel the qi is strong at your fingers.

Then breathe naturally, and use your fingers to untie the knots. As you untie the knots, image that the knots are acupuncture points and/or joints on the human body. After you have untied the rope, make 9 more dead knots and again untie them, two more times.

When you are done untying 27 knots, relax your hands and lead qi to your fingers to *wash* them with qi.

Step 2. Stand in a Horse Stance. Squeeze your thumb, index, and middle fingers together. Lead the energy from all over your body to the tips of the three fingers on each hand. Hold for one minute.

Continue squeezing your fingers together and point the three fingers towards the ground. Rub your thumb on your index and middle fingers 9 revolutions in one direction, then reverse for 18 revolutions, and again reverse for 9 more revolutions. Then repeat the rubbing training, two more times.

Step 3. Find a bucket and fill it with moon beans (green beans). Stand in a Horse Stance in front of the bucket. Alternate spearing your hands into the beans. When spearing down, lead the qi from your *dantian* to your fingers. Use all your power to thrust your fingers into the bucket as deep as possible. Practice spearing down 50 to 100 times each training session. However, you may have to start with less repetitions to avoid rupturing your skin. Gradually increase the repetitions.

Stage 2.

Procedure:

Step 1. *Untying Rope*: The same procedure as in Untying Rope in Stage 1, except immerse the rope in water before untying the knots to increase the difficulty.

Step 2. The same procedure as in Stage 1, Step 2, except increase the time of squeezing your fingers together to 2 minutes. When rubbing your thumbs on your index and middle fingers, place a penny between your fingers before rubbing.

Step 3. Spear your fingers towards a sand bag, rug, or grassy area. Practice spearing 100 times each session. You must lead the qi from your *dantian* to your fingers each time you spear down.

Stage 3.

Procedure:

Step 1. *Untying Rope*: The same procedure as in Untying Rope in Stage 1, except immerse the rope in oil before untying the knots to increase the difficulty.

Step 2. The same procedure as in Stage 1, Step 2, except increase the time of squeezing your fingers together to 3 minutes. When rubbing your thumb on your index and middle fingers, place a soy bean, chalk, or a small rock between your fingers before rubbing your fingers.

Step 3. Spear your fingers toward tree trunks, wooden boards, roofing tiles, and bricks. Start spearing softer material. As your fingers get stronger, gradually begin to spear harder material. Start from light to heavy spearing. Each session, train until your fingers are hot and sore, but before causing injury to your fingers.

6. IRON FOREARM TRAINING

Preparation:

Do the *Qigong for Developing Incredible Strength* before all Stages in this training.

Stage 1.

Procedure:

Step 1. *Push the Bricks*: Follow the same procedure as in Stage 3, Step 3 in Eagle Claw Training.

Step 2. *Striking the Tree*: Use the different surfaces of your forearm to strike the tree. Do 100 times on each forearm.

Step 3. *Elbow Striking a Sand Bag*: Use your elbow to strike a sand bag. Use sideways, and up and down striking movements to hit the bag. Do 100 times on each side.

Step 4. *Training with a Partner*: Stand facing your partner. Both of you swing your right arm in and down, contacting each other on the surface of your forearm at abdomen level.

Then pull your arms away from each other and swing up and out to your right, contacting each other's forearm at head level. Next, swing your arms down and out to your right, contacting each other's forearm at abdomen level.

Repeat Step 4 with your left arm. Keep alternating arms 50-100 times.

| Figure 5-66 | Figure 5-67 | Figure 5-68 |

Stage 2.

Procedure:

Step 1. *Circling the Bricks*: Hold on to two bricks with your hands. Use the distance between your *shanzhong* and your *dantian* as the diameter of the circle, move the bricks 36 to 72 times clockwise (Figure 5-66). Then reverse the direction, 36-72 times counterclockwise.

Inhale when you raise the bricks and place your mind at your *shanzhong* point. Exhale when you lower the bricks and place your mind at your *dantian*.

Step 2. *Strike the Arm with a Rod*: Hold a rod in one hand and hit the other arm. When striking, use your mind to lead the qi from your *dantian* to the arm being hit. Hit until your arm is sore and can't take it any more (Figure 5-67). Then change arms.

Step 3. *Elbow Strike Layers of Paper*: Stabilize the paper on a wall, post, or place it on a sturdy table. Use the front and back of your elbow to hit the paper.

Step 4. *Training with a Partner*: Same as in Stage 1, Step 4.

Stage 3.

Procedure:

Step 1. *Large Circling with the Bricks*: Hold on to two bricks. Circle the bricks over your head and down to your *huiyin* level 36 to

Figure 5-69   Figure 5-70   Figure 5-71

72 times clockwise (Figure 5-68). Then reverse the direction, 36-72 times counterclockwise.

Inhale when you raise the bricks, hold up your *huiyin* area, and place your mind at your *baihui* point. Exhale when you lower the bricks, relax your *huiyin* area, and place your mind at your *huiyin* point.

Step 2. *Rolling the Cylinder*: Find a cylindrical container about 3-5 feet long fill it with sand. The weight could be 30 to 100 plus pounds depending on an individual's condition. Stand in a Horse Stance and place the cylinder on your hands with your palms facing up (Figure 5-69).

Raise your forearms up and allow the cylinder to roll up your arms until your upper arm (Figure 5-70). (Tuck your chin in slightly to prevent the cylinder from hitting your throat). Straighten your arms and allow the cylinder to roll back down the inside of your arms to your hands (Figure 5-71).

Then, toss the cylinder up, rotate your arms until your palms are facing down, and catch the cylinder with the back side of your forearm (Figures 5-72 and 5-73).

Next, raise your forearms and allow the cylinder to roll back up to your upper arm (Figure 5-74). Straighten your arms and allow the cylinder to roll back down the back side of your arms to the back of your hands (Figure 5-75).

Then toss the cylinder up, rotate your arms until your palms are facing up, and catch the cylinder with the inside of your forearm (Figures 5-76 and 5-77).

Figure 5-72

Figure 5-73

Figure 5-74

Figure 5-75

Figure 5-76

Figure 5-77

Repeat Step 2, as many times as you can.

Step 3. *Elbow Strike a Tree Trunk*: Use the front and back of your elbow to strike a tree trunk. Use sideways, and up and down striking movements to hit the tree trunk.

Step 4. *Training with a Partner*: Same as in Stage 1, Step 4.

7. IRON KNEE TRAINING

Procedure:

Step 1. Sit cross legged or on a chair. Keep your body erect, gently touch your teeth together, relax your shoulders, and place your hands at your *dantian* level. Sit for 5 minutes and pay attention to your knees.

Next, use your fists to hit around your knees. Start gently and gradually increase the power until your knee area is hot and slightly numb. Then place your palms over your knees and rub in a circle 36-72 times, then 36 to 72 times in the other direction.

Again use your fists to hit your knee area, then rub. Repeat several times. After a period of time, when your knees no longer feel the pain from your fists hitting your knees, change to hitting your knees with a wooden rod or wooden hammer. Start gently and gradually increase the power of the hit.

Step 2. Hang a sand bag at abdomen level. Knee the sand bag from the front, side, and bottom. As you hit the sand bag, exhale, and lead the qi from your *dantian* to your knee. Practice 36 to 72 times on each knee, in each direction. Start with a regular sand bag. Gradually change the sand bag to a rock bag or iron sand bag

Step 3. Kneel on a rug, sand, or a grassy area. Alternate lifting one knee up and down to hit the floor. Practice kneeing the rug 100 times on each side, then rest for a while and repeat one or more time. After practicing for a period of time, start from a standing position and hit the rug with both knees at the same time. When your knees get stronger, gradually change to kneeing a wooden board and on concrete.

Notes:

A. As with all other Hard Qigong training, you must proceed gradually. You should not be impatient in your training progress, or else you will injure your knees.

B. After every training session, massage your knees with your hands until they are hot.

C. If your goal is not for martial arts and you only want to strengthen your knees for healing arthritis, practice Step 1 and Step 3. In Step 3, only practice kneeling on the rug.

Appendix A:

Acupuncture Charts

Chart A-1: Lung Channel (P)
Chart A-2: Large Intestine Channel (IC)
Chart A-3: Stomach Channel (G)
Chart A-4: Spleen Channel (LP)
Chart A-5: Heart Channel (C)
Chart A-6: Small Intestine Channel (IT)
Chart A-7: Urinary Bladder Channel (VU)
Chart A-8: Kidney Channel (R)
Chart A-9: Pericardium Channel (PC)
Chart A-10: Triple Burner Channel (T)
Chart A-11: Gall Bladder Channel (VF)
Chart A-12: Liver Channel (H)
Chart A-13: Governing Vessel (TM)
Chart A-14: Conception Vessel (JM)
Chart A-15: Thrusting Vessel
Chart A-16: Girdle Vessel
Chart A-17: Yang-Activation Vessel
Chart A-18: Yin-Activation Vessel
Chart A-19: Yang-Maintenance Vessel
Chart A-20: Yin-Maintenance Vessel

Symbols

——————— Main energy pathway

— — — — — Branch, collaterals, or internal energy pathways

— — · — — · Indicates the continuation of the pathway at a different angle

✖ Interacts with the pertinent organ

✸ Communication with other internal organs

• Acupuncture point on the energy pathway

△ Location where the energy pathway meets another pathway

1. The Lung Channel

◆ The Lung Channel starts at the Middle Burner (the middle portion of the torso, stomach region).

◆ Pertains to the Lungs.

◆ Communicates with the large intestine and Middle Burner.

◆ Passes through the trachea and the throat.

◆ Qi cycles in from the Liver Channel to the Lung Channel in the lungs.

◆ Qi cycles out of the Lung Channel to the Large Intestine Channel at the lower medial corner of the index fingernail at the *shangyang* (IC1) point.

zhongfu (P1)
yunmen (P2)
tianfu (P3)
xiabai (P4)
chize (P5)
kongzui (P6)
lieque (P7)
jingqu (P8)
taiyuan (P9)
yuji (P10)
shaoshang (P11)

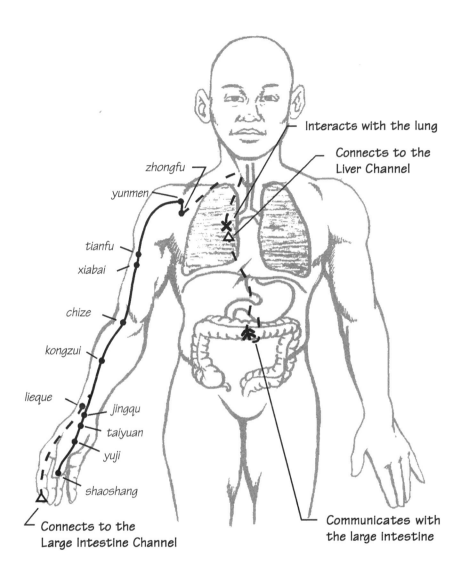

zhongfu

yunmen

tianfu

xiabai

chize

kongzui

lieque

jingqu

taiyuan

yuji

shaoshang

Interacts with the lung

Connects to the
Liver Channel

Communicates with
the large intestine

Connects to the
Large Intestine Channel

Chart A-1: Lung Channel

2. The Large Intestine Channel

◆ The Large Intestine Channel starts from the lower medial corner of the index fingernail (*shangyang* point, IC1).

◆ Pertains to the large intestine.

◆ Communicates with the lungs.

◆ Passes through the mouth, the lower teeth, and the nose.

◆ Connects to the Small Intestine Channel at the *bingfeng* point (IT12); to the Stomach Channel at the *dicang* (G4) and *juliao-face* (G3) points; to the Gall Bladder Channel at the *yangbai* (VF14) point; to the Governing Vessel at the *dazhui* (TM14) and *renzhong* (TM26) points.

◆ Qi cycles in from the Lung Channel to the Large Intestine Channel at the lower medial corner of the index finger at the *shangyang* (IC1) point.

◆ Qi cycles out from the Large Intestine Channel to the Stomach Channel at the corner of the nose at the *yingxiang* (IC20) point.

shangyang (IC1)
erjian (IC2)
sanjian (IC3)
hegu (IC4)
yangxi (IC5)
pianli (IC6)
wenliu (IC7)
xialian (IC8)
shanglian (IC9)
shousanli (IC10)
quchi (IC11)
zhouliao (IC12)
shouwuli (IC13)
binao (IC14)
jianyu (IC15)
jugu (IC16)
tianding (IC17)
futu (neck) (IC18)
heliao (nose) (IC19)
yingxiang (IC20)

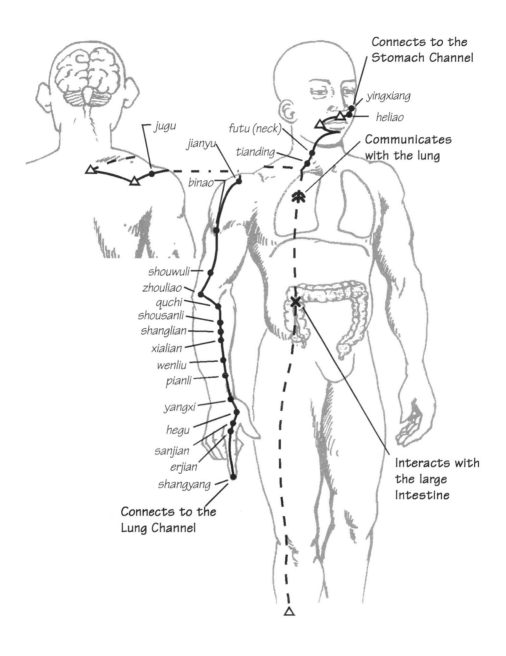

Connects to the
Stomach Channel

yingxiang

heliao

Communicates
with the lung

jugu

futu (neck)

jianyu

tianding

binao

shouwuli

zhouliao

quchi

shousanli

shanglian

xialian

wenliu

pianli

yangxi

hegu

sanjian

erjian

shangyang

Interacts with
the large
Intestine

Connects to the
Lung Channel

Chart A-2: Large Intestine Channel

3. The Stomach Channel

◆ The Stomach Channel starts from the *yingxiang* (IC20) point, to the side of the nose.

◆ Pertains to the stomach.

◆ Communicates with the spleen, large intestine, and small intestine.

◆ Passes through the nose, eyes, mouth, upper teeth, and nipples.

◆ Connects to the Stomach Channel at the *yingxiang* (IC20) point; to the Urinary Bladder Channel at the *jingming* (VU1) point; to the Gall Bladder Channel at the *shangguan* (VF3), *xuanli* (VF6), *xuanlu* (VF5), *hanyan* (VF4), and *yangbai* (VF14) points; to the Governing Vessel at the *renzhong* (TM26), *yinjiao-mouth* (TM28), *shenting* (TM24), and *dazhui* (TM14) points; to the Conception Vessel at the *chengjiang* (JM24), *shangwan* (JM13), and *zhongwan* (JM12) points.

◆ Qi cycles in from the Large Intestine Channel to the Stomach Channel at the *yingxiang* (IC20) point.

◆ Qi cycles out of the Stomach Channel to the Spleen Channel at the lower medial side of the big toe at the *yinbai* (LP1) point.

chengqi (G1)	yingchuang (G16)	biguan (G31)
sibai (G2)	ruzhong (G17)	futu (femur) (G32)
juliao (face) (G3)	rugen (G18)	yinshi (G33)
dicang (G4)	burong (G19)	liangqiu (G34)
daying (G5)	chengman (G20)	dubi (G35)
jiache (G6)	liangmen (G21)	zusanli (G36)
xiaguan (G7)	guanmen (G22)	shangjuxu (G37)
touwei (G8)	taiyi (G23)	tiaokou (G38)
renying (G9)	huaroumen (G24)	xiajuxu (G39)
shuitu (G10)	tianshu (G25)	fenglong (G40)
qishe (G11)	wailing (G26)	jiexi (G41)
quepen (G12)	daju (G27)	chongyang (G42)
qihu (G13)	shuidao (G28)	xiangu (G43)
kufang (G14)	guilai (G29)	neiting (G44)
wuyi (G15)	qichong (G30)	lidui (G45)

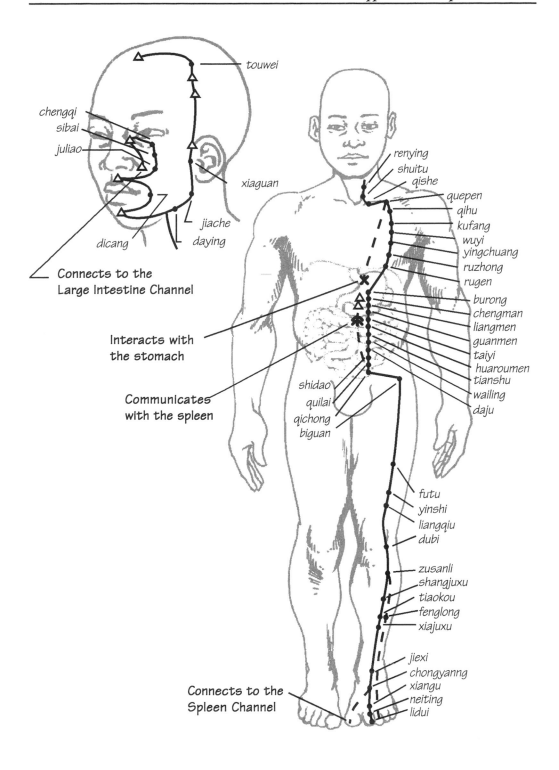

touwei

chengqi
sibai
juliao

xiaguan

jiache
daying

dicang

Connects to the
Large Intestine Channel

renying
shuitu
qishe
quepen
qihu
kufang
wuyi
yingchuang
ruzhong
rugen
burong
chengman
liangmen
guanmen
taiyi
huaroumen
tianshu
wailing
daju

Interacts with
the stomach

Communicates
with the spleen

shidao
quilai
qichong
biguan

futu
yinshi
liangqiu
dubi

zusanli
shangjuxu
tiaokou
fenglong
xiajuxu

jiexi
chongyanng
xiangu
neiting
lidui

Connects to the
Spleen Channel

Chart A-3: Stomach Channel

4. The Spleen Channel

◆ The Spleen Channel starts at the *yinbai* (LP1) point, located on the lower medial side of the big toenail.

◆ Pertains to the spleen.

◆ Communicates with the stomach and the heart.

◆ Passes through the tongue and esophagus.

◆ Connects to the Conception Vessel at the *zhongji* (JM3), *guanyuan* (JM4), and *xiawan* (JM10) points; to the Gall Bladder Channel at the *riyue* (VF24) point; to the Liver Channel at the *qimen* (H14) point; to the Lung Channel at the *zhongfu* (P1) point.

◆ Qi cycles in from the Stomach Channel to the Spleen Channel at the *yinbai* (LP1) point.

◆ Qi cycles out from the Spleen Channel to the Heart Channel in the heart.

yinbai (LP1)
dadu (LP2)
taibai (LP3)
gongsun (LP4)
shangqiu (LP5)
sanyinjiao (LP6)
lougu (LP7)
diji (LP8)
yinlingquan (LP9)
xuehai (LP10)
jimen (LP11)
chongmen (LP12)
fushe (LP13)
fujie (LP14)
daheng (LP15)
fuai (LP16)
shidou (LP17)
tianxi (LP18)
xiongxiang (LP19)
zhourong (LP20)
dabao (LP21)

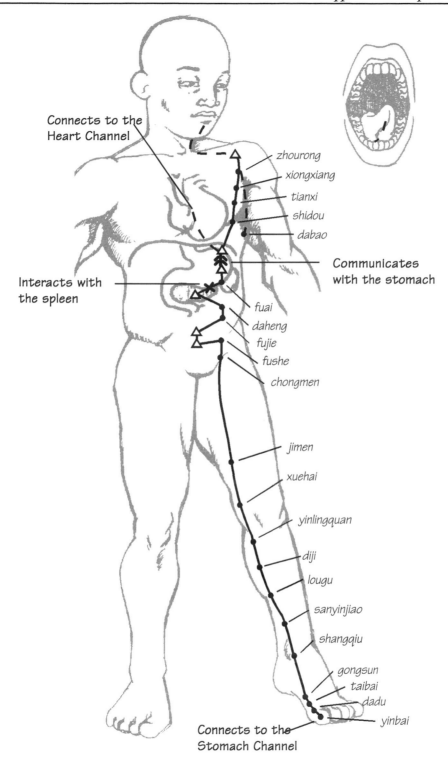

Connects to the
Heart Channel

Interacts with
the spleen

Communicates
with the stomach

zhourong
xiongxiang
tianxi
shidou
dabao

fuai
daheng
fujie
fushe
chongmen

jimen

xuehai

yinlingquan

diji

lougu

sanyinjiao

shangqiu

gongsun
taibai
dadu
yinbai

Connects to the
Stomach Channel

Chart A-4: Spleen Channel

5. The Heart Channel

◆ The Heart Channel starts from the heart.

◆ Pertains to the heart.

◆ Communicates with the small intestine and the lungs.

◆ Passes through the aorta, esophagus and the eye.

◆ Qi cycles in from the Spleen Channel to the Heart Channel in the heart.

◆ Qi cycles out from the Heart Channel to the Small Intestine Channel at the *shaochong* (C9) point, located on the lower medial corner of the small fingernail.

jiquan (C1)
qingling (C2)
shaohai (C3)
lingdao (C4)
tongli (C5)
yinxi C6)
shenmen (C7)
shaofu (C8)
shaochong (C9)

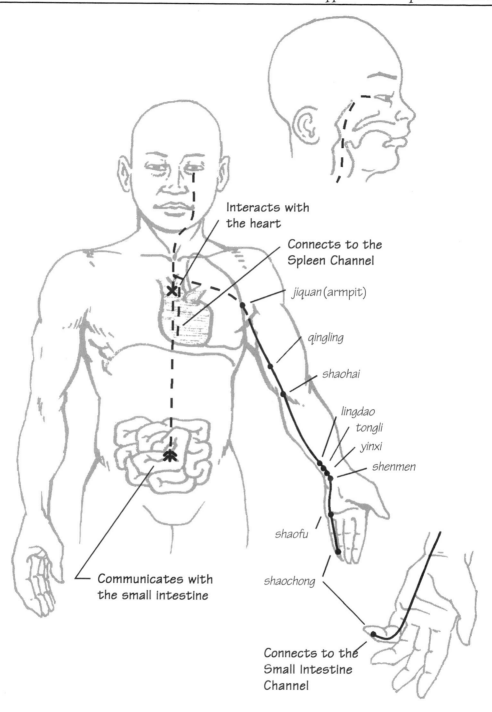

Interacts with
the heart

Connects to the
Spleen Channel

jiquan (armpit)

qingling

shaohai

lingdao

tongli

yinxi

shenmen

Communicates with
the small intestine

shaofu

shaochong

Connects to the
Small Intestine
Channel

Chart A-5: Heart Channel

289

6. The Small Intestine Channel

◆ The Small Intestine Channel starts from the *shaoze* (IT1) point, located on the lateral side of the tip of the small fingernail

◆ Pertains to the small intestine.

◆ Communicates with the heart and stomach.

◆ Passes through the esophagus, eyes, ears, and nose.

◆ Connects to the Urinary Bladder Channel at the *fufen* (VU41), *dashu* (VU11), and *jingming* (VU1) points; to the Gall Bladder at the *tongziliao* (VF1) point; to the Triple Burner at the *heliao-ear* (T22) and *jiaosun* (T20) points; to the Conception Vessel at the *shanzhong* (JM17), *shangwan* (JM13), and *zhongwan* (JM12) points; to the Governing Vessel at the *dashui* (TM14) point.

◆ Qi cycles in from the Heart Channel to the Small Intestine Channel at the *shaochong* (C9) point.

◆ Qi cycles out from the Small Intestine Channel to the Urinary Bladder Channel at the *jingming* (VU1) point, located on the medial corner of the eye.

shaoze (IT1)
qiangu (IT2)
houxi (IT3)
wangu (hand) (IT4)
yanggu (IT5)
yanglao (IT6)
zhizheng (IT7)
xiaohai (IT8)
jianzhen (IT9)
naoshu (IT10)
tianzong (IT11)
bingfeng (IT12)
quyuan (IT13)
jianwaishu (IT14)
jianzhongshu (IT15)
tianchuang (IT16)
tianrong (IT17)
quanliao (IT18)
tinggong (IT19)

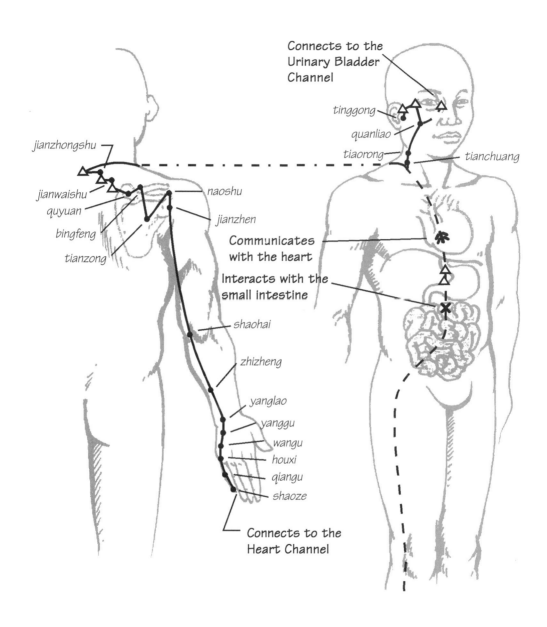

Connects to the
Urinary Bladder
Channel

tinggong

quanliao

tiaorong

tianchuang

jianzhongshu

jianwaishu

quyuan

bingfeng

tianzong

naoshu

jianzhen

Communicates
with the heart

Interacts with the
small intestine

shaohai

zhizheng

yanglao

yanggu

wangu

houxi

qiangu

shaoze

Connects to the
Heart Channel

Chart A-6: Small Intestine Channel

7. The Urinary Bladder Channel

◆ The Urinary Bladder Channel starts from the medial corner of the eye at the *jingming* (VU1) point.

◆ Pertains to the urinary bladder.

◆ Communicates with the brain and kidneys, and all other organs and bowels in the torso cavity.

◆ Passes through the eyes and nose.

◆ Connects to the Gall Bladder Channel at the *linqi-head* (VF15), *shuaigu* (VF8), *tianchong* (VF9), *fubai* (VF10), *qiaoyin-head* (VF11), *wangu-head* (VF12), *qubin* (VF7), and *huantiao* (VF30) points; to the Governing Vessel at the *shenting* (TM24), *baihui* (TM20), *naohu* (TM17), *fengfu* (TM16), *dazhui* (TM14), *taodao* (TM13) points.

◆ Qi cycles in from the Small Intestine Channel to the Urinary Bladder Channel at the *jingming* (VU1) point, located on the inner side of the eye.

◆ Qi cycles out of the Urinary Bladder Channel to the Kidney Channel at the *zhiyin* (VU67) point, located on the lower lateral corner of the small toenail.

jingming (VU1)	ganshu (VU18)	huiyang (VU35)	zhishi (VU52)
zanzhu (VU2)	danshu (VU19)	chengfu (VU36)	baohuang (VU53)
meichong (VU3)	pishu (VU20)	yinmen (VU37)	zhibian (VU54)
quchai (VU4)	weishu (VU21)	fuxi (VU38)	heyang (VU55)
wuchu (VU5)	sanjiaoshu (VU22)	weiyang (VU39)	chengjin (VU56)
chengguang (VU6)	shenshu (VU23)	weizhong (VU40)	chengshan (VU57)
tongtian (VU7)	qihaishu (VU24)	fufen (VU41)	feiyang (VU58)
luoque (VU8)	dachangshu (VU25)	pohu (VU42)	fuyang (VU59)
yuzhen (VU9)	guanyuanshu (VU26)	gaohuang (VU43)	kunlun (VU60)
tianzhu (VU10)	xiaochangshu (VU27)	shentang (VU44)	pushen (VU61)
dashu (VU11)	pangguangshu (VU28)	yixi (VU45)	shenmai (VU62)
fengmen (VU12)	zhonglushu (VU29)	geguan (VU46)	jinmen (VU63)
feishu (VU13)	baihuanshu (VU30)	hunmen (VU47)	jinggu (VU64)
jueyinshu (VU14)	shangliao (VU31)	yanggang (VU48)	shugu (VU65)
xinshu (VU15)	ciliao (VU32)	yishe (VU49)	tonggu (VU66)
dushu (VU16)	zhongliao (VU33)	weicang (VU50)	zhiyin (VU67)
geshu (VU17)	xialiao (VU34)	huangmen (VU51)	

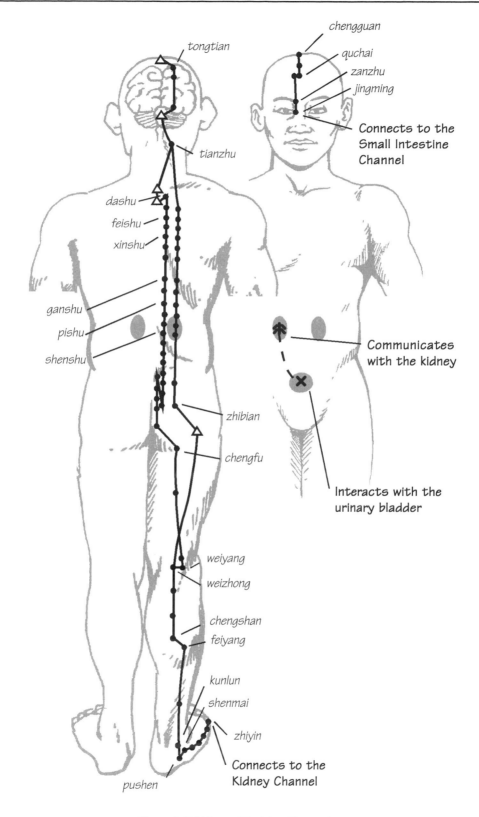

Chart A-7: Urinary Bladder Channel

8. The Kidney Channel

◆ The Kidney Channel starts from the bottom of the small toe towards the *yongquan* (R1) point.

◆ Pertains to the kidneys.

◆ Communicates with the urinary bladder, liver, lungs, heart and the spinal cord.

◆ Passes through the tongue and throat.

◆ Connects to the Spleen Channel at the *sanyinjiao* (LP6) point; to the Governing Vessel at the *changqiang* (TM1) point; to the Conception Vessel at the *zhongji* (JM3), *guanyuan* (JM4), and *shanzhong* (JM17) points.

◆ Qi cycles in from the Urinary Bladder Channel to the Kidney Channel at the *zhiyin* (VU67) point.

◆ Qi cycles out from the Kidney Channel to the Pericardium Channel at the pericardium.

yongquan (R1)	zhongzhu (abdomen) (R15)
rangu (R2)	huangshu (R16)
taixi (R3)	shangqu (R17)
dazhong (R4)	shiguan (R18)
shuiquan (R5)	yindu (R19)
zhaohai (R6)	tonggu (abdomen) (R20)
fuliu (R7)	youmen (R21)
jiaoxin (R8)	bulang (R22)
zhubin (R9)	shenfeng (R23)
yingu (R10)	lingxu (R24)
henggu (R11)	shencang (R25)
dahe (R12)	yuzhong (R26)
qixue (R13)	shufu (R27)
siman (R14)	

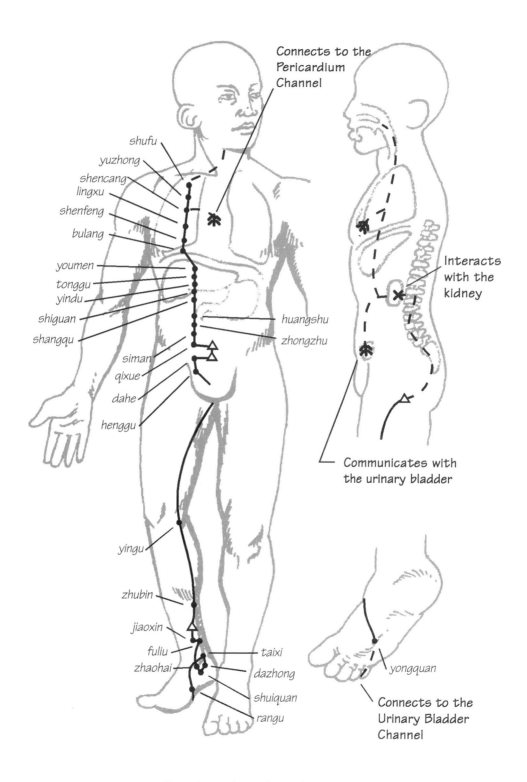

Connects to the
Pericardium
Channel

shufu

yuzhong

shencang

lingxu

shenfeng

bulang

youmen

tonggu

yindu

shiguan

shangqu

siman

qixue

dahe

henggu

huangshu

zhongzhu

Interacts
with the
kidney

Communicates with
the urinary bladder

yingu

zhubin

jiaoxin

fuliu

zhaohai

taixi

dazhong

shuiquan

rangu

yongquan

Connects to the
Urinary Bladder
Channel

Chart A-8: Kidney Channel

295

9. The Pericardium Channel

◆ The Pericardium Channel starts from the pericardium.

◆ Pertains to the pericardium.

◆ Communicates with the Triple Burner.

◆ Qi cycles in from the Kidney Channel to the Pericardium Channel at the pericardium.

◆ Qi cycles out of the Pericardium Channel to the Triple Burner at the *guanchong* (T1) point, located on the lower lateral corner of the fourth fingernail.

> tianchi (PC1)
> tianquan (PC2)
> quze (PC3)
> ximen (PC4)
> jianshi (PC5)
> neiguan (PC6)
> daling (PC7)
> laogong (PC8)
> zhongchong (PC9)

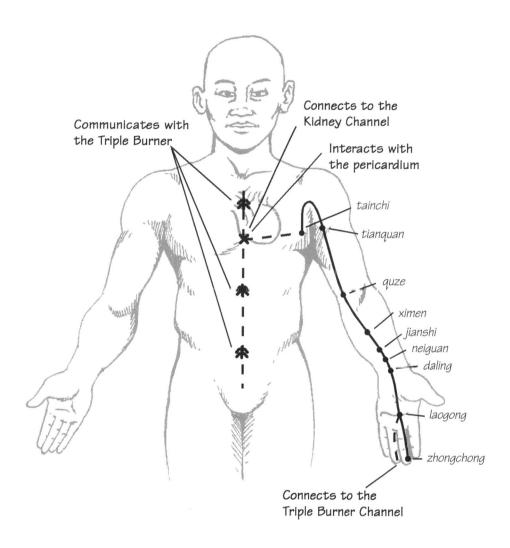

Communicates with
the Triple Burner

Connects to the
Kidney Channel

Interacts with
the pericardium

tainchi

tianquan

quze

ximen

jianshi

neiguan

daling

laogong

zhongchong

Connects to the
Triple Burner Channel

Chart A-9: Pericardium Channel

10. The Triple Burner Channel

◆ The Triple Burner Channel starts at the *guanchong* (T1) point, located at the lower lateral corner of the fourth fingernail.

◆ Pertains to the Triple Burner.

◆ Communicates with the pericardium.

◆ Passes through the ears and eyes.

◆ Connects to the Pericardium Channel at the *tianchi* (PC1) point; to the Small Intestine Channel at the *bingfeng* (IT12), *tinggong* (IT19), *quanliao* (IT18) points; to the Gall Bladder Channel at the *jianjing* (VF21), *fengchi* (VF20), *qiaoyin-head* (VF11), *shangguan* (VF3), *xuanlu* (VF5), *xuanli* (VF6), *hanyan* (VF4), *yangbai* (VF14), *tongziliao* (VF1) points; to the Urinary Bladder Channel at the *dashu* (VU11) point; to the Conception Vessel at the *zhongwan* (JM12), and *shanzhong* (JM17) points; to the Governing Vessel at the *dashui* (TM14) point.

◆ Qi cycles in from the Pericardium Channel to the Triple Burner Channel at the *guanchong* (T1) point, located at the lateral tip of the fourth finger.

◆ Qi cycles out from the Triple Burner to the Gall Bladder Channel at the *tongziliao* (VF1) point, located on the lateral side of the eye.

guanchong (T1)	naohui (T13)
yemen (T2)	jianliao (T14)
zhongzhu (hand) (T3)	tianliao (T15)
yangchi (T4)	tianyou (T16)
waiguan (T5)	yifeng (T17)
zhigou (T6)	qimai (T18)
huizong (T7)	luxi (T19)
sanyangluo (T8)	jiaosun (T20)
sidu (T9)	ermen (T21)
tianjing (T10)	heliao (ear) (T22)
qinglengyuan (T11)	sizhukong (T23)
xiaoluo (T12)	

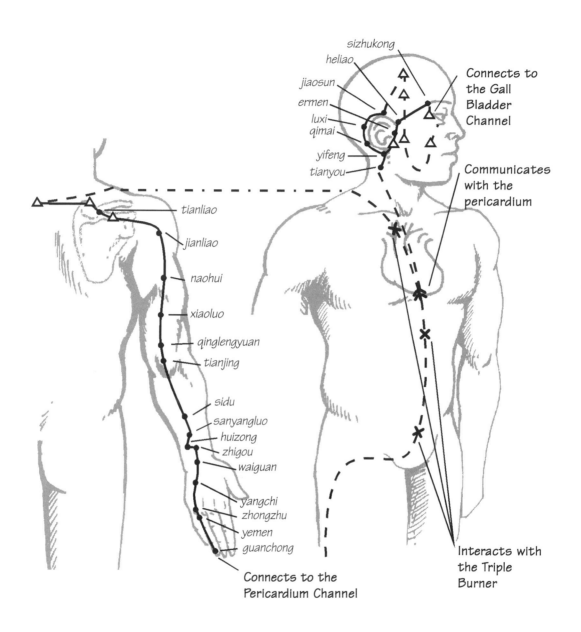

sizhukong
heliao
jiaosun
ermen
luxi
qimai
yifeng
tianyou

Connects to the Gall Bladder Channel

Communicates with the pericardium

tianliao
jianliao
naohui
xiaoluo
qinglengyuan
tianjing
sidu
sanyangluo
huizong
zhigou
waiguan
yangchi
zhongzhu
yemen
guanchong

Connects to the Pericardium Channel

Interacts with the Triple Burner

Chart A-10: Triple Burner Channel

11. The Gall Bladder Channel

◆ The Gall Bladder Channel starts at the *tongziliao* (VF1) point, located on the lateral side of the eye.

◆ Pertains to the gall bladder.

◆ Communicates with the liver.

◆ Passes through the eyes and ears.

◆ Connects to the Stomach Channel at the *touwei* (G8), *xiaguan* (G7), and *renyin* (G9) points; to the Urinary Bladder Channel at the *dashu* (VU11), *shangliao* (31), *zhongliao* (VU33), and *xialiao* (VU34) points; to the Small Intestine Channel at the *tinggong* (IT19) *bingfeng* (IT12), and *tianrong* (IT17) points; to the Triple Burner Channel at the *yifeng* (T17), *jiaosun* (T20), *heliao-ear* (T22), *tianliao* (T15) points; to the Governing Vessel at the *dazhui* (TM14) and *changqiang* (TM1) points; to the Liver Channel at the *zhangmen* (H13) point; to the Pericardium Channel at the *tianchi* (PC1) point.

◆ Qi cycles in from the Triple Burner Channel to the Gall Bladder Channel at the *tongziliao* (VF1) point.

◆ Qi cycles out from the Gall Bladder Channel to the Liver Channel at the *dadun* (H1) point, located on the lower lateral corner of the big toenail.

tongziliao (VF1)	muchuang (VF16)	fengshi (VF31)
tinghui (VF2)	zhengying (VF17)	zhongdu (femur) (VF32)
shangguan (VF3)	chengling (VF18)	xiyangguan (VF33)
hanyan (VF4)	naokong (VF19)	yanglingquan (VF34)
xuanlu (VF5)	fengchi (VF20)	yangjiao (VF35)
xuanli (VF6)	jianjing (VF21)	waiqiu (VF36)
qubin (VF7)	yuanye (VF22)	guanming (VF37)
shuaigu (VF8)	zhejin (VF23)	yangfu (VF38)
tianchong (VF9)	riyue (VF24)	xuanzhong (VF39)
fubai (VF10)	jingmen (VF25)	qiuxu (VF40)
qiaoyin (head) (VF11)	daimai (VF26)	linqi (foot) (VF41)
wangu (head) (VF12)	wushu (VF27)	diwuhui (VF42)
benshen (VF13)	weidao (VF28)	xiaxi (VF43)
yangbai (VF14)	juliao (femur) (VF29)	qiaoyin (foot) (VF44)
linqi (head) (VF15)	huantiao (VF30)	

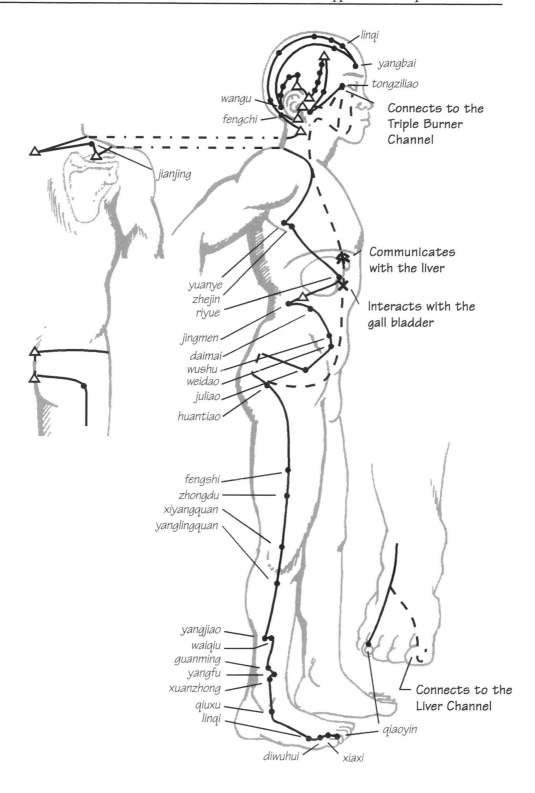

linqi
yangbai
tongziliao
wangu
fengchi

Connects to the Triple Burner Channel

jianjing

Communicates with the liver

Interacts with the gall bladder

yuanye
zhejin
riyue
jingmen
daimai
wushu
weidao
juliao
huantiao

fengshi
zhongdu
xiyangquan
yanglingquan

yangjiao
waiqiu
guanming
yangfu
xuanzhong
qiuxu
linqi
diwuhui
xiaxi

qiaoyin

Connects to the Liver Channel

Chart A-11: Gall Bladder Channel

12. The Liver Channel

◆ The Liver Channel starts at the *dadun* (H1) point, located on the lower lateral corner of the big toenail.

◆ Pertains to the liver.

◆ Communicates with the gall bladder, stomach, and lungs.

◆ Passes through the reproductive organs, throat, eyes, cheeks, and inner side of the lips.

◆ Connects to the Pericardium Channel at the *tianchi* (PC1) point; to the Spleen Channel at the *sanyinjiao* (LP6), *chongmen* (LP12), and *fushe* (LP13) points; to the Conception Vessel at the *qugu* (JM2), *zhongji* (JM3), and *guanyuan* (JM4) points.

◆ Qi cycles in from the Gall Bladder Channel to the Liver Channel at the *dadun* (H1) point, located on the lateral corner of the big toenail.

◆ Qi cycles out of the Liver Channel to the Lung Channel in the lungs.

dadun (H1)
xingjian (H2)
taichong (H3)
zhongfeng (H4)
ligou (H5)
zhongdu (tibia) (H6)
xiguan (H7)
ququan (H8)
yinbao (H9)
zuwuli (H10)
yinlian (H11)
jimai (H12)
zhangmen (H13)
qimen (H14)

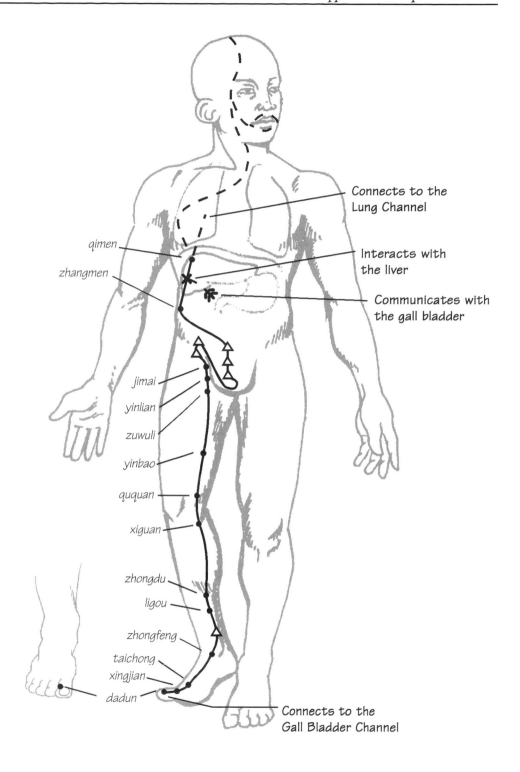

Connects to the
Lung Channel

Interacts with
the liver

Communicates with
the gall bladder

qimen

zhangmen

jimai

yinlian

zuwuli

yinbao

ququan

xiguan

zhongdu

ligou

zhongfeng

taichong

xingjian

dadun

Connects to the
Gall Bladder Channel

Chart A-12: Liver Channel

13. The Governing Vessel

◆ The Governing Vessel starts at the pelvic cavity, emerges at the perineum, and continues up to the *changqiang* (TM1) point.

◆ Communicates with the brain, spinal cord, kidneys, uterus, nose, eyes, mouth and lips.

changqiang (TM1)
yaoshu (TM2)
yaoyangguan (TM3)
mingmen (TM4)
xuanshu (TM5)
jizhong (TM6)
zhongshu (TM7)
jinsuo (TM8)
zhiyang (TM9)
lingtai (TM10)
shendao (TM11)
shenzhu (TM12)
taodao (TM13)
dazhui (TM14)
yamen (TM15)
fengfu (TM16)
naohu (TM17)
qiangjian (TM18)
houding (TM19)
baihui (TM20)
qianding (TM21)
xinhui (TM22)
shangxing (TM23)
shenting (TM24)
suliao (TM25)
renzhong (aka shuigou)
(TM26)
duiduan (TM27)
yinjiao (mouth) (TM28)

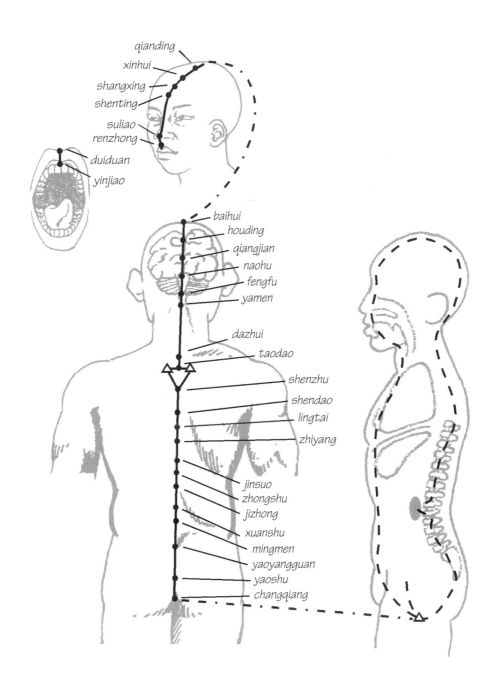

qianding
xinhui
shangxing
shenting
suliao
renzhong
duiduan
yinjiao

baihui
houding
qiangjian
naohu
fengfu
yamen

dazhui
taodao
shenzhu
shendao
lingtai
zhiyang
jinsuo
zhongshu
jizhong
xuanshu
mingmen
yaoyangguan
yaoshu
changqiang

Chart A-13: Governing Vessel

14. The Conception Vessel

◆ The Conception Vessel starts at the pelvic cavity and emerges at the *huiyin* (JM1) point.

◆ Communicates with the eye lids, mouth, lips, and eyes.

huiyin (JM1)
qugu (JM2)
zhongji (JM3)
guanyuan (aka dantian) (JM4)
shimen (JM5)
qihai (JM6)
yinjiao (abdomen) (JM7)
shenque (JM8)
shuifen (JM9)
xiawan (JM10)
jianli (JM11)
zhongwan (JM12)
shangwan (JM13)
juque (JM14)
jiuwei (JM15)
zhongting (JM16)
shanzhong (JM17)
yutang (JM18)
zigong (chest) (JM19)
huagai (JM20)
xuanji (JM21)
tiantu (JM22)
lianquan (JM23)
chengjiang (JM24)

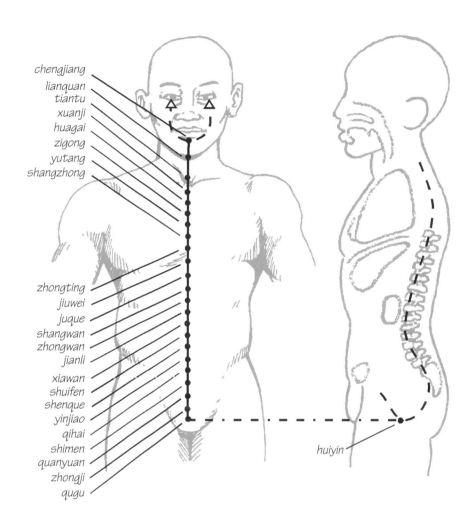

chengjiang
lianquan
tiantu
xuanji
huagai
zigong
yutang
shangzhong

zhongting
jiuwei
juque
shangwan
zhongwan
jianli
xiawan
shuifen
shenque
yinjiao
qihai
shimen
quanyuan
zhongji
qugu

huiyin

Chart A-13: Conception Vessel

15. Thrusting Vessel

◆ The Thrusting Vessel starts at the *qichong* (G30) point.

◆ Communicates with the eye lids, uterus, kidneys, mouth, lips, and eyes.

16. Girdle Vessel

◆ The Girdle Vessel starts at the floating rib and connects to the *daimai* (VF26), *wushu* (VF27), and *weidao* (VF28) points.

◆ Communicates with the kidneys and the reproductive organs.

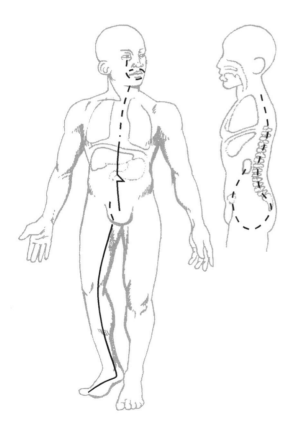

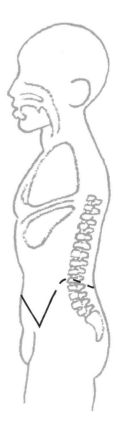

Chart A-15: Thrusting Vessel   Chart A-16: Girdle Vessel

17. Yang-Activation Vessel

◆ The Yang Activation Vessel starts at the lateral side of the heel.

◆ Communicates with the brain, eyes, and mouth.

◆ Connects to the Urinary Bladder Channel at the *shenmai* (VU62), *pushen* (VU61), *fuyang* (VU59), and *jingming* (VU1) points; to the Gall Bladder Channel at the *juliao-femur* (VF29) point; to the Stomach Channel at the *dicang* (G4), *juliao-face* (G3), and *chengqi* (G1) points; to the Large Intestine Channel at the *jianyu* (IC15) and *jugu* (IC16) points; to the Small Intestine Channel at the *naoshu* (IT10) point.

18. Yin-Activation Vessel

◆ The Yin-Activation Vessel starts at the medial side of the heel.

◆ Communicates with the brain, eyes, and the reproductive organs.

◆ Connects to the Kidney Channel at the *zhaohai* (R6), *jiaoxin* (R8) points; to the Urinary Bladder Channel at the *jingming* (VU1) point.

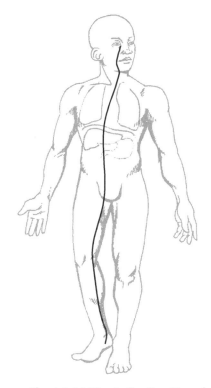

Chart A-17: Yang-Activation Vessel   Chart A-18: Yin-Activation Vessel

19. Yang-Maintenance Vessel

◆ The Yang-Maintenance Vessel starts at the convergence of the Yang Channels.

◆ Connects to the Gall Bladder Channel at the *yangjiao* (VF35), *riyue* (VF24), *jianjing* (VF21), *fengchi* (VF20), *naokong* (VF19), *zhengying* (VF17), *muchuang* (VF16), *linqi-head* (VF15), *yangbai* (VF14), and *benshen* (VF13) points; to the Stomach Channel at the *touwei* (G8) point; to the Small Intestine Channel at the *naoshu* (IT10) point; to the Triple Burner Channel at the *tianliao* (T15) and *naohui* (T13) points; to the Large Intestine Channel at the *binao* (IC14) point; and to the Governing Vessel at the *fengfu* (TM16) and *yamen* (TM15) points.

20. Yin-Maintenance Vessel

◆ The Yin-Maintenance Vessel starts at the convergence of the Yin Channels.

◆ Connects to the Kidney Channel at the *zhubin* (R9) point; to the Spleen Channel at the *chongmen* (LP12), *fushe* (LP13), *daheng* (LP15), and *fuai* (LP16) points; to the Liver Channel at the *qimen* (H14) point; to the Conception Vessel at the *tiantu* (JM22) and *lianquan* (JM23) points.

 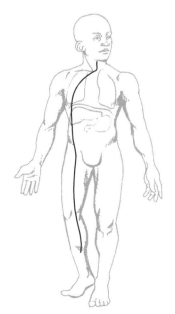

Chart A-19: Yang-Maintenance Vessel   Chart A-20: Yin-Maintenance Vessel

Appendix B:

Corrective Methods

During qigong training, if a practitioner is overeager in trying to attain certain qigong sensations, training without proper guidance, or training improperly, some problems may occur. The Corrective Methods are techniques to remedy problems that result from improper qigong training.

The qigong methods introduced in this book are presented in their proper sequential steps with the training requirements outlined. As long as you follow the requirements and let your progress take its natural course, you will not have any problems. From the many years of experience in which the authors have been teaching the qigong methods presented in this book, there have not been any problems. They have, however, encountered many practitioners with qigong problems from practicing other qigong improperly and had to help them correct the problems.

Many of these people had problems due to a lack of understanding the qigong methods they were practicing, they were too eager, and/or too stubborn in their learning approach. Some individuals had problems because they were practicing methods presented in movies, television, and Chinese martial arts novels. They failed to realize that information presented in movies, TV, and novels are only stories. Even though many of the training methods presented in those mediums make sense, they are not intended as instructional materials.

In China, there were actual cases of people that followed the methods they read in novels about superhuman feats, and resulted in life threatening injuries or death. Some blindly followed novels and improperly fasted for many days as a way to reach an understanding of the Dao (Tao), to reach enlightenment, or to become immortal. Many died of starvation because of improper fasting methods. There were also cases of people training *Iron Shirt*, *Golden Bell Cover*, or *Spiritual Striking* methods without proper guidance, and resulted in serious bodily injuries or death.

Improper training can also result in a cold body, constant shivering, exhaustion, and/or a mental breakdown. Cases of death or serious injuries due to unwise attempts to do superhuman tasks were not unheard of in China. These results are generally due to a lack of proper guidance — students not following the instructor's guidance, due to stubbornness, and overeagerness, and/or searching for what is insignificant and not present.

It is imperative that you study from a knowledgeable qigong instructor. Don't be stubborn and don't pursue any strange or odd sensations. Simply let your training take its natural course. So long as you follow and respond naturally and exercise common sense, you will not have any problem.

However, if problems should occur, you will need to know how to correct it. The correction or amending method is also known as Daoyin. Daoyin uses the mind and the movements of the body to lead qi back to the origin. It consists of two components, the Internal Scenery and the External Scenery Daoyin methods. Internal Scenery Daoyin method uses a set of exercise patterns that circulate, calm, and return the qi to the origin. External Scenery Daoyin method usually requires that an assistant administer cavity presses to regulate, calm, and return scattered qi.

The following are some common problem areas and conditions, and the ways to correct them:

1. Forehead

During training, some people may feel qi stagnation in the forehead and are unable to get it to flow downward. It feels like a medicated plaster is sticking to the forehead. The way to correct this problem is to relax and let the stagnating qi dissipate. Place your thumbs on your eye bridge and the other fingers on the back of your head. Next push your thumbs towards your *Taiyang* points (temple) and massage 3 to 5 times in a circular pattern in each direction. Repeat the push and massage technique about 10 times. This will allow the stagnating qi to release from your *Taiyang* points.

Then put both index or middle fingers on the upper inside corner of the eye. Massage it for a few seconds, then massage the upper inside corner of your eyebrow. This will smooth out the stagnation of qi in your forehead.

2. Top of the Head

Some people may have qi stagnating on the top of their head and are unable to circulate it down. It feels like you have a hat on the top of your head or the top of head is aching and swelling. To remedy this problem, use your thumbs to push down while making a half turn on your *baihui* and release. Stabilize your thumbs by positioning your index fingers under your thumbs, before pushing down with your thumbs. This technique is known as the Duck's Beak Technique.

3. Back of the Head

Some people may not have strong enough qi to circulate through the Jade Pillow Gate during the Microcosmic and Macrocosmic Circulation training. If you have this problem, place your attention on the top of your head and use your mind to lead the qi up, to pass through the Jade Pillow Gate. Once through, stop using this technique.

4. The Sideburn Area

Some people may feel qi stagnating at their sideburn area and are unable to move it forward or backward; and have a swelling, and a slight aching feeling. Sometimes qi is stuck on both sides; sometimes just on one side. To remedy this problem, squeeze your thumb and index fingers together and push on the area of stagnation. Vibrate your fingers twenty to thirty times. Do this only once. This technique is known as the Crane's Beak Technique.

5. Head Shaking

Some people when they enter into a meditative state, their body will begin shaking uncontrollably. The turning of their neck may even go beyond what is naturally possible, as far back, as facing back. If you have this problem, place your middle fingers in your ears and gently turn your head forward, then to the sides, a couple of times. Next vibrate your fingers to make a drumming sound inside your ears. Then pull your fingers out rapidly. This will stop the shaking of your head. Practicing this technique daily can also help refresh your head.

6. Dizziness

Some people may feel dizzy or sleepy during training. If this happens, the practitioner should stop the training and take a nap. Wait until you don't feel tired before resuming practice.

7. Loss of Control of Body Movements

In some of the qi activation training exercises, your body will move or vibrate by itself. Some people may even dance, jump, perform fluid Taijiquan, smile, laugh, or even cry. This is due to the redistribution and rebalancing of your qi, by releasing worries and/or unpleasant tensions from your body. Don't be scared. These are your body's normal reactions. The movements will stop by itself after a short while. While listening to a qigong master who lectures with qi emission, some people may also move, due to the qi interactions between the master and the student.

All these automatic movements can be controlled by you. When you want to stop the movements, simply use your mind to stop the movements. The movements will gradually stop. Some training doesn't want you to use your mind to stop the movements. This type of training requires that you allow your body to stop the movements by itself, to completely finish a training session.

There are, however, a small number of individuals that may be unable to stop the movements for several hours. This is an indication of loss of control. To remedy this problem, you can do the steps below or ask a partner to apply techniques on your *quchi, hegu, dazhui,* and *jianjing* points.

Step 1. Use your thumb and index or middle fingers to grab on to your *quchi* point on your right arm. Then grab a hold of the thick tendon, lift it up and then let it go. (*Quchi* is located on the outside tip of the elbow line when you bend your elbow.)

Step 2. Use your left thumb and index or middle fingers of one hand to grab onto your *hegu* point. Then hold onto the tendon, rub and pull it before you release your hold. (*Hegu* is located on the back of your palm between the shaft of your index finger and thumb.)

Step 3. Next repeat Steps 1 and 2 on the left arm and hand. It is important that you start with your right arm, then left arm. This is because the right arm is where the *lung-qi* enters. After you have stabilized the qi in your right arm, the left arm will respond and stop moving. Then apply the technique on your left arm and hand to even the qi and blood.

At times, your partner may also need to grab a hold of, push on, and massage your *dazhui* and *jianjing* points. (*Dazhui* is located between the 7th cervical vertebra and the 1st thoracic vertebra. *Jianjing* points are located on either side of the shoulder, midway between your *dazhui* point and the edge of the shoulder.)

8. Chills or Heat in the Chest or Back

If you should feel an unbearable heat sensation on your back or in your chest during sitting meditation, regulate your body temperature by opening your mouth and make the *ha* sound as you exhale (as many times as necessary). This will gradually reduce the heat sensation in your body or eliminate the problem.

If you should feel chills and or shivering, make the *om* sound as you exhale. This will invigorate your qi and spread it throughout your back and chest, and up to your head. All seven openings (mouth, tongue, two eyes, two ears, and nose) on your head will be filled with harmonious *yang-qi*, and chilliness eliminated.

Individuals that feel a qi burning sensation all over their body, a dry mouth, and dry hot lips are experiencing symptoms resulting from qi knots. Some individuals may be burned to the point that their eyes are red and body filled with excess qi. To remedy this problem stop training and lie down. Relax your body and do Relaxation Qigong to dissipate the heat. Heat will naturally reduce.

To help others with this condition, locate the two *xinshu* points and the two *geshu* points on the individual's back. Push your thumbs into the points at the same time and use the other four fingers to grab a hold of the tendon next to the points. Then pull and rub the tendon, before releasing your hold. Repeat

3 to 4 times. This will adjust the chill or heat sensations due to an imbalance of *yin-yang*. The individual will feel very comfortable. Then press your index and middle fingers on the individual's *dazhui* point. Use your qi to release the individual's fire down his or her spine to reduce the heat.

(*Xinshu* points are located at the level of the 5th thoracic vertebra, two finger widths from the centerline of the spine, one on each side. The *geshu* points are located at the level of the 7th thoracic vertebra, two finger widths from the centerline of the spine, one on each side. The *dazhui* point is located between the 7th cervical vertebra and the 1st thoracic vertebra.)

10. Qi Thrusting with Breath

During training, some individuals may feel qi thrusting in and out of their body with their breathing. It may feel like a snake thrusting out of your mouth one to two meters away, during exhalation, and thrusting back into your *dantian*, during inhalation. To stop this problem, push your middle finger on your *quepen* point and vibrate your finger. Then move your middle fingers back and forth on the tendon next to the *quepen* point. Stop training the qigong that caused this problem. Don't do it anymore. (*Quepen* is located on the midpoint of the indentation above the collar bone.)

11. Qi Knots in the Dantian

Some people visualize and pay attention to their *dantian* with too strong a focus. They look for qi sensations with excessive eagerness. After training, due to the excessive focus of qi at the *dantian*, qi is unable to dissipate. This may cause a swelling of the abdomen. Serious cases may even cause lower abdominal pain and digestive problems. To correct the problem associated with qi knots, the most important emphasis is on relaxation, releasing qi, and using your mind along with hand techniques to lead the qi.

Step 1. If this happens, gently press the middle finger of your right hand on your *dantian*. Then use your mind to lead the stagnating qi down, as you push down with your finger. In a little while, you will feel qi begin to flow down, and you will let out gas. The swelling of your abdomen will naturally reduce.

Step 2. If you are unable to correct the problem yourself, another method will be necessary. Ask someone that can emit qi (your instructor) to use their thumbs and index fingers to pull on the tendons on both sides of your belly button. The instructor can use his or her qi to lead your qi outward. When you hear sounds from gas releasing, the swelling in your stomach will reduce and return to normal.

12. Qi Leakage

Some people feel qi leaking out their urethral orifice and anus during training. If this situation persists after a period of training and is not corrected, qi will still leak out of their body even when they are not training. Even though there is no grave danger associated with the leakage, it could cause frequent seminal emission which could affect their vitality.

Step 1. Have the individual with this problem lie down. Push your middle finger into his or her navel. Start with your palm facing down, then rotate your palm until facing up. Keep rotating your palm facing up to facing down, several times, while maintaining constant contact between your middle finger and the individual's navel.

Step 2. Locate the Yangjiao Gate on the gap between the first and the second section of your sacrum. Continuously push down with your index or middle finger on that spot, until the spot feels sore and aching.

Step 3. Individuals with this problem should regularly rub their hands together until they are warm. Then place their palms on their *mingmen* point. Let the warmth of your palms enter into your *mingmen* point, while holding up the *huiyin* area gently.

12. Constant Erection

If you become sexually aroused during training and have an erection and the erection persists even when you are not training, grab the second joint on your fourth finger with the thumb and index finger of the other hand. Move your thumb back and forth on the second joint of your fourth finger. You will feel the tiny tendons on the medial side of your fourth finger, and slight pain being generated. This technique can help dissipate the fire in you and correct the problem of a constant erection.

13. Numb Legs from Crossed Leg Meditation

Beginners are often faced with the problem of numb legs from sitting crossed leg during meditation. With practice the numbness will gradually reduce and cease. However, some beginners may have unbearable numbness and can not walk for several minutes, after meditating. If this should happen to you, use your hands to stretch your legs from the crossed position. Put your shoes on and place a pen or pencil like object in your shoe on the inside edge of your foot and your shoe, towards the middle of your foot. When the pen is inserted, you will feel the numbness reduce from your legs, one section at a time. Next, insert the pen in your other shoe.

Appendix C:

Glossary

This glossary contains many of the important terms used in this volume. Most of the terms are translations from Chinese. The terms used in this volume are translated to the closest English meaning possible. Some terms are used directly, and are romanized into the Roman alphabet. There are several different standards used in the romanization of Chinese characters to the Roman alphabet. They include *pinyin*, Wade-Giles, Yale, Gouyu, and Hong Kong. The romanization system used in this volume is the *pinyin* system. *Pinyin* is the official romanization system of the People's Republic of China which was adopted in the 1950's. It is now widely adopted and accepted in China and abroad. The pinyin system of romanization is generally more phonetically spelled than other romanization systems.

China is a vast country with over fifty ethnic groups. Each group has their unique dialects of Chinese. Even though the dialects may differ from one region of China to the next, the written language is the same. In the pinyin romanization of the Chinese characters, we have used the official dialect, Mandarin — *putonghua* or *guoyu*. When there is another commonly used romanization that differs from the pinyin spelling, it is usually placed in parenthesis next to the pinyin romanization. If you should have any confusion regarding the romanization of the Chinese characters using the other systems, look up the term in this glossary. It will direct you to the romanization used under the pinyin system. For individuals that can read Chinese characters, we have included most of the Chinese characters in this glossary. The characters are placed next to the translated terms or the pinyin, in alphabetical order.

Unlike the common English way of writing and addressing people by their name, Chinese surnames are placed ahead of the given name. This sometimes causes confusion to readers. Many people are unable to tell which is the first name and which is the surname. Most Chinese names are three syllables long, one for the surname and two for the first name. There are, of course, exceptions. The given name (first name) is either romanized with a hyphen (-) with each of the syllables in the given name capitalized; or is lumped together in romanized form with only the first letter capitalized. Although Chinese names all have a significant meaning to the individual, each syllable in the name can be a word. The combination of syllables could add to the meaning of the individual words, or have a totally different meaning than if written separately or in a different context.

A

Absorb Qi to Make up for the Leakage 探氣補漏法 A qigong method.

Achieving Through Dreams 夢觀成就法 A Buddhist Qigong method.

Achieving Through Middle Yin 中陰成就法 A Buddhist Qigong method.

Achieving Through Pure Light 淨光成就法 A Buddhist Qigong method.

Achieving Through Reverse View 轉識成就法 A Buddhist Qigong method.

Achieving Through Spiritual Flame 靈熱成就法 A Buddhist Qigong method.

Achieving Through Visualization 幻觀成就法 A Buddhist Qigong method.

Achok Trungpa (Azong Zhuba) 阿宗竹巴上師 The lama of Angzang Temple in Sichuan Province, who taught The Great Perfection — The Heart Essence Buddhist Qigong method.

acupuncture 針治 A traditional Chinese healing method whereby needles are inserted into specific points on the acupuncture channels and vessels to assist the patient in balancing their qi.

acupuncture chart A chart indicating the qi pathways and points.

acupuncture point 穴位 A location on the qi pathways where there is either a high concentration of qi, a major passageway of energy, or a location for nourishing or draining qi.

Apparent Virtue 顯德 Virtue that is visible to others, and rewarded with material and/ or verbal gratitude, and even exchange of energy.

Armor Protection from Negative Energies 披甲護身法 A Buddhist Qigong method.

Arrow Technique 射息 A term used in Precious Vessel Qigong.

aura An emanation or manifestation of energy; can be perceived as colors by gifted and trained individuals.

Avalokiteshvara 觀世音 The Bodhisattva of compassion.

B

Baopuzi 抱朴子 1. Another name of Ge Hong. 2. A book on alchemy, diets, and mystical practices.

Basic Relaxation Technique 放鬆功 A qigong technique used for relaxation.

biological midnight 正子時 In the evening during the end of extreme yin energy and the beginning of rising yang energy; in a healthy male, it is indicated by the stiffening of his sexual organ, without sexual thoughts.

bowels 腑 Refers to the gall bladder, stomach, large intestine, small intestine, urinary bladder, and Triple Burner; organs that transform food into jing, but do not store them.

branches 絡脈 The sub-channels of the 12 acupuncture channels, the Conception Vessel, and the Governing Vessel: including the 12 branches of the acupuncture channels, plus one branch from the Conception Vessel, one branch from the Governing Vessel, and an additional one from the Spleen Channel. There are a total of 15 main branches.

Brief Introduction to Rainbow Body Documentary of Tibetan Buddhism 《西藏佛教虹化事遺簡介》 A book mentioned in this volume.

Brimming the Breath 滿息 A term used in Precious Vessel Qigong.

bubbling well 湧泉 A translation of the yongquan point on the Kidney Channel.

Buddha 佛〔覺者〕1. It literally means awakened, developed, and enlightened. 2. Sakyamuni.

buddhahood Enlightenment, realization; the attainment of Buddha.

Buddhism 佛教 A religion originating in ancient India, from the teachings of the first Buddha, Sakyamuni.

Buddhist A person who follows the Buddhist philosophy in their life and pursuit of greater understanding.

Buddhist Qigong 佛家氣功 1. Energy cultivation for health, healing, longevity, and spiritual cultivation developed by the Buddhist society. 2. Energy cultivation methods to assist individuals in purifying the three karma causing sources to attain enlightenment.

C

cavity (see acupuncture point)

Chan 禪 A Buddhist practice following the Sutrayana practices of Mahayana Vehicle.

chakra (see energy center)

channels 經 1. In TCM, it refers to the qi pathways that connect to the organs internally and extend to the limbs externally, and have accessible acupuncture points on the surface of the body along the pathways, 12 in all. 2. In Buddhist Qigong, it refers to one of the three energy pathways: the Middle, Left, and Right Channels

Chuang Tzu (see Zhuangzi) Wade-Giles romanization of Zhuangzi

Chi Kung (see qigong) Wade-Giles romanization of qigong.

Clearing Technique 失 A term used in Precious Vessel Qigong

collateral 絡 The smaller net like energy pathways, branching out from the main energy pathways.

Conception Vessel 任脈 One of the Eight Extraordinary Vessels in the human body.

Converting Bone Marrow to Qi 練神還虛髓化炁 A qigong method.

creative midnight 活子時 An ideal condition achieved by an individual for Microcosmic circulation.

Cross Space Power Qigong 空勁功 A qigong method.

Crown Energy Center 頂輪 One of the seven energy centers involved in Tantric Buddhist

Qigong, located on the soft spot on top of the head.

D

dampness 濕 1. One of the six atmospheric influences on the body. 2. The retention of water due to impaired water circulation and distribution.

dantian 丹田 1. A qi center in the area within the lower abdomen; inside-dantian 2. Guanyuan point; outside-dantian. 3. Inside of the head; upper-dantian. 4. Energy center.

Dao 道 1. Nature Wisdom. 2. The Way. 3. A reluctantly used term to refer to Origin, the Source, and the Law of the cosmos. 4. Void, Emptiness, Undefinable. 5. The path which one walks and experiences. The Chinese character for Dao is sometimes written in the calligraphic form that resembles a human footprint, implying that the Dao is the experience on one's journey in life.

Daodejing 道德經 A philosophical text written by Laozi; it is regarded as one of the most influential books ever written in the history of human civilization. This book contains two parts: Dao and De. Dao and De are one with different explanations — "when Dao is in me, it is De". "De is the foundation of Dao." That is, if one wishes to attain the Dao, one must first accumulate abundance of De. Literally, De can be translated as morality or virtue. Both Dao and De are the principles of Daoism. They are the focal points of Daoist belief and actions.

Daoist 道士 1. A person who follows the Daoist School of Thought in their thinking and action. 2. A person who believes in the Daoist Religion and follows its beliefs and rituals. 3. A person with high moral values who has accomplished a definite understanding in the pursuit of the Dao.

Daoist Qigong 道家氣功 1. Energy cultivation for health, healing, and longevity developed by the Daoist society. 2. An energy cultivation that attempts to figure out the mystery of life and its relationship with nature, so as to attain the highest possible goal of existence. 3. Energy cultivation that fosters the practitioner's jing into qi, qi into shen, and shen into the Void, and finally shatter the Void to become one with the Dao.

daojiao 道教 1. Use the Dao to teach. 2. Daoist Religion.

Daoyin 導引 1. Guiding and stretching; methods used to guide qi to achieve harmony. 2. Another name for qigong. 3. Methods used to correct problems resulting from improper practice.

Dapeng Qigong (see Emei Dapeng Qigong)

deficient-yin 陰虛 Usually refers to a condition of the kidney, associated with the production of internal heat. Some of the common symptoms are low fever, feverishness of the palms and soles, furless tongue, and fine and rapid pulse.

Distributing the Breath 均息 A term used in Precious Vessel Qigong.

Dongmi 東密 A subdivision within Japanese Tantric Buddhism.

Dorsal Gate 夾脊 The second of the Three Gates located on the back between the shoulder blades.

dou 斗 A peck, Chinese unit of dry measurement approximately equal to 10 pints.

E

Eight Extraordinary Vessel Circulation 奇經八脈 A qigong method.

Eighteen Sensory Levels 色界十八天 The more definitive term referring to the Middle Planes. These levels are visible to the human eye; consist of senses but no desire; no yin and yang interaction; and spirit is able to evolve.

Emei 峨嵋 Refers to Emei Mountain, located in Sichuan Province, it is the highest mountain within Sichuan Province, with an elevation of 3,099 meters; well-known as a Buddhist, qigong, and martial arts center in China.

Emei Dapeng Qigong 峨嵋大鵬氣功 A qigong training that develops incredible

physical and energetic potential in the practitioners for health, as well as, for martial arts. It was passed down from the Emei Mountain area, and is one of Master Shou-Yu Liang's many areas of expertise. Master Liang learned this qigong from his grandfather beginning at age 6.

Emei Dapeng Qigong was passed down from General Yue Fei (1103-1142 A.D.) during the Song Dynasty. Yue Fei was one of the most respected people, patriot, and martial artist in Chinese history. Yue Fei's teacher, Master Zhou Tong, was the most famous martial arts teacher at the time. Most of his students later became highly accomplished generals or respected martial arts heroes. While Yue Fei was in his youth and studying under Zhou Tong, Zhou Tong introduced him to a Buddhist hermit to study Dapeng Qigong. The amazing power and abilities of Yue Fei were attributed to his training in Dapeng Qigong.

Dapeng is a great big bird that lived in ancient China. Legend has it, that Dapeng was the guardian that stayed above the head of the first Buddha, Sakyamuni. Dapeng could get rid of all evil in any area. Even the Monkey King was no match for it. During the Song Dynasty the government was corrupt and foreigners were constantly invading China. Sakyamuni sent Dapeng down to earth to protect China. Dapeng descended to earth and was born as Yue Fei.

Yue Fei began learning martial arts in his early childhood from Zhou Tong, mastering many martial arts systems and all 18 primary weapons. He was a fighting champion in all of China in his youth. He joined the military as a low rank soldier and became the Commander in Chief of the armed forces after numerous victories in protecting the nation from foreign invaders. There are many legends and novels written about Yue Fei. Many of the well-known martial arts styles available today are also credited to have been passed down by Yue Fei. Some of these stories about Yue Fei are just legends, which may or may not be true. However, Yue Fei was a real historical figure in Chinese history, who was loved and respected by all.

Dapeng Qigong seems to be indigenous to Sichuan Province. In Master Liang's extensive travels throughout China, he is yet to see this qigong training in any other part of China, nor has he seen it in any writing on the training of Dapeng Qigong. Even in Sichuan Province, it is a well-guarded training method for a few.

The complete name for Dapeng Qigong is *Clearing the Impurity Dapeng Qigong.* Clearing the Impurity refers to the training that absorbs the pure essence of the universe and eliminates impurities from the body. There are a total of 12 parts in this training. Every part includes several movements. It will generally take an individual about 2 hours to complete each session of the training, many people are unable to last. Due to the length and extensive nature of this training, to write it down would result in a book by itself. The authors have decided not to include this training in this volume. Individuals interested in this training should contact the authors.

Emei Dragon Qigong 峨嵋龍形氣功 Qigong training derived from the Emei Mountain area.

Emei Fire Dragon Rotating Qi Ball 峨嵋火龍氣功滾球法 A qigong method.

endogenous causes 內因 An internal pathogenic influence, referring mainly to emotional trauma; including excesses of joy, anger, pensiveness, worry, sorrow, fear, and shock.

energy center 氣輪 A location in or on the body with a high concentration of energy.

Esoteric Abilities of the Body 身密 The training that utilizes hand and body seals to unlock the hidden abilities within and achieve a union of human and cosmos, and attain realization.

Esoteric Abilities of the Mind 意密 The training that utilizes visualization to purify the mind.

Esoteric Abilities of the Speech 口密 The training that sincerely recites the mantra of

realization to attain unlimited merit; when chanting mantras, the sound wave of the chant also makes the energy in the body respond to it.

excess-fire 上火 Excessive internal heat with symptoms such as, constipation, and inflammation of the nasal and oral cavity.

excessive symptom-complex 實證 It is a result of an infection due to external pathogenic factors or by the accumulation of pathologic products due to a dysfunction of the organs.

exogenous causes 外因 External pathogenic influence, referring mainly to wind, cold, heat, dampness, dryness, and fire.

Extending the Wings 展翅式 A term used in Wushu Qigong.

External Binding Seal 外縛印 The fifth of the Nine Esoteric Seals, represented by the character Jie.

External Lion Seal 外獅子印 The third of the Nine Esoteric Seals, represented by the character Dou.

F

Final Level 大羅天 One of the Four Infinite Levels.

fire-qi 火氣 A manifestation of intense heat such as, a flushed face, bloodshot eyes, etc.

Five Element Theory 五行學說 1. A theory used to explain the characteristics, classifications, and the law of mutual nourishment and mutual restraint. 2. In TCM, it is used to expound on the unity of the human body and the environment, and the physiological and pathological relationship between the internal organs.

Five Unit of Rice Dao 五斗米道 The first religious organization that used the *Daodejing* as the theoretical foundation for their beliefs.

Four Enlightened Levels 四梵天 The levels of spirit evolution beyond the Three Planes.

Four Infinite Levels 聖境四天 The levels of spirit evolution beyond the Four Enlightened Levels.

Four Mental Levels 無色界四天 The more definitive term referring to the Upper Plane. These levels are not visible to the human eye and there are no physical forms, desires or emotions, only pure mentality.

Foster Jing into Qi 練精化氣 A stage in Daoist Qigong training.

Foster Qi into Shen 練氣化神 A stage in Daoist Qigong training.

Foster Shen into Void 練神還虛 A stage in Daoist Qigong training. In this stage of training, one is attempting to transcend duality, in a state of Wuji, back to the Dao.

Full Lotus 蓮花坐 A sitting meditation posture where an individual crosses his or her legs with their feet facing up.

Fourteen Meridian Circulation 十四經功法 A qigong method.

G

Gall Bladder Channel 足少陽膽經 An abbreviation for the Foot Minimum Yang Gall Bladder Channel.

Gathering Qi Method 聚氣法 A Daoist Qigong method.

Gathering Spirit Method 聚靈法 A Daoist Qigong method.

Ge Hong 葛洪 (281-341 A.D.) The author of *Baopuzi*; a famous physician and well-known alchemist.

Gelug 格魯派（黃教）A tradition under Tibetan Tantric Buddhism; the Yellow Sect.

genuine-qi 眞氣 The combination of innate-qi with acquired-qi serving as the dynamic force of all vital functions.

Genuine Virtue 眞德 Natural and uncontrived, without any formulated mental process. The genuine and natural expression of the harmony of Dao and De.

Girdle Vessel 帶脈 One of the Eight Extraordinary Vessels in the human body.

Golden Bell Cover 金鐘罩 Another name for Iron Shirt.

Golden Light Method 金光法 A Daoist Qigong method.

Golden Ox Lows the Field 金牛耕地 A term used in Wushu Qigong.

gong 功 1. The power to produce an effect. 2. An attainment or an accomplishment that is achieved with steady practice.

gongfu 功夫 1. Chinese martial arts. 2. An attainment gained through the input of time and energy into a particular discipline.

Governing Vessel 督脈 One of the Eight Extraordinary Vessels in the human body.

Grand Purity Level 太清境 One of the Four Infinite Levels.

Great Cosmos 天地（宇宙）1. The universe. 2. The complete, orderly, and harmonious universe.

Great Grand Purity Level 上清境 One of the Four Infinite Levels.

Great Luminosity of the Cosmos 宇宙明點 A term used in Buddhist Qigong cultivation.

Great Vajrasattva Seal 大金鋼輪印 The second of the Nine Esoteric Seals, represented by the character Bin.

guardian-qi 衛氣 The energy that permeates on the surface of the body, functions as the superficial layer of resistance against external pathogenic influences.

H

Half Lotus 半蓮花坐 A sitting meditation posture where an individual crosses one leg over the other leg.

Heart Channel 手少陰心經 An abbreviation for the Hand Minimum Yin Heart Channel.

Heart Energy Center 心輪 One of the seven energy centers involved in Tantric Buddhist Qigong, located around the heart.

heart-fire 心火 The flaring up of fire in the heart, which may cause ulcers on the tongue, irritability, insomnia, etc.

heart-qi 心氣 The energy that flows in the Heart Channel.

Hinayana 小乘 One of the two vehicles in Buddhism; with its motivation emphasis placed on an individual's own liberation.

Historical Records 史記 The official Chinese historical record with historical information beginning from the Yellow Emperor (2697-2597 B.C.) to the Earlier Han Dynasty (206 B.C.-7 A.D.).

Holding the Heaven 托天式 A term used in Wushu Qigong.

Huang Zhe-Xi 黃哲西 Master Shou-Yu Liang's mother.

Huimu 慧目 Eye of wisdom; another descriptive term for Huizhong.

Huizhong 慧中 The center of wisdom, located at the indentation of the forehead right above the eye bridge.

I

Immovable Foundation Seal 不動根本印 The first of the Nine Esoteric Seals, represented by the character Lin.

insufficiency symptom-complex 虛證 Deficiency of yin (vital essence), yang (vital function), qi and blood caused by prolonged illness.

Intensive Iron Shirt Qigong 速成鐵布衫功法 A qigong method.

Internal Binding Seal 內縛印 The sixth of the Nine Esoteric Seals, represented by the character Zhen.

Internal Lion Seal 內獅子印 The fourth of the Nine Esoteric Seals, represented by the character Zhe.

Iron Shirt 鐵布衫 A training method in Chinese martial arts that develops a practitioner's ability to withstand attacks; making the practitioner so strong that it is like the practitioner is wearing a shirt made of iron.

J

Jade Pillow Gate 玉枕關 The third of the Three Gates located at the base of the skull.

Jade Purity Level 玉清境 One of the Four Infinite Levels.

jing 精 Essence-of-life, the fundamental material that makes up the human body, the material foundation of life; derived from innate and acquired sources.

K

Kagyu 噶舉派（白教）A tradition under Tibetan Tantric Buddhism; the White Sect.

kan-water 坎水 (see kidney-yang)

karma 因果 Cause and effect.

Kidney Channel 足少陰腎經 An abbreviation for the Foot Minimum Yin Kidney Channel.

kidney-jing 腎精 The essence stored in the kidneys.

kidney-qi 腎氣 A descriptive term referring to the energy that flows in the Kidney Channel.

kidney-yang 腎陽 The original vital function, believed to be the source of heat energy in the body.

kidney-yin 腎陰 The original essence, the material basis from vital functioning of the kidneys.

Kung Fu (see gongfu) A commonly used romanization for gongfu.

L

lama 喇嘛 A spiritual teacher, a mentor.

Lao Tzu (see Laozi) Wade-Giles romanization of Laozi.

Laozi 老子 1. Another name for the *Daodejing*. 2. The honorary name given to the author of the *Daodejing*. 3. Li Er.

Large Intestine Channel 手陽明大腸經 An abbreviation for the Hand Yang Equilibrium Large Intestine Channel.

Leading the Breath 引息 A term used in Precious Vessel Qigong.

Left Channel 左脈 One of the three energy channels involved in the Tantric Buddhist Qigong cultivation located on the left side of the Middle Channel; color red.

Li Er 李耳 1. The real name of Laozi (604-531 B.C.); the author of the Daodejing.

Liang Shou-Yu 梁守渝 (1943-) The coauthor of this volume; one of Wen-Ching Wu's teachers.

Liang Zhi-Xiang 梁芷箱 Master Liang's grandfather.

life-fire 命火 (see kidney-yang) The same as kidney-yang.

light-qi 光炁 A purer form of qi with a higher vibration that is not restricted by time and space.

Lin Bin Dou Zhe Jie Zhen Lie Qian Xing 臨兵斗者皆陣列前行 The nine key words originating from Baopuzi used in training the Nine Esoteric Seals.

Lin Bin Dou Zhe Jie Zhen Lie Zai Qian 臨兵斗者皆陣列在前 A variation of the nine key words used in the training of the Nine Esoteric Seals.

Liu Han-Wen 劉漢文 A qigong master who documented and presented a method of unification with the cosmos in his work on Chan and Tantric Buddhist Qigong in China (under the chapter called *Wisdom Qigong*).

Liver Channel 足厥陰肝經 An abbreviation for the Foot Equilibrium Yin Liver Channel.

lower astral planes 陰性空間 Refers to the space that the Yin Spirit travels to.

Lower Burner 下焦 Refers to the area in the lower portion of the torso below the navel; it contains the kidneys, urinary bladder, small intestine, large intestine, and the liver; it is responsible for eliminating waste through the filter passages of the kidneys, urinary bladder, and large intestine.

Lower Plane 下界 The lowermost of the Three Planes. (also see Six Physical Levels)

Luminous Spot 明點 A term used in Buddhist Qigong cultivation.

Lung Channel 手太陰肺經 An abbreviation for the Hand Maximum Yin Lung Channel.

lung-qi 肺氣 A descriptive term referring to the energy that flows in the Lung Channel.

M

Ma Li-Tang 馬禮堂 (1903-1989 A.D.) A well-known qigong master.

Macrocosmic Circulation 大周天功法 A qigong method.

Mahayana 大乘 One of the two vehicles in Buddhism; with its motivation emphasis placed on the humanitarian intention to attain enlightenment for the benefit of others.

mantra 眞言 1. Pledge and wishes without any pretense. 2. Truth; the internal unspoken real thoughts in the mind. 3. Special tones that can vibrate the qi channels in the body to bring about the hidden potential within.

Medical Qigong 醫療氣功 1. An energy practice for health, healing, and longevity developed by the Medical society. 2. An energy practice for healing illness, to build qi to counteract pathogenic influences, to regulate the balance of qi, to prevent illness, and to attain longevity.

Microcosmic Circulation 小周天功法 A qigong method; a training for Fostering Jing into Qi, the first of the three primary Daoist training. The circulation of energy resembling the circulation of the earth around the sun, thereby, the name Microcosmic Circulation.

Middle Burner 中焦 The area of the torso between the diaphragm and the navel; it contains the spleen and the stomach; it is responsible for digesting food and transforming it into nutrients through the fermentation process of the stomach and the spleen.

Middle Channel中脈 One of the three energy channels involved in Tantric Buddhist Qigong cultivation located inside the spinal cord; color blue.

Middle Plane 中界 The middle of the Three Planes. (also see Eighteen Sensory Levels)

Mizong 密宗 The Chinese term for Tantric Buddhism; it literally means the Secret Doctrine.

moxa 灸 Artemisia vulgaris; an herb used in the treatment of diseases in TCM; it is usually made into a cone shape or a stick shape.

moxibustion An application of moxa either indirectly above the skin surface or indirectly with something (ginger, garlic, salt, etc.) between the skin and the moxa.

Mystical Virtue玄德 An expression of Virtue by cultivators in the process of nurturing the spirit. They are knowingly and unknowingly helping others and society by healing the sick, helping people in trouble, protecting the balance of nature, etc.

N

Navel Energy Center 臍輪 One of the seven energy centers involved in Tantric Buddhist Qigong, located around the belly button.

Nectar The nourishing fluid generated in the Achieving Through Spiritual Flame qigong. 菩提心月液﹝甘露水，天庭水﹞

Nine Esoteric Seals A Buddhist Qigong method. 念力開發一九字密令

Nine Rotations to Bring Back the Spiritual Elixir 九轉還魂丹 A qigong method.

Nine Segment Buddhist Breathing 九節佛風 A Buddhist Qigong method.

Nourishing Qi Method 養氣法 A Daoist Qigong method.

Nourishing Your Qi 養氣 A term used in Wushu Qigong.

Nyingma 寧瑪派﹝紅教﹞A tradition under Tibetan Tantric Buddhism; the Red Sect.

O

OM AH HUM 唵阿吽﹝嗡阿吽﹞The mantra that contains the principle syllables of Sanskrit; OM is the fundamental sound of the energy behind the origin of the cosmos; AH is the fundamental sound of the growth of life in the beginning of the cosmos; HUM is the fundamental sound of the hidden potential of life.

OM BORULAN ZHELI A mantra used in the training of the Nine Esoteric Seals and the Armor Protection from Negative Energies. 嗡 • 波汝藍者利

OM FURILUO SADUOFU AH KANG 唵 • 縛日羅 • 薩埵縛 • 阿 • 康 A mantra used in the training of the Nine Esoteric Seals.

OM MA NI PAD ME HUM 唵 • 嘛 • 呢 • 叭 • 咪 • 吽 The mantra of Avalokiteshvara.

OM NAMO BENZI Sakyamunifo and all the Enlightened Families A mantra used in the training of the Nine Esoteric Seals. 嗡 • 南無本師釋伽牟尼佛及眾聖眷

One Finger Chan 一指禪 1. A qigong method. 2. A martial arts hard qigong training that conditions one finger for cavity strikes.

Opening and Closing Your Pores 毛孔開合功 A term used in Wushu Qigong.

original-qi 原氣﹝元氣﹞The dynamic of visceral functions; vitality.

Original Qi 混然一氣﹝宇宙原氣﹞The purest undifferentiated energy at the beginning of the cosmos. According to Daoist philosophy when the universe was first formed, it came from the Dao, from the Dao came the One, from the One came the Two, from the Two came the Three, and from the Three came all things in the universe. In the cultivation of the Dao, the One refers to the undifferentiated Original Qi; the Two refers to the differentiated pure forms of Yin-Qi and Yang-Qi; the Three refers to the Yin-Qi, Yang-Qi, and the interaction of the Two.

Original Spirit 元神（性体）One of the two components of human spirit, containing information from past lifetimes. It is further classified into two parts — Yin and Yang Spirits. (also see Personality)

P

pathogenic influence 邪氣 Any cause of illness, including exogenous, endogenous, and those that are neither exogenous nor endogenous causes.

Pericardium Channel 手厥陰心包經 An abbreviation for the Hand Equilibrium Yin Pericardium Channel.

Personality 識神（欲神）One of the two components of human spirit, containing information we have learned in this lifetime. The Post-Birth Spirit. (also see Original Spirit)

point (see acupuncture point)

Pratyekabuddhas A subdivision of the Hinayana Vehicle; a solitary realizer, one who attains realization without relying on a teacher, by following one's natural inclination.

Priceless Vessel Seal 寶瓶印 One of the hand seals used in Buddhist Qigong training; the ninth of the Nine Esoteric Seals, represented by the character Qian.

Precious Vessel Qigong 寶瓶氣 A Buddhist Qigong method.

pure essence 精氣 All the positive and good energy of the universe; including the sun, the moon, the earth, and the stars that are advantageous to the human body.

Push the Ground 按地式 A term used in Wushu Qigong.

Push the Mountain 推山式 A term used in Wushu Qigong.

Q

qi 氣 1. Energy. 2. The intrinsic substance that makes up the cosmos. 3. In TCM, it refers to the intrinsic substance that flows in the human body and is the impelling force for all living activities.

Qi Permeating Technique 貫氣法 A qigong method.

Qi Shi 綺石 A Ming Dynasty (1368-1644 A.D.) medical expert.

qi-deficincy 氣虛 In TCM, it refers to a weakness in the functioning of the body or the organ systems.

qigong 氣功 1. Any set of breathing and energy circulation techniques that are capable of improving health, preventing illness, strengthening the body, and for spiritual development. 2. The attainment of qi.

Qigong for Developing Incredible Strength 養氣神力功 A qigong method.

qi-stagnation 氣滯 In TCM, it refers to the restricted flow of qi in the body.

R

rainbow body 虹化 The spontaneous manifestation of light and a rainbow of colors, when a highly accomplished Buddhist cultivator chooses to leave this physical plane.

Relaxing the Body and Calming the Mind 鬆靜健身功 An advanced relaxation technique.

Reproductive Energy Center 生殖輪 One of the seven energy centers involved in Tantric Buddhist Qigong, located at the root of the reproductive organ.

Return the Void Back to the Dao 還虛合道 The final stage of the Daoist cultivation to attain the unification with the Dao. (also see Shatter the Void)

Right Channel 右輪 One of the three energy channels involved in Tantric Buddhist Qigong cultivation located on the right side of the Middle Channel; color white.

Root Chakra (see Sea Bottom Energy Center)

S

Sanskrit An ancient Indian language, noted for its complex grammar and rich vocabulary.

Sakya 薩迦派﹝花教﹞A tradition under Tibetan Tantric Buddhism; the Flower Sect.

Sakyamuni 釋伽牟尼佛 (620-543 B.C.) The name of the first Buddha, from whom the teachings of Buddhism originated.

School of Thought 學派 The thinking of a particular group of people following the philosophy and practice of the group; including Daoist, Confucius, Mohist, etc. Philosophical studies from all schools of thought in China, including an understanding of humans and their nature. This is because humans are part of the universe, so our involvement in the study of anything, will be influenced by our presence. For a school of thought to exist, it must include the study of humans and their nature, as well as, the particular emphasis of the study.

Sea Bottom Energy Center 海底輪 One of the seven energy centers involved in Tantric Buddhist Qigong, located at the huiyin area.

seven baser spirits 七魄 The yin components of the Original Spirit that must rely on the physical body to exist and travel in the lower astral planes.

Shaolin 少林 1. Refers to the Shaolin Temple, a Buddhist monastery known for its martial arts and Buddhist teaching. 2. Refers to Shaolin Kung Fu, the martial arts that came from the Shaolin Temple.

Shaolin Internal Power Qigong 少林內勁功 A training of qigong derived from the Shaolin Temple.

Shatter the Void 粉碎虛空 The completion of Daoist cultivation, where the concept of the Void is also given up to attain the ultimate goal — one with the Dao.

shen 神 1. Spirit. 2. The manifestation of life. 3. In TCM, it refers to the mental faculties, and the expression of one's vitality of spirit; it is the individual's expression of consciousness and living activities. 4. God.

Shravakas A subdivision of Hinayana Vehicle.

shunyata Emptiness; Void; no inherent existence by itself.

Six Healing Sounds for Nourishing Life 六字訣養身功 A qigong method.

Six Physical Levels 欲界六天 The more definitive term referring to the Lower Plane. These levels are visible to the human eye, consists of all physical forms, desires, senses, and emotions; yin and yang are interacting; and humans are reborn.

Small Cosmos 小天地 1. Human body. 2. The complete, orderly, harmonious human body that mirrors the Great Cosmos.

Small Intestine Channel 手太陽小腸經 An abbreviation for the Hand Maximum Yang Small Intestine Channel.

Soyal Tulku 索朗頓珠 (Suolang Dunzhu) The author of *The Brief Introduction to Rainbow Body Documentary of Tibetan Buddhism.*

spiritual-breath 靈息 A term used in this volume.

Spiritual Connections 神通 Extraordinary ability, either as a by-product of the evolution of the spirit or channeled.

Spiritual Guides 空間大師 The guides or entities that help people on the Physical Plane with their tasks and spiritual development; astral teachers.

Spiritual Luminance 靈光﹝元性﹞The luminance that enters the womb prior to the birth of a baby, it combines with innate-qi and innate-jing to become the Original Spirit.

Spiritual Movement 靈動 The involuntary movements of the physical body while training the Gathering the Spirit Method.

spiritual-qi 靈氣 A term used in this volume.

Spleen Channel 足太陰脾經 An abbreviation for the Foot Maximum Yin Spleen Channel.

Stomach Channel 足陽明胃經 An abbreviation for the Foot Yang Equilibrium Stomach Channel.

Sun Chakra Seal 日輪印 The eighth of the Nine Esoteric Seals, represented by the character Zai.

Sun Si-Miao 孫思邈 (561-682 A.D.) A prominent physician in the Tang Dynasty.

Sunrise and Sunset Circulation 卯酉周天功法 A qigong method.

Sutrayana A subdivision of the Mahayana Vehicle, with a practice that includes a rational, intellectual, and systematic approach to mental training.

T

Tai Chi (see Taiji) The Wade-Giles romanization of Taiji.

Tai Chi Chuan (see Taijiquan) The Wade-Giles romanization of Taijiquan.

Taiji 太極 1. The grand ultimate; the term referring to the dynamic interactions of yin-yang. 2. The name of the yin-yang symbol.

Taiji Cord 太極弦 1. The curvature within the Taiji Symbol. 2. A representation of the philosophy and obstacles in the attainment of immortality. 3. The highest cultivation in all the schools of Daoism, is to achieve the ability to reverse the twist in the Taiji Cord, thereby returning to Wuji, and the eventual unification with the Dao.

Taijiquan 太極拳 1. An internal style Chinese martial arts characterized by a soft and subtle appearance, with its training philosophy based on the Yin-Yang Theory. 2. A self-healing exercise known and practiced for its healing and illness prevention potential.

Tailbone Gate 長強關 The first of the Three Gates, located at the tailbone area.

Taimi 台密 A subdivision within the Japanese Tantric Buddhism.

Tantra The unbroken stream or continuum, flowing from ignorance to realization.

Tantrayana 密宗佛法 A subdivision of the Mahayana Vehicle; also known as Vajrayana, because this vehicle is characterized by the realization of the indestructible reality of the Three Esoterics.

Tantric Buddhism 密宗佛教 (see Tantrayana)

Tao (see Dao) The Wade-Giles romanization of Dao.

Tao Teh Ching (see *Daodejing*) The Wade-Giles romanization of *Daodejing*.

Taoist (see Daoist) The Wade-Giles romanization of Daoist.

Taoist Chi Kung (see Daoist Qigong) The Wade-Giles romanization of Daoist Qigong.

TCM An abbreviation for Traditional Chinese Medicine.

The Advanced Method of Unification with the Cosmos 天人合一法（二）A qigong method.

The Basic Method of Unification with the Cosmos 天人合一法（一）A qigong method.

The Great Perfection — The Heart Essence 大圓滿心髓 A Buddhist Qigong method.

Third Eye The area between the eye brows.

Third Eye Energy Center 眉間輪 One of the seven energy centers involved in Tantric Buddhist Qigong, located around the eye bridge area.

Three Check Points 三關 The three areas on the Governing Vessel that tend to restrict the flow of qi during Microcosmic and Macrocosmic Circulation: the Tailbone Gate, Dorsal Gate, and Jade Pillow Gate.

Three Esoterics 三密 The Esoteric Abilities of the Body, Speech, and Mind; also known as buddha-body, buddha-speech, and buddha-mind, respectively

three finer spirits 三魂 The yang components of the Original Spirit that is able to leave the physical body and travel in the higher astral planes.

Three Gates (see Three Check Points) Another translation for the Three Check Points.

Three Karmas 三業 The three karmic causing agents: body, speech, and mind.

Three Planes 三界 Part of the cosmos, including the Lower, Middle, and Upper Planes.

Throat Energy Center 喉輪 One of the seven energy centers involved in Tantric Buddhist Qigong, located at the throat.

Thrusting Vessel 沖脈 One of the Eight Extraordinary Vessels in the human body.

Tiantai 天台 A Buddhist sect.

tiger's mouth 虎口 The area of the hand between the index finger and the thumb.

Traditional Chinese Medicine 傳統中醫學 A medical practice that inherited and continued classical diagnosis and treatment methods.

Tranquil Hand Seal 定印 One of the hand seals used in Buddhist Qigong training; accomplished by overlapping one hand on top of the other and the tip of the, thumbs touching each other; men with left hand on top, women with right hand on top.

Triple Burner Channel 三焦 An abbreviation for the Hand Minimum Yang Triple Burner Channel.

U

Upper Burner 上焦 The area of the torso above the diaphragm; which contains the heart and lungs; it is responsible for taking in air, and functions as a sprayer by distributing nutrients and qi throughout the body.

Upper Plane 上界 The highest of the Three Planes. (also see Four Mental Levels)

Urinary Bladder Channel 足太陽膀胱經 An abbreviation for the Foot Maximum Yang Urinary Bladder Channel

Use Movements to Purify Jing 動以化精 The fundamental step in Daoist cultivation, including training to discipline the mind and repair physical damage.

V

Vairocana 大日如來 The Buddha of one of the five Enlightened Families; usually depicted as white in color; literally means the *Illuminator*.

vajra A ritual object representing an indestructible reality.

Vajrasattva 金剛薩埵 The indestructible, brave, and courageous Bodhisattva, with an earnest effort to cultivate virtue and to get rid of evil; also known as the Bodhisattva of the Three Indestructibles.

Vanishing Technique 消 A term used in Precious Vessel Qigong.

Vehicle 乘（經）Scripture; yana; sutra; classics; cannon.

vessels 脈 Qi pathways in the human body that connect to the acupuncture channels in the body.

Virtue 德 De, the second component of the *Daodejing*, the expression of the Dao in human action.

viscera 臟 Refers to the heart, liver, spleen, lungs, and kidneys; organs that store, but don't discharge jing, qi, blood, or body fluids.

visualization 1. The training that leads the practitioner into a state of Void in thought, to enter a calm abiding meditative state; usually by concentrating on one thought or process, such as breathing or an object, to eliminate all other thoughts. 2. The training of concentration to reduce conscious thoughts, to give the subconscious a chance to work.

vital-qi 正氣 A general term referring to the ability of the human body to defend against the pathogenic influences which cause disease.

Void 無 1. A term often used as a synonym for the Dao when describing the parallels between the Great Cosmos and the human body. 2. A generic term used to mean the undefinable, the Truth, or the Dao; it is beyond the comprehension of our limited mind and beyond our limited language to describe.

W

Wang Ju-Rong 王菊蓉 (1928-) A highly respected and accomplished Chinese martial arts expert; one of Wen-Ching Wu's teachers.

Wang Wei-Yi 王維一 (987-1067 A.D.) A distinguished acupuncture doctor responsible for the casting of the two life-size bronze acupuncture figures, and was in charge of compiling the *Manual of the Illustrated Points for Acupuncture and Moxibustion*, published in 1207 A.D.

water-qi 水氣 Water retention caused by a dysfunction of the *spleen* and *kidney*.

Wisdom Fist Seal 智拳印 The seventh of the Nine Esoteric Seals, represented by the character Lie (pronounce lee-a).

Wu Cheng-De 吳誠德 (1930-) A highly acclaimed Traditional Chinese Medical doctor and professor, and a highly respected and accomplished Chinese martial artist; one of Wen-Ching Wu's teachers.

Wu Wen-Ching 吳文慶 (1964-) The coauthor of this volume.

Wuji 無極 1. The state one achieves when one becomes one with the Dao, the state after transcending the duality of yin-yang. 2. The original nature of the Dao.

Wushu 武術 The proper Chinese term for martial arts.

Wushu Qigong 武術氣功 A part of the martial arts' internal energy training that develops the physical body's ability to withstand attacks, and develops a strong offensive application potential.

X

Y

yang 陽 1. One of the two fundamental forces in the cosmos; the counterpart of yin. 2. The active aspect or functional aspect of the human system.

Yang-Activation Vessel 陽蹻脈 One of the Eight Extraordinary Vessels in the human body.

Yang-Maintenance Vessel 陽維脈 One of the Eight Extraordinary Vessels in the human body.

yang-qi 陽氣 Refers to the circulation of qi in the body where the energy is moving towards a more yang state; following a 24 hour cycle, yang-qi rises at 12 midnight and reaches its maximum at 12 noon.

Yang Spirit 陽神 The yang component of the Original Spirit. (also see *three finer spirits*)

Yangtze River 楊子江〔長江〕 Also known as Changjiang, the longest river in China, and the fourth longest in the world. It is the most important water transportation route in China.

Yellow Emperor 黃帝 the father of Chinese civilization who governed ancient China between 2697-2597 B.C.

Yellow Emperor's Internal Classic 《黃帝內經》 Also known as *Cannon of Medicine*, the oldest and greatest Chinese medical text; ascribed to the Yellow Emperor. In actuality, it was written by numerous unknown authors in the Warring Kingdom Period. This book has two parts: the *Plain Questions* and *Miraculous Pivot (Cannon of Acupuncture)*.

yin 陰 1. One of the two fundamental forces in the cosmos; the counterpart of yang. 2. The structure or the material aspect of the human system.

Yin-Activation Vessel 陰蹻脈 One of the Eight Extraordinary Vessels in the human body.

Yin-Maintenance Vessel 陰維脈 One of the Eight Extraordinary Vessels in the human body.

yin-qi 陰氣 Refers to the circulation of qi in the body where the energy is moving towards a more yin state; following a 24 hour cycle, yin-qi rises at 12 noon and reaches its maximum at midnight.

Yin Spirit 陰神 The yin component of the Original Spirit. (also see *seven baser spirits*)

Yintang 印堂 The midpoint between the eyebrow.

Yin Virtue 陰德 An expression of Virtue while in the physical body. Doing kind deeds without expecting rewards, and doing kind deeds without leaving names.

yin-yang 陰陽 The two fundamental forces in the cosmos that have an opposing, yet dependent nature.

Yin-Yang Theory 陰陽學說 1. A basic reasoning behind all ancient Chinese natural science; primarily used to describe the opposing, interdependent, waxing and waning, and transformational nature of all things in the cosmos. 2. In TCM, it refers to the various antitheses in the human body which occur in the anatomy, physiology, pathology, diagnosis, and treatment.

Z

Zen (see Chan) The Japanese romanization of Chan.

Zhang Dao-Ling 張道陵 (張陵) The founder of the Five Unit of Rice Dao, the first religious organization that used the *Daodejing* as the theoretical foundation for their beliefs.

Zhi Zhuan 智顗 A Tiantai Buddhist high priest during the Sui Dynasty (590-618 B.C.).

Zhuangzi 莊子 1. The title of the book written by Zhuan Zhou. 2. The honorary name given to Zhuan Zhou (369-295 B.C.).

About the Author:

Master Liang, Shou-Yu

Master Liang, Shou-Yu was born in 1943 in Sichuan, China. At age six, he began his training in qigong, under the tutelage of his renowned grandfather, the late Liang Zhi-Xiang. He was taught esoteric qigong and the martial arts of the Emei Mountain region, including Emei Dapeng Qigong. At age eight, his grandfather also made special arrangements for him to begin training Emei Qigong and Wushu with other well-known masters of the time.

By the time he was twenty, Master Liang had already received instruction from 10 of the most well-known legendary grandmasters of both Southern and Northern origin. His curiosity inspired him to learn more than one hundred sequences from many different styles. As he grew older, through and beyond his college years, his wide background in various martial arts helped form his present character, and led him to achieve a high level of martial arts and qigong skills. Some of the training he concentrated on included: the Emei Styles, Shaolin Long Fist, Praying Mantis, Chuojiao, Qinna, vital point striking, many weapons systems, and qigong methods presented in this volume.

Master Liang received a university degree in biology and physiology in 1964 and taught high school in a remote village in China. This was part of his *reeducation* program enforced on him for being born in a bourgeois family, by the government during the political structure of the time. His dedication to his own training and helping others to excel didn't stop during the years he was in the remote village. He begin to organize Wushu and wrestling teams to compete in the provincial tournaments.

During the years of the Cultural Revolution (1966-1974), all forms of martial arts and qigong were suppressed. To avoid conflict with the Red Guards, Master Liang left his teaching position and used this opportunity to tour various parts of the country. During his travel, he visited and studied with great masters in Wushu and qigong, and made friends with people who shared his devotion. During these years, he made many Wushu and qigong friends, and met many great masters. His mastery of qigong and martial arts, both technically and philosophically grew to new horizons.

Master Liang went through numerous provinces and cities, visiting many renowned and revered places where Wushu and qigong originated, was developed, and refined. Among the many places he visited were Emei Mountain, Wudang Mountain, Hua Mountain, Qingcheng Mountain, Chen's Village in Henan, the Changzhou Territory in Hebei Province, Beijing, and Shanghai.

At the end of the Cultural Revolution, the Chinese government again began to support the martial arts and qigong. During the reorganization and categorizing of the existing martial arts, research projects were set up to seek out living masters and preserve their knowledge. It was at this time that the Sichuan government appointed Master Liang as a coach for the city, the territory, and the province. Many of Master Liang's students were among the top martial artists of China. In 1979, he received the title of *Coach of Excellence* since 1949, by the People's Republic of China.

With his wealth of knowledge, Master Liang was inspired at an early age to compete in martial arts tournaments, in which he was many times a noted gold medalist. During his adolescence, Master Liang won titles in Chinese wrestling (Shuaijiao), various other martial arts, and weight lifting. After the Cultural Revolution, despite his many official duties Master Liang continued to participate actively in competitions both at the provincial and national level. Between 1974 and 1981, he won numerous medals, including four gold medals. His students also performed superbly both in national and provincial open tournaments, winning many medals. Many of these students are now professional Wushu coaches in colleges, in the armed forces, or have become movie stars. In 1979, Master Liang received several appointments, including committee membership in the Sichuan Chapter of the Chinese National Wushu Committee and Coaches Committee.

In 1981, Master Liang visited Seattle, Washington. This trip marked another new era in the course of his life. His ability immediately impressed Wushu devotees. The Wushu and Taiji Club of the Student Association, at the University of Washington, retained him as a Wushu Coach. At the same time, Master Liang taught at the Taiji Association in Seattle. In the following year, Master Liang went to Vancouver, Canada, and was appointed Taiji Coach by the Villa Cathy Care Home. The same year, he was appointed Honorary Chairman and Head Coach by the North American Taiji Athletic Association. He also began to teach classes in the Physical Education Department at the University of British Columbia (UBC).

In 1984, Master Liang was certified as a national First Class Ranking Judge by China. He was also appointed Chairperson and Wushu Coach by the University of British Columbia. In 1985, Master Liang was elected coach of the First Canadian National Wushu Team, which was invited to participate in the 1985 World Wushu Invitational Competition that took place in Xian, China. The Canadian team took the Team Third Place after competing against teams from 13 other countries.

The following year, Master Liang was again elected coach of the Second Canadian National Wushu Team, that competed in the 1986 World Wushu Invitational Competition held in Teintsin, China. A total of 28 countries participated. This time, the Canadian team took Team Second Place which was only second to China. Master Liang and the Canadian success story shocked the Chinese nation, and news of their outstanding accomplishment spread throughout China.

In 1994, Master Liang led the North American Martial Arts Exhibition Team for a friendship performance tour to ten major cities in China. His team received a warm welcome by the people and government of China. While in China, the team also competed in the International Wushu Competition held in Shanghai. This competition was represented by 32 nations. Master Liang's team received 42 gold medals awarded to the competitors. Canadian premier, Mr. Jean Chretien, also wrote a letter of encouragement to the team. Many Chinese television stations, radio stations, and newspapers spread the news of the Exhibition Team all over China.

Master Liang has not limited his contributions of Wushu to Vancouver, Canada. He has also given numerous seminars and demonstrations to Wushu students and instructors in the United States and Europe, including instructors and professionals from Karate, Taiji, and Shaolin Kung Fu disciplines. Students in Boston, Denver, Houston, New York, Providence, and around the globe have benefited greatly from Master Liang's personal touch. Since the beginning of his advantageous martial arts life, he has been featured by scores of newspapers and magazines in China, Europe, USA, and Canada; as well as, has been interviewed by several television stations in China, USA, and Canada. Master Liang has published instructional video programs teaching Liangong Shr Ba Fa, and coauthored three other books: *A Guide to Taijiquan*, *Hsing Yi Chuan*, and *Baguazhang*.

About the Author:

Mr. Wu, Wen-Ching

Mr. Wu was born in Taiwan, China in 1964, in a little farming village named Establishing Peace, located on the northern part of the Beautiful Island. He attended an international high school in West Africa for three years, then came to the U.S. for college. In five years, Mr. Wu completed the cooperative and academic requirements to receive his BSME Degree with honors from Northeastern University. While in college Mr. Wu studied Kung Fu and Taijiquan from Dr. Jwing-Ming Yang. After graduation, Mr. Wu began working as a mechanical engineer during the day and teaching Shaolin Kung Fu and Taijiquan in the evenings.

In 1986, Mr. Wu began studying with Master Shou-Yu Liang. For the past 10 years Master Liang has willingly shared much of his vast knowledge with him. Mr. Wu has learned Xingyiquan, Taijiquan, Baguazhang, White Ape Sword, Kung Fu, Liuhe Bafa, and Qigong from Master Liang.

In 1989, Mr. Wu began studying with Professor Ju-Rong Wang and Dr. Cheng-De Wu. For the past 7 years, Mr. Wu has been privileged to study Chaquan, Taijiquan, Qigong, and Chinese medicine from Professor Wang and Dr. Wu.

In 1990, Mr. Wu competed in eight events in the United States National Chinese Martial Arts Competition held in Houston, Texas. Mr. Wu was ranked first nationally in every event he competed in. He was awarded two of the highest awards in the competition: Men's All-Around Internal Style and External Style Grand Champion.

In 1991, Mr. Wu and his wife, Denise, founded The Way of the Dragon — School for Health Healing and Martial arts, in Rhode Island. In less than five years the school has established a solid foundation, attracting students from Rhode Island and other neighboring states.

Since 1991, Mr. Wu has traveled to other states and countries to offer seminars. He has been featured on a several TV shows. He is also a part-time instructor at the University of Massachusetts where he teaches Taijiquan and Qigong. He has produced a *Qigong: Qi Permeating* audiotape, *The Complete Tai Chi Chuan Workout* videotape, and has coauthored two other books: *A Guide to Taijiquan* and *Baguazhang*.

Bibliography

(Chinese References)

1. 《中國功法百家》董剛昭，廣東高丹教育出版社，一九八八年。

2. 《中國年鑑》京士威國際出版有限公司，一九八一年。

3. 《中國佛教與傳統文化》方立天，上海人民出版社，一九八八年。

4. 《中國禪密功》劉漢文，黑龍江人民出版社，一九八八年。

5. 《中華宗教編》程杰 等，天津人民出版社，一九九二年。

6. 《中醫按摩療法》曹錫珍，人民出版社，一九七九年。

7. 《中醫常用術語集註》王家出版社。

8. 《中醫學概論》孟景春•周仲瑛，知音出版社，一九九一年。

9. 《中醫學診法大全》麻仲學，臺灣中華書局印行，一九九一年。

10. 《中醫學療法大全》麻仲學，三東科學技術出版社，一九九零年。

11. 《玉蟾硬氣功》唐景祥，江西科學技術出版社，一九九一年。

12. 《全國氣功匯編》全國氣功交流大會，中國大百科全書出版社，一九八四年。

13. 《金剛指點穴術》殷永洲，廣東科學出版社，一九九零年。

14. 《武術匯宗》萬賴聲，香港錦華出版社。

15. 《神密的密宗》桐山靖雄，大方文化事業公司。

16. 《氣功密旨》莫文丹，廣西科學技術出版社，一九八九年。

17. 《密宗密法》印陵，北京工業大學出版社，一九八九年。

18. 《密宗百問百答》菩提學社，一九九零年。

19. 《密教眞言宗入門必讀》菩提學社，一九八七年。

20. 《密宗與密法》菩提學社

21. 《超能力氣功法》高藤聰一郎，武陵出版社，一九八七年。

22. 《硬氣功技擊術》安在峰，北京體育出版社，一九九零年。

23. 《硬氣功點穴術》安在峰，北京體育學院出版社，一九九零年。

24. 《道教氣功百問》陳兵，佛光出版社，一九九一年。

25. 《傷科學》上海中醫學院，商務印書館有限公司，一九七六年。

26. 《實用臨床腧穴彩色圖譜》陳志榮，一九八六年。

27. 《實用中國針灸經穴學》郭家樑•郭靖海，眾文圖書出版社，一九九一年。

28. 《養氣功問答與實踐》馬禮堂，人民體育出版社，一九八八年。

29. 《儒佛道三家氣功精義》林樹滋•李韶敏，重慶大學出版社，一九九四年。

30. 《禪與道槪論》南懷瑾，老古文化事業公司，一九九零年。

31. 《藏密修法精粹》印陵，北京工業大學出版社，一九九一年。

Bibliography

(English References)

1. Barrett, Abramoff, Kumaran, & Millington. *Biology*. Englewood Cliffs, NJ: Prentice-Hall, 1986.

2. Coleman, Graham. *A Handbook of Tibetan Culture*. Boston, MA: Shambhala, 1994.

3. Editors. *Dictionary of Traditional Chinese Medicine*. Taipei, Taiwan: Southern Materials Center, Inc., 1985.

4. Memmler & Wood. *The Human Body in Health and Disease*, Sixth Ed. Philadelphia, PA: J.B. Lippincott Company, 1987.

5. Sieg, Kay & Adams, Sandra. *Illustrated Essentials of Musculoskeletal Anatomy*, Second Ed. Gainesville, FL: Megabooks Inc., 1985.

6. Sogyal Rinpoche. *Tibetan Book of Living & Dying*. San Francisco, CA: Harper Collins,1992.

Index

L

laogong (PC8) 296
Laozi 79
large intestine *68*
   Channel 282
Laryngitis *75*
Later Han Dynasty 78
law *30*
Left Channel 130
Li Er 79
Liang, Shou-Yu 14, 333
Liang Zhi-Xiang 333
liangmen (G21) 284
liangqiu (G34) 284
lianquan (JM23) 306
liberation 134
lidui (G45) 284
Lie Seal 159
lieque (P7) 280
life-fire *48*
light *See* aura
light-qi 122
ligou (H5) 302
Lin Bing Dou Zhe Jie Zhen
   Lie Zai Qian 157
Lin Seal 157
lingdao (C4) 288
lingtai (TM10) 304
lingxu (R24) 294
linqi (foot) (VF41) 300
linqi (head) (VF15) 300
Liu Han-Wen 182
Liuhebafa 238
liver *28, 52, 68, 70*
   Ailments *73*
   Channel 302
   Diseases 210
   Qigong *52*
longevity 77, 79, 84
loss of control 313
lougu (LP7) 286
Low Temperature and Low
   Thrombocyte 211
lower back pain *74*
Lower Burner *36, 68*
Lower Plane 85
Lucky Posture 156
Luminous Spot 148

Lung *28, 41, 47, 68, 70*
   Channel 280
   Qigong *41*
lung-qi *41*
luoque (VU8) 292
luxi (T19) 298

M

Ma Li-Tang *71*
Macrocosmic 21
Mahayana 127
Mandarin 317
mantras 130, 132
martial arts 19, 237
massage 18
Medical Qigong 20, *23, 31*
Medical Restorative Qigong
   41
meichong (VU3) 292
memory *47*
mental diseases 210
meridians *23*
metal *28, 70*
Microcosmic 21
Middle Burner *68*
Middle Channel 130
Middle Plane 85
mind 20
Ming Dynasty *47*
mingmen (TM4) 304
Mizong 128
Mongolia 128
moxibustion 18
muchuang (VF16) 300
Mutual Burdening *28*
Mutual Nourishment *28*
Mutual Over-Restraint *28*
Mutual Restraint *28*

N

naohu (TM17) 304
naohui (T13) 298
naokong (VF19) 300
naoshu (IT10) 290
Navel Energy Center 131
nectar 132
negative energy 236
negativity 155

neiguan (PC6) 296
neiting (G44) 284
Nepal 128
neurasthenia *60*
night sweats *60*
nirvana 128, 130
nocturnal emission *48*
Northern Dynasty *23*
numb legs 316
Nyingma 128

O

om 314
OM AH HUM 132
OM BORULAN ZHELI
   155, 156, 164
OM FURILUO SADUOFU
   AH KANG
   164, 166, 168
OM MA NI PAD ME HUM
   156, 167, 168
OM NAMO BENZI
   Sakyamunifo and all
   the Enlightened
   Families 160, 172
opposing *30*
Origin 80
original-qi *42*, 94
ox pace 94

P

palpitation *59, 60*
pangguangshu (VU28) 292
pangs *60*
panicky *60*
pathogenic influences
   18, *25, 27, 31, 41*, 155
pensiveness *27*
Pericardium Channel 296
philosophy of being natural
   79
philosophy of freedom 79
pineal gland 122
pinyin 317
pishu (VU20) 292
pituitary gland 132
pledge 130
pohu (VU42) 292

Order Form

For additional copies, please send a check, money order, or credit card number for $34.95/copy plus shipping and handling, *(for orders shipped to Rhode Island addresses, please add 7% sales tax)* along with your name and address to:

The Way of the Dragon Publishing
Shipping Department
P. O. Box 14561
East Providence, RI 02914-0561
U.S.A.

Tel: (401) 435-6502
Fax: (401) 435-3743

Shipping and Handling per Copy:

U.S.: *Priority Mail* $4.00 for the first copy, $2.00 for each additional copy.

U.S.: *Book Rate* $2.50 for the first copy, $1.50 for each additional copy.

Canada: *Air Mail* $6.50, *Surface Mail* $3.00

Mexico: *Air Mail* $8.00, *Surface Mail* $4.00

Europe: *Air Mail* $13.00, *Surface Mail* $4.00

Surface mail may take several weeks.

Qigong Empowerment

Name _____

Address _____ Apt. # _____

City _____ State _____ Zip _____

Telephone # ( ) _____

Credit Card # _____ Exp. / _____

Signature _____

$34.95 X __ copies = $ _____

S&H: __ copies = $ _____

Tax (7% RI only) $ _____

Total $ _____

I'm enclosing $_____

❏ *Check*   ❏ *Money Order*

❏ *VISA*   ❏ *Master Card*

payable to:

The Way of the Dragon Publishing

Gift Order Form

Qigong Empowerment — The Gift that Keeps on Giving

To send a copy to a friend, please send a check, money order, or credit card number for $34.95/copy plus shipping and handling, (*for orders shipped to Rhode Island addresses, please add 7% sales tax*) along with your name and address and your friend's name and address to:

The Way of the Dragon Publishing
Shipping Department
P. O. Box 14561
East Providence, RI 02914-0561
U.S.A.

Tel: (401) 435-6502
Fax: (401) 435-3743

Shipping and Handling per Copy:

U.S.: *Priority Mail* $4.00 for the first copy, $2.00 for each additional copy.

U.S.: *Book Rate* $2.50 for the first copy, $1.50 for each additional copy.

Canada: *Air Mail* $6.50, *Surface Mail* $3.00

Mexico: *Air Mail* $8.00, *Surface Mail* $4.00

Europe: *Air Mail* $13.00, *Surface Mail* $4.00

Surface mail may take several weeks.

Your Name _____

Address _____ Apt. # _____

City _____ State ____ Zip ____

Telephone # (___) _____

Credit Card # _____ Exp. ___ / ___

Signature _____

Ship to:

Name _____

Address _____ Apt. # _____

City _____ State ____ Zip ____

Qigong Empowerment

$34.95 X ____ copies = $ _____

S&H: ____ copies = $ _____

Tax (7% RI only) $ _____

Total $ _____

I'm enclosing $ _____

❏ *Check*   ❏ *Money Order*

❏ *VISA*   ❏ *Master Card*

payable to:

The Way of the Dragon Publishing